Told through the lives of the American Century's most talented and stubborn dissidents, *Flights* is the archetypal hero's journey of a group of progressives whose struggle for truth, and for freedom from persecution, sent them into exile, both literal and metaphorical.

Wanted for a crime she did not commit, Professor Angela Davis went on the run in 1970, describing the struggle against panic in her nightly safehouse transfers: "Living as a fugitive means resisting hysteria, distinguishing between the creations of a frightened imagination and the real signs that the enemy is near." In her quest "to elude him, outsmart him," she recalled, "Thousands of my ancestors had waited, as I had . . . for nightfall to cover their steps . . ."

Davis is just one of a rich array of refugees portrayed here by Joel Whitney, all forced to flee homes and/or friends because of their progressive stance. In these pages are compelling profiles of Seymour Hersh, Lorraine Hansberry, Graham Greene, Paul Robeson, Gabriel García Márquez, George and Mary Oppen, Frances Stonor Saunders, Malcolm X, Octavio Paz, Diego Rivera, Leonard Peltier, N. Scott Momaday, Miguel Ángel Asturias, Guatemalan guerrilla fighter Everado and his American wife, Jennifer Harbury, Nobel Peace laureate Rigoberta Menchú, deposed Honduran President Manuel "Mel" Zelaya, and murdered Lenca environmentalist Berta Cáceres.

At once a group portrait of these geniuses of creative escape, *Flights* is also a prehistory (and indictment) of American mass surveillance culminating in Edward Snowden's revelations, of torture culminating in Abu Ghraib, of censorship culminating in the incarceration of journalist Julian Assange, of fascism culminating in January 6, and of political murder culminating in the Bush-Obama-Trump air assassination program.

FLIGHTS

FLIGHTS

Radicals on the Run

JOEL WHITNEY

OR Books
New York · London

© 2024 Joel Whitney

Published by OR Books, New York and London

Visit our website at www.orbooks.com

All rights information: rights@orbooks.com

All rights reserved. No part of this book may be reproduced or transmitted in any form or by any means, electronic or mechanical, including photocopy, recording, or any information storage retrieval system, without permission in writing from the publisher, except brief passages for review purposes.

First printing 2024

Library of Congress Cataloging-in-Publication Data: A catalog record for this book is available from the Library of Congress.
British Library Cataloging in Publication Data: A catalog record for this book is available from the British Library.

Typeset by Lapiz Digital.
Cover and interior illustration design by Everything Studio.

paperback ISBN 978-1-68219-431-7 • ebook ISBN 978-1-68219-432-4

for Peter Tolman Whitney
(1944–2023)

The mystery for me begins where it begins for Aquinas: The individual encounters the world, and . . . . registers the existence of what is not himself, what is totally independent of him, can exist without him, as it must have existed before him, as it will exist after him, and is totally free of nothingness and death (which is, for Aquinas, the intuition of God. It is at any rate the intuition of the indestructible).

—George Oppen

CONTENTS

I

Prologue: My Father's House:
Seymour Hersh and James Risen in Washington
4

Amplifier:
Lorraine Hansberry in Midtown
22

Nonsense of All These Years:
Graham Greene in Vietnam
42

Wake Up, America!: Paul Robeson†* in Peekskill
56

Fifty Years of Disquietude:
Gabriel García Márquez in *Mundo Nuevo*
70

Indestructible:
George and Mary Oppen in Mexico City
90

†*   indicates a possible attempt on the subject's life. In Robeson's case, his mysterious decline while visiting Russia led his son to question whether Robeson was poisoned. He required hospitalization; journalists framed it as a possibility. (See "Did the CIA Poison Paul Robeson?" Alexander Cockburn and Jeffrey St. Clair, *Counterpunch*, April 1, 1999, https://www.counterpunch.org/1999/04/01/did-the-cia-poison-paul-robeson/).

†   denotes the subject was, in fact, killed.

II

Silver Spoons:
Frances Stonor Saunders in Kansas
126

Infiltrated:
Malcolm X† at the Audubon
138

Ars Politica:
Octavio Paz at 100
166

For All Mankind:
Diego Rivera in San Francisco and Detroit
190

Embodiment of the Enemy:
Angela Davis in California
202

Militant:
Leonard Peltier and Anna Mae Aquash in Pine Ridge
216

III

Blood Memory:
N. Scott Momaday on Rainy Mountain
236

Anachronistic:
Miguel Ángel Asturias on his grandparents' finca
258

Clarification:
Rigoberta Menchú in Oslo
274

Unearthed:
Jennifer, Efraín† and the CIA in Guatemala
292

Hard Choices:
Manuel Zelaya and Berta Cáceres† on the Run
316

Acknowledgements
341

Endnotes
345

I

2021

Prologue: My Father's House:
Seymour Hersh and James Risen in Washington

or an impromptu definition of public interest journalism
after a flight from a chair

1.

Seymour Hersh pulls up to the Cleveland Park Metro Station, telling me brusquely to get in. "I'm vaccinated and I assume you are," he says, alluding to my mask. Climbing into his taupe Volvo, I unmask. Hersh is wearing khakis and a plaid button-down, with large, iconic 1980s-style metal specs—Christopher Reeves's Clark Kent. He parallel parks, locks the car, and we walk a block to a restaurant. Hunching forward, he's tall, shaped a bit like a basketball player. In a slight rush to get to his afternoon meetings and a game of tennis, he talks a blue streak. He is out of the house after a pandemic has lifted, hopefully for good.

After moving to D.C., I invited him to my summer class, then asked him to lunch. Could I come to him? he asked. I didn't mind. He leads us to an art deco diner. We take a long table on the sidewalk. It is acorn season, warm enough to sit outside but best not to sit under an oak tree. Unknown to us both, Hersh's chair—safe from acorns—sits on a manhole cover. It is about to give out.

Hersh broke many famous stories in the decades since his exposé of the My Lai massacre, which reported that American soldiers unleashed their fury in a massive war crime on a small Vietnamese village, killing over 500 civilians, mostly women and children. The piece earned Hersh the 1970 Pulitzer Prize for International Reporting. Even then journalists attacked.

In a *New York Times* op-ed, James Reston (revealed later to have links to the CIA) wrote, "Whatever happened in the massacre, should it be reported . . . since clearly reporting the murder of civilians by American soldiers helps the enemy, divides the people of this country, and damages the ideal of America in the world?"[1] It could only have girded him against fellow journalists. Hersh went on to earn many other awards. Many of his stories were too hot for editors.

In May 2015, he reported for the *London Review of Books* that Osama bin Laden was not hunted down by intrepid CIA interrogations and heroic trail sniffing—nor had the necessary evil of pro-democracy torture administered by savvy, model-pretty redheads been decisive. Instead, bin Laden had been a stone's throw from a Pakistani military base the entire time, holed up under US allies' noses with his hosts holding him in an upscale jail.

Instead of the massive expenditure in signals, paramilitary and HUMINTEL that this operation would later go on to justify, Hersh revealed that bin Laden's assassination came via a quieter process: a walk-in. An informant hoping to earn the ample reward for the liquidation of the US-backed[2] eminence gris of terror, *walked in*to the local CIA station, *surprise!*, as if checking into a hotel.

His message? Osama and his entourage are in a house very close. Locals knew he was there. This is what $18 billion[3] in aid earns you: when they are playing a double game, the silence of your allies is the most you can purchase. The story displeased US foreign policy mandarins. The more heroic version had become a feather in Obama's cap and the administration's key foreign policy narrative in its bid for reelection.

The Agency, too, had staked its reputation on this plotline out of Fox's *24*. CIA officers had received Rolex watches from the producers of *Zero Dark Thirty*. That they were fake didn't make the gifts any more legal. While the film dramatically depicted the torture and other unsavory measures that supposedly led to bin Laden's arrest and death, its falsifications rose to fantasy. California Senator Dianne Feinstein stormed out of the theater during a screening. "In fact, the use of 'enhanced interrogation techniques' on" detainees "like Khalid Sheik Mohammed produced false and misleading information," griped torture victim, Senator John McCain.

When Hersh's story appeared, Obama loyalists tweeted conspiracy theories like: "Obviously, this ran in the *London Review* and not the *New Yorker* because the piece was a mess, right?" To discredit the story, the administration's media bloodhounds shouted and murmured a familiar critique of the maestro's work. Hersh uses anonymous sources (a practice government agencies take for granted when leaking propaganda that flatters). Writing in *Vox*, Max Fisher added that Hersh "has appeared increasingly to have gone off the rails."[4]

Hersh's editor at *The New Yorker*, David Remnick, had in the past been adamant: "I know every single source that is in his pieces . . . Every 'retired intelligence officer,' every general with reason to know, and all those phrases that one has to use, alas, by necessity, I say, 'Who is it? What's his interest?' We talk it through."[5] "As much as I liked David," writes Hersh in his memoir, *Reporter*, "I was troubled by what I saw as his closeness to Barack Obama . . . and the fact that he was planning to write a biography of him."[6]

Long before the bin Laden piece was a question, Hersh resigned—on good terms with Remnick. Remnick kept the door open, offering to read whatever he sent. Later, Hersh begrudgingly offered Remnick the story. Remnick dithered, confessing that he was planning to run a story "from the point of view of the SEALs who did the mission, and the killing," Hersh recalls.[7] This was "Getting Bin Laden," by Nicholas Schmidle, fed to the journalists, Hersh suggests, over long fact-check calls with then-counterintelligence advisor John Brennan and with Dennis McDonough, deputy national security director.[8]

After it ran, readers and media watchdogs complained about lack of clarity over Schmidle's anonymous sources—and no clear notice to readers that *none* of the 23 SEALs who captured and assassinated bin Laden spoke to the author of the piece.[9]

Enraged, Hersh re-resigned. Remnick mollified him, asking to see the piece when it was done. Hersh cooled off, shrugged, and sent it. In the end, Remnick passed on Hersh's "walk-in" story, "The Killing of Osama Bin Laden." It would have been difficult to run a piece using unattributed sources after the SEALs piece had been attacked over this very question. When it came to a story countering the administration's narrative, Hersh needed on-the-record sourcing.

After the bin Laden piece became a book, *The Killing of Bin Laden*, I interviewed Hersh onstage in Brooklyn in 2016. He was very talkative, but also jet lagged, having flown in from London. And I couldn't keep the talk focused. His vignettes were amusing, but he pivoted to subvert my attempts to underline propaganda components of the bin Laden narrative in the mainstream.

When Hersh came to my class, "National Security Reporting: Secrets, Leaks & Whistleblowers," in 2021 for the School of *The New York Times*—a course for rising college freshmen—he was sharp, focused, and said something surprising. In the Q&A with students that followed his delightfully cranky talk, he offered advice to the students: don't take him too seriously. He himself doesn't. This charmed me. Yet it was what he said next that haunted me.

With each article, he holds back key information.

"Insurance," he called it.

One man's insurance, another man's lead. Was he serious? Was there something splashy that might *not* have made it into his memoir?

2.

Out on the sidewalk, before our food comes, I quote the "insurance" bit back to him. He launches into a stream-of-consciousness monologue, a mix of charm and sleight of hand. He's recounting—or self-positioning—a career of blockbuster stories. Each contains (I realize amidst the speed of his thoughts) hints of what he held back. This might also be material that could fill several more chapters of his memoir, which I hadn't yet finished.

The first bit of intel he asks me to keep secret. Later, I can't stop thinking about it. It was grim, involving brutal things done to a minor. Reminding myself to keep it off the record, I see that every single one of his asides and bon mots is also on his Wikipedia page.

Such as the theory that the My Lai massacre was a CIA operation. Though Second Lieutenant William Calley was treated as if he was the proverbial *one bad apple*, the operation was actually an assassination program anticipating the likes of Operation Phoenix (and the drone assassination program that killed an estimated 14,000 people in its second decade alone, under Obama and Trump).[10]

He also said something offhand that is common speculation among spy-watchers and hardly secret: that since it was formed in 1947, the CIA had been operating domestically (violating its charter). What was it doing? Spying on the left, of course, chasing journalists, poets, and whistleblowers into flight—over borders, out of print, or into their early graves.

I try a joke on him.

"Sy," I say, like I'm his friend. "How do you know a CIA agent is lying?"

"How?" he asks, looking bored.

"His lips are moving." I continue, "How do you know he's telling the truth?"

"How?"

"He's dead!"

He pauses.

"Actually, not bad," he says as a tomato soup and grilled cheese are set before him.

I sit across from him at a long table that we share with other diners. Pecking at his grilled cheese, he returns to his monologue about those insurance items left in the vault. (I will read in his memoir: "discriminating readers will know how much more I know—and did not tell.")[11]

Hersh adjusts his chair. The manhole cover he has been sitting on has a thumbhole in it, for lifting. Hersh's front chair leg falls into the thumbhole. As the chair gives way, Hersh shoots forward, falls half out of the seat. He's pinned between the table and chairback.

Unable to get around the table fast enough, I make useless gestures, standing over my chair. Finally, a few diners on his side of the table help him. Once upright, Hersh recovers his poise, calling for management.

When the manager arrives, Hersh points out the danger, telling the manager that it isn't his fault. But he also lets him know that if it happens again to someone else, it will be. It's a Freudian pratfall. A Freudian slip is when you confess to something you don't mean to; Hersh's stumble has that effect. "If it happens to someone else" is Hersh honoring his sources.

Through constant informational, soft power and physical warfare throughout the Cold War and since, the left's ideas are mooted and modified. Called radical, they're co-opted and cut in half, making their way—repurposed and domesticated—to the center, converted into half-measures. This has involved a network of interlocking campaigns, flows of information and other resources between big media, administration-friendly journalists, NGOs, intelligence staffers, corporate owners, all of which are arrayed against the urgency of the left—against stories like Hersh's. It's not a conspiracy. It's careerist, done in the open.

But Hersh recalls, too, in *Reporter* that his career would not be possible without civil servants who take their patriotic oath to serve the country and Constitution seriously. I'd forgotten this. Again and again during his long career, these are his sources. Rather than doing performative battle, we should keep an ear to the ground for honest leakers, he suggests.

When he joins me for another lunch after the depressing Ukraine war starts, he lets me out at the same station, shouting: "Give me a call when you figure out what you want to do with your life." In one of his first Substack scoops after mainstream media exile, he reports on the CIA's sabotage of the Nord Stream pipeline,[12] an act of environmental terrorism that President Biden had long before promised to do in a recorded speech,[13] but then blamed on Russia.[14]

The *real* story is how America's greatest reporter is now largely ignored by the mainstream media. As one former NYPD officer puts it in the pages to come: "It's like a baseball team depriving itself of its greatest slugger. How much better does it get than that?"

3.

The next day I ride out to Rockville for lunch with James Risen. Over Uruguayan tapas, he recalls a litany of Hersh's reportorial heroism. When I first met him six years before, Risen was at *The New York Times* and going through his own pushback crisis from the White House and the editors they were intimidating. He had been subpoenaed by the Obama administration over a source in what should have been a blockbuster story. He faced jail. The story in question reported on how a CIA operation backfired. The agency had falsified a nuclear weapons plan and slipped it to the Iranians. Scientists in Iran quickly spotted the fake segment of the plan and rewrote it correctly. The goal had been to misdirect the Iranian scientists, but this little taxpayer-funded slip took them closer than they had been to possessing a nuclear weapon. Never mind that hawks said Iran already had a nuke, hoping to use the fake weapon to invade.

Threatening him with jail time, the Obama Justice Department ordered Risen to reveal his source. The soft-spoken reporter remained stubborn, defending his source from the DOJ's unprecedented breaches of press freedom. As *Vanity Fair* put it: "The track record of the Obama administration—which has invoked the rarely utilized 1917 Espionage Act, enacted during World War I to deal with spies, to prosecute current and former government employees for sharing information with the press—is a surprising one for a team that in its early days promised increased openness and stronger protections for whistle-blowers."[15]

Laid back and soft spoken, Risen is deadpan and gently skeptical. He dons a sweatshirt and khakis and slouches as he sits. I order a Cuban sandwich, Risen orders a flatbread

PROLOGUE: MY FATHER'S HOUSE 13

panini, which he also enjoyed the last time he was here. He's spent the pandemic in his large house on a hundred acres not far from here.

He's just turned in his next book, *The Last Honest Man*, on Frank Church, the senator from Idaho. It will focus a great deal on the Church Committee, which investigated the CIA, its assassinations, coups, domestic operations, and other crimes, but through a common character in Church. He reminds me that Hersh's 1974 story on the CIA's illegal domestic operations led to the Church Committee hearings. Cheers to Sy. Then Risen tells me something like a joke about Gary Hart, senator from Colorado, and Jim Angleton, chief of CIA counterintelligence.

Hart infamously lost the 1988 primary for the Democratic nomination for president over an extramarital affair. But a decade before, he was investigating the Kennedy assassination for the Church Committee. Meaning, his work was enabled by Hersh and by freedom of the press. The Freedom of Information Act, or FOIA, ensuring that journalists can petition government agencies for their day-to-day doings, came from similar public interest journalism a decade before and Hersh and Church strengthened it. It meant to keep creeps like Angleton in line. As did the FISA Court, a court created to approve (or not) secret government surveillance requests. At one point, working for this transparency and this committee, Hart asked Angleton, the counterintelligence chief, to dinner, Risen recalls in a half-amused whisper. This is the setup.

In spy circles, thrillers and espionage studies, James Jesus Angleton is both legendary and obscure. He spoke in riddles; his impassive obsession with rare orchids, while quietly driving himself crazy with paranoia, became a Hollywood cliché: it was a *poetic* paranoia. What drove him was the question: which of his defector-spies was in fact a double agent for the Soviets?

To illustrate the contractions and contradictions of Angleton's mind, someone slapped T. S. Eliot's image onto it: "Wilderness of mirrors," also a cliché in espionage studies. In truth, Angleton was gullible. Vain: he let British spy Kim Philby operate as a double agent under his nose, simply because he liked him. He gave unwarranted credence to a Russian defector (who said all subsequent defectors would be moles, reporting to Moscow) and tortured one defector nearly to death, to get him to admit a fable: that he was a mole. But he wasn't.

Beyond this quaint, counterproductive paranoia shot through with inconsistent, badly aimed bouts of gullible trust, Angleton, also an Idaho native, maintained a sophisticated ineffability, answering officials as if he had been the spy-world's riddle of the Sphinx. It made him one of the most fictionalized (Mailer's *Harlot's Ghost*) and mythologized (his paranoia inspired Le Carre's *Tinker Tailor Soldier Spy*) of the first generation of CIA conmen, dissemblers, and prevaricators who posed as swashbucklers and heroes and who got dubbed, in half-sarcastic corrective, "the best and the brightest." It was *this* Angleton an earnest Gary Hart invited to dinner, under Church Committee auspices.

Hart asked Angleton—patriot to patriot—if Angleton's counterintelligence apparatus knew more than they had said on the Kennedy assassination. Many still thought of the killing as Fidel's retaliation for the agency's many attempts on his own life. (No evidence for this.) But according to Risen, Angleton sat across from Hart at a Washington restaurant, glanced at him noncommittally. In a soft-spoken deadpan, quoting John, 14:2, he said:

"In my father's house, there are many mansions."

4.

Risen's so-called "warrantless wiretapping" story, originally reported with Eric Lichtblau in fall 2004,[16] was delayed. As he has written and told interviewers (including me onstage in Brooklyn), their reporting revealed that the Bush administration was using extraordinary powers to spy on Americans, tapping our phones illegally, dragnet-style, without seeking approval from the FISA court put in place after the Church Committee in 1978.

It was a blockbuster that would likely have affected the Bush team's 2004 bid for reelection, turning the White House back to Democrats. Instead, Risen and Lichtblau's editors sent the story to the Bush administration for vetting, a long practice at the paper, in some cases to ensure a story not be discredited for small errors.[17]

What happened next is tragic: The administration warned that the *Times* leadership would have "blood on [their] hands" if the story ran. The editors held it until long after the election, only publishing it when Risen told them how silly the paper would look if the story ran in his book *State of War* before it ran under his *Times* byline. The warning worked, and the *Times* finally ran it, but far too late to impact voters.[18]

Incidentally, Edward Snowden remembered this when he deliberated over where to leak a follow-up revelation nine years later. In thousands of files, he revealed that this dragnet surveillance expanded exponentially into our virtual lives, amounting to hundreds of thousands of felonies by the federal government as they spied on us. For what they did to Risen's story, he ruled out *The Times*. To Snowden, it was no longer the *Times* of *The Pentagon Papers*, of Sy Hersh's heyday.[19]

Understanding his frustration, I sit across from Risen and am confronted again by his curiosity and affability. I tell him I was impressed with his reporting for *Pay Any Price*, which followed the transit of American dollars, billions of greenbacks piled onto wooden crates that landed in an Iraqi cave, then in Jordan, stacks of which found their way home in loot nabbed by American soldiers. It was an unforgettable image of war as a corruption super-spreader, of broken American institutions. I add that he's clever to tell the story of runaway corruption at the CIA through a figure like Frank Church. A singular character to follow makes a story sing.

Nodding, he asks what I'm doing. I tell him of my pandemic research on Indonesia's Pramoedya Ananta Toer, whose fourteen years in an anticommunist gulag, from which he smuggled out seven novels, was underwritten by the United States. The propaganda version of the Cold War insists that the US supported human rights and freedom of expression. But anyone who reads history knows that, in the immortal words of the Gospel of John, as quoted by super-spy Jim Angleton, himself quoted by Gary Hart, subsequently quoted by Jim Risen:

My father's house has many mansions.

When acts of routine American censorship—passport denial, disinformation, public lying, and blacklisting—boil over into something more toxic—including financial persecution, arrest, and execution—honest figures like those highlighted in this book are forced into flight.

In cars, on horseback, by air, or on foot, these archetypal progressives—facing persecution—must focus their energies on survival at borders, in deserts, before they can return to democracy and freedom. They are impeded on all sides by bigots of both stripes—the boorish reactionaries and the centrist liberals who appease, or preempt, them. These are flights, also, because any cure for this miserable American psychosis involves mental and spiritual motion. As Toni Morrison observed, "You wanna fly, you got to give up the shit that weighs you down."[20]

After the brick is flung through her window, Lorraine is running, ducking. As a result of the lies spread about him and his book, Graham is running, punching back, laughing. From a mob, Paul is running, ducking, standing, singing. From death threats made on behalf of General Gustavo Rojas Pinilla, Gabo is running, fleeing into exile. From federal agents parked outside their house, grilling their neighbors, poets George and Mary are running, and then driving through the scorching desert. Their blue parakeet pants in the heat.

*

From a gaslighting neocon, Frances is running—with her notebook hidden as he drinks himself honest on cheap wine. From the NYC secret police and the FBI, from his bodyguard-informant, and his "honorable" teacher, from a bomb planted in his house and his newfound pennilessness, Malcolm is running, cursing. From brutal October 2 killings in the plaza, Octavio is running. From Stalin's assassins, Mexican police, the Rockefellers' security guards, and Detroit's right-wing protests, Diego is running. From agents lurking in her hotels, interviewing staff, searching the cushions for her abandoned film, Angela is running. From the largest manhunt in FBI history, Leonard is running, heading north.

*

From the memory of a negative birth-rate, repression of the Sun Dance, from his grandmother's vision of deicide, Scott is running; from the death of his grandfather, Scott's protagonist, too, is running. From lies spread in The New World and The New York Times, Miguel is running. From lies spread about her, and the horror of her father and brother's death, both by fire, Rigoberta is running. From stonewalling generals, the State Department, Jennifer is running, starving herself. From a posse of gunmen on the eve of her birthday, Berta is running. But neither she, nor Everardo, can run now. From their horror, their PTSD, we are running. We, too, are running for their lives.

1952

Amplifier: Lorraine Hansberry in Midtown

and how she was almost killed by a brick, before her parents
fled Yankee racism to Mexico

In May 1963, in a Kennedy family living room on Central Park South, Lorraine Hansberry tried to defend civil rights activists from being beaten. The *Raisin in the Sun* playwright had come along with actor Harry Belafonte, author James Baldwin, and other luminaries at the invitation of Robert F. Kennedy. She listened as activist Jerome Smith tried to impress upon the attorney general the level of violence protesters were facing in the South. Smith had been beaten in Birmingham and had come straight from the Freedom Rides for medical treatment on his jaw and head.

Among the more prestigious attendees, it was this young activist who spoke first. He chided Kennedy for not doing enough to protect protesters. On television and in newspapers around the world, it was clear that African American protesters were routinely punched, kicked, spat upon, clubbed, hosed, and had police dogs sicced on them. For what? Wanting to vote? Equal protection? Just being there, he said, made him sick at the administration's inaction. When Kennedy turned away from Smith—as if to say, "I'll talk to all of you, who are civilized. But who is he?"—Hansberry "unleashed," Imani Perry writes in her recent biography. There were many accomplished individuals in the room, Hansberry said. But Smith's was the "voice of twenty-two million people."[1] Kennedy should not only listen; he should give his "moral commitment" to protect those like Smith.

The meeting ended abruptly. Hansberry invited Smith to speak at a fundraiser a week later in Westchester, which raised $5,000. Part of that amount purchased a Ford station wagon[2] that turned up in the news a year later: empty, burned, and three civil rights workers missing.[3] A month after the car was found, the activists were discovered dead in a ditch. What if Bobby Kennedy had listened to Smith and Hansberry? The oft-told vignette is given new urgency in Perry's *Looking for Lorraine*, a powerful retelling of Hansberry's short but dazzling life. (Perry offers insights in Tracy Heather Strain's visually beautiful 2017 documentary *Sighted Eyes/ Feeling Heart*,[4] too.)

The first Black woman playwright to produce a play on Broadway and the daughter of the first Black family to move into white Chicago, Hansberry grew distrustful of the cult of firsts, as well as of celebrity activism and liberal incrementalism. Though she died at thirty-four and only produced two plays during her lifetime, her work and ideas continue to reverberate; since her 1965 death, a Hollywood, Broadway, or other large-scale adaptation of *A Raisin in the Sun* has come out at least once per decade, along with a stream of posthumous plays and prose. Almost 60 years after her death, *The Sign in Sidney Brustein's Window* has just debuted on Broadway. But like her friend James Baldwin, it is Hansberry's political pronouncements that resonate most profoundly. These are scattered but potent arrows that, as Perry writes, gave "public voice to her belief that the Black working class [was] at the center of the struggle for liberation, and that she must be an amplifier, not a figurehead."[5]

A Brick

Lorraine Hansberry's father's successes, and failures, rushed into her consciousness one afternoon, piggybacking on a brick* that flew through her window, almost crushing her.

---

* A chunk of mortar in other tellings.

Carl Hansberry migrated from Mississippi, where he had studied at Alcorn State. Her mother, Nannie, migrated from Tennessee. The youngest of four, Lorraine came into the world on May 19, 1930 (sharing a birthday with Malcolm X). Her mother gave birth in "Provident, the first Black-owned and operated hospital in the nation."[6]

Carl was in real estate. As Black transplants crowded into Chicago, Hansberry ("the Kitchenette King") cut larger apartments into smaller units. "The kitchenettes allowed Carl . . . to provide housing for Black residents who, due to discrimination, were squished into far too small a terrain."[7] With the considerable money he made from real estate, Carl gave to organizations that sought to end racial discrimination. He became secretary of the local NAACP chapter, donating $10,000 to endow the Hansberry Foundation.[8] Lorraine looked up to him—by some accounts, worshiped him.

As a girl, Lorraine spent time alone, thinking, observing. "The honesty of their living is there in the shabbiness," she wrote of the poor Black families surrounding her, "scrubbed porches that sag and look their danger. Dirty gray wood steps. And always a line of white and pink clothes . . . waving in the dirty wind of the city. . . . Our south side is a place apart . . . each piece of our living is a protest."[9]

In spring 1937, Carl bought a house in the South Side neighborhood of Woodlawn, expecting a legal battle. The house, at 6140 South Rhodes Avenue, was just inside the "white section" enforced by restrictive covenants. One day, the family bodyguard saw a crowd outside. He led Lorraine and her sister, Mamie, inside, "and that's when they threw this huge piece of mortar," Mamie recalls in *Sighted Eyes/Feeling Heart*. "That mortar lodged in the wall. And just missed [Lorraine]," who was seven.

As Perry notes on-screen, "It's in that moment that she recognizes that notwithstanding her family's prosperity, she was still going to be subjected to racial violence like every other Black American." Hansberry recalled "my desperate and courageous mother patrolling our house all night with a loaded German Luger, doggedly guarding her four children."[10]

These battles were not unique. "There were literally hundreds of cases across the Midwest of white mob violence in response to individual efforts to integrate," Perry writes. "The consequences were destroyed property, lost homes, trauma, and sometimes death." While in the South racial apartheid meant segregated public transportation and lynching, up north, "real estate was the border of racial status."[11]

Around when the brick landed in the drywall, Nannie and Carl took the children on a trip to Nannie's mother's Tennessee. While driving, they passed the hills of Kentucky, where Nannie "directed her children, from the car, to look at the hills." Nannie recalled:

> that her father, their grandfather, had escaped to [those hills] when he was a boy. A runaway slave as a child, he was protected by his own mother. She kept him alive by wandering into the forested hills in the middle of the night, leaving food and other provisions. Lorraine found the hills beautiful.[12]

"I Must Perhaps Go To Jail"

Soon after moving, a court ruling forced the Hansberrys out of their new house. Carl appealed the case all the way to the Supreme Court, yielding a partial victory three years later.

While the court upheld the restrictive covenant, it deemed that the contracts were poorly written: the Hansberrys could stay at 6140 South Rhodes Avenue. The court also opened up five hundred new properties to Black residents.

Through the NAACP and other civil rights groups, Carl and Nannie attacked segregation in travel and in the military. But they began to feel that little had been gained. After years of striving, they recognized with bitterness that Chicago was still segregated. They decided to move to Mexico City. Carl felt free for the first time in his life.

Lorraine stayed in Chicago to complete her schooling, where, despite segregation, an efflorescence of cultural and artistic expression had taken place in Lorraine's youth, a Black Renaissance. Black writers' collectives grew out of the Communist Party. "Perhaps the most important project in the 1930s for Black Chicagoans," writes Perry, "was the Negro in Illinois project of the [New Deal's Works Progress Administration],"

> which enlisted dozens of workers to study the world of Black Chicago under the directorship of Black sociologists . . . Among the writers who worked on the Negro in Illinois were future literary luminaries Gwendolyn Brooks, Richard Wright, and Margaret Walker.[13]

Two months before her sixteenth birthday, Lorraine received a devastating telegram: her father had died of a cerebral hemorrhage. "In reflection years later," writes Perry, "Lorraine would describe her father as a 'real American type American,' who believed in struggling for equality 'the respectable way.' And yet it was clear . . . that such efforts were rarely rewarded in kind." Lorraine would later write that "the cost in emotional turmoil, time and money" of his battles against segregation "led to my father's early death."[14] She added, "Daddy felt that this country was hopeless ... [and] became a refugee from America. He bought a house in ... a suburb of Mexico City, and we were planning to move there when he died."[15]

After two years at the University of Wisconsin, Hansberry arrived in New York, seeking "an education of another kind."[16] She moved uptown to take a job at a new magazine in Harlem called *Freedom*, launched by left-wing actor, singer, and activist Paul Robeson. At *Freedom*, she amassed a number of bylines, reviewing Richard Wright's *The Outsider* ("exalts brutality"), Howard Fast's *Spartacus* (should have been told through the eyes of the enslaved), and the Japanese film *Hiroshima* (defending it both as propaganda and art).[17] Described by her editor in chief as "the girl who could do everything,"[18] she joined the Communist Party and Labor Youth League and wore many hats, thinking and writing on a broader, more global canvas.

Hansberry wrote on independence movements in Africa, praised her renowned uncle Leo's former student, Kwame Nkrumah, who fought for Ghanaian independence, and began to see the fight against Jim Crow in the United States as part of an international struggle of Black and brown people. She took up poetry, publishing in *Masses and Men* on topics such as life in poor Chicago and the execution of Willie McGee, a Black man falsely accused of raping a white woman.

In exchanges with friends from college, Hansberry fully embraced her leftism, writing: "I am sick of poverty, lynching, stupid wars and the universal maltreatment of my people and obsessed with a rather desperate desire for a new world for me and my brothers. So dear friend, I must perhaps go to jail. Please at the next painting session you have . . . remember this 'Communist!'"[19]

Condemned by the State

Around the same time, Hansberry began studying at the Jefferson School of Social Science, a Communist Party–affiliated center for adult education in Harlem, where she befriended one of its luminary instructors, W. E. B. Du Bois. The famed radical "recognized Lorraine's gifts, and . . . she became his favorite student . . . gifted enough to teach others as well as study under his tutelage."[20]

The admiration was mutual. In her diary, Hansberry praised Du Bois's mind and manner. "Tenderly noting his idiosyncrasies alongside the enormity of his influence," writes Perry, "she distilled Du Bois [as] freedom's passion personified. . . . Her own admiration of beauty and elegance, her own aspirations toward the life of the mind, sat there in front of her."[21] Jotting down his bon mots—"Somehow you have got to know more than what you experience individually"[22]—she conceived a moral and political action plan, a politics based on understanding the way that needs of others intersect with one's own.

But she also saw that however influential Du Bois was on the Left, McCarthyism had rendered him persona non grata. He and Robeson "were prime targets within an intellectual and political community of Black socialists and communists who were under surveillance," writes Perry. "Being a communist wasn't strange back then." But it did make "you vulnerable to steady attack from the powerful."[23] Du Bois had circulated a petition against nuclear weapons, "and in response he was arrested and indicted for being an agent of the Soviet Union."[24]

Efforts to discredit Black activists and leftists as agents of the Soviet Union, particularly during the Korean War, was a standard ploy. Du Bois's peace and anti-nuclear weapons organization, the Peace Information Center, was forced to register as a foreign agent. When Du Bois and his comrades refused, they were arrested. "As a result of the trial," writes Perry,

> he became a pariah in many circles. At the time when Lorraine sat before him as a student, he was so stigmatized that he found himself struggling to buy groceries. And in 1952, his passport was revoked. The State Department claimed they took it because they could not authorize him to attend a peace conference in Canada, but it had the effect of limiting his connections and political influence and potentially his moving abroad.[25]

The case was dismissed when his defense attorney announced that Albert Einstein would appear as a character witness. Yet while other luminaries, like Langston Hughes, stood by him, Du Bois was embittered by those who wouldn't. The NAACP, which Du Bois had cofounded in 1909 (and for whom Lorraine's father had worked), refused to issue even a mild statement of support.

Meanwhile, Robeson's passport had already been revoked, blocking his work as a global entertainer and activist. As a result of the ban, Lorraine agreed to go as his proxy to the Inter-American Peace Conference in Montevideo, Uruguay, in March 1952, which was held underground to avoid repression. At the 280-delegate conference, Hansberry was one of five US delegates who witnessed the organizers' necessary subterfuge, which "consisted of delegates pretending they were having parties by playing loud music and dancing outdoors... Whenever they retreated indoors:

> they delivered conference papers. On Lorraine's first full day of the conference, she attended a women's meeting ... and listened to an address by a former woman deputy of the Uruguayan Parliament. After the address there was some communication in Spanish that Lorraine didn't understand. . . . A woman approached her and said, in English, that Lorraine had been one of the honored women who should sit on the presidium and speak. Stunned, Lorraine stepped up to deliver her report.[26]

Soon interrupted by police, Hansberry watched the gathering camouflage itself as a prissy ladies' tea. When the police left, Hansberry continued. The Brazilian delegate honored her with red carnations; she was moved, thinking "of the women who had been jailed and terrorized in the U.S. for their activism ... of her people suffering, and she was honored to be selected, the sole Black American woman at the conference, to represent them all."[27]

That summer, after Lorraine continued to teach at the Jefferson School, an officer from the State Department knocked on the door of her mother's house and confiscated her passport. She was twenty-two.

The Communist Line?

Two years after Hansberry moved to New York, a comrade from the Labor Youth League, Robert Nemiroff, began courting her. When the relationship threatened to get serious, she wrote him a firm reminder of her priorities, admitting that "I *do* love you, you wide-eyed immature unsophisticated revolutionary," adding,

1. *I am a writer. I am going to write.*
2. *I am going to become a writer.*
3. *Any real contribution I make to the movement can only be the result of a disciplined life. I am going to institute discipline in my life.*
4. *I can paint. I am going to paint.*

THE END.[28]

They married on the same sweltering weekend in June 1953 that Julius and Ethel Rosenberg were executed for espionage. The specter haunted their wedding. Hansberry recalled a ceremony overshadowed by "the desire . . . to thrust one's arms into the air . . . screaming at one's countrymen to come . . . down from the houses, to get up from the television sets, from the dinner tables." The bride, she wrote, "sits a moment in the corner, alone . . . she thinks . . . And what shall I say to my children?"[29]

This was rhetorical. Hansberry would never have children. But after reading Simone de Beauvoir's *The Second Sex,* "her mind afire . . . with ideas from France,"[30] she also doubted marriage. The book shaped her and Nemiroff's anything-but-conventional partnership. Like his wife, Nemiroff also hoped to write, but repeatedly committed himself to supporting her work.

After Lorraine left *Freedom*, both of them took odd jobs. Nemiroff wrote a pop love song adapted from a Calypso standard. It became a hit, and the windfall allowed Hansberry to write full time. The pressure could sometimes overwhelm her. *Sighted Eyes* reenacts a moment when she tosses the *Raisin in the Sun* manuscript in the air.

Nemiroff quietly collects pages from the floor and sets them aside. A few days later, he places them before her; she nods and gets back to work.³¹

"Here was a family living in the Chicago South Side ghetto," writes Perry of the play's story. "Armed with a $10,000 life insurance check after the death of the father, they hope to move out of their tiny kitchenette apartment and into a house in a segregated white neighborhood. The adult son, Walter Lee, dreams of becoming a businessman. His sister, Beneatha, aspires to become a doctor. The matriarch, Lena, and her daughter-in-law are most of all hoping for a home of their own."³² When it was done, Hansberry and Nemiroff invited producer Phil Rose to spaghetti. Hansberry read her play aloud after serving banana cream pie.

Rose telephoned in the morning. "I want to produce your play," he said.³³ But Sidney Poitier, cast as Walter Lee Younger, told Strain that investors were scared that no audience would come. Hoping to prove that "greed [might] triumph over bigotry," they put the play up in New Haven, Philadelphia, and Chicago.³⁴ A thousand Black actors lined up to audition. The early buzz caught the eye and ear of FBI director J. Edgar Hoover.

When casting began, the agency had already been tailing Hansberry for years. But before looking over her literary work, they reviewed her style, noting in one memo her "Italian cut" hairstyle.³⁵ The media did the same, also conflating Hansberry's looks with her politics. "Her physical beauty and grace added to their confusion about *who* she actually was, politically speaking," writes Perry.³⁶ *Vogue* depicted Hansberry "as a woman still dressed in the 'collegiate style.'"³⁷ After the local New Haven branch missed its run there, Hoover ordered a New York–based special agent "to conduct a necessary investigation to establish whether the play . . . is controlled or influenced by the Communist Party [or] in any way follows the Communist line."[38]

Their definition was capacious: any figure or material critical of US Cold War policy could be deemed beyond the pale. After the peace conference in Uruguay, the agency had placed Hansberry on its Security Index, a list of supposedly dangerous and presumably disloyal Americans who were to be rounded up in camps in the event of war or some other emergency.

For the country's top law enforcement agency, reviews and clippings of the play weren't enough to gauge whether it toed the Communist line. So a Philadelphia special agent was sent to the Walnut Street Theater. "The play contains no comments of any nature about Communism as such," the agent deadpanned. And he went on, across four pages, to describe the play's views on "negro aspirations, the problems inherent in their efforts to advance themselves."[39]

In the same February 5, 1959 memo, the agent explained that he opted not to follow through with an interview of Hansberry since "the subject and her play have received considerable notoriety in the NY press . . . and the Bureau could be placed in an embarrassing position if it became known . . . that the Bureau"[40] was investigating writers like Hansberry.

A Keynote, Erased

On March 1, 1959, Hansberry was invited to deliver the keynote at the First Conference of Negro Writers at New York's Hudson Hotel. Almost certainly unknown to her, the CIA had set up the sponsoring organization, the American Society of African Culture, to counter the Black radicalism and anti-imperialism of the day, replicating what it had done with cultural movements like the Congress for Cultural Freedom, student groups like the National Students Association, and many others.

Although Langston Hughes was among the attendees, the group arrayed at the Hudson that March day was more conservative in its makeup than the activists Hansberry had met in Montevideo. Her radical talk struck a discordant note. "One cannot live with sighted eyes and feeling heart and not know the miseries which afflict this world," she told the crowd:

> Let no Negro artist who thinks himself deserving of the title take pen to paper . . . if in doing so the content of that which he presents or performs suggests to the nations of the world that our people do not yet languish under privation and hatred and brutality and political oppression in every state of the forty-eight.[41]

Speaking of art as a "war against illusions," Hansberry suggested that "whatever the corruption within our people," artists must "tear it out and expose it and let us then take the measure of what is left . . . the most painful exigency of cultural and social life will not be exempt from exploration by my mind or pen." Arguing for self-criticism and radical truth-telling, Hansberry added that any necessary exposure by artists of oversights "of our people will not result in a denigrated image" but will "only heighten and make more real the inescapable image of their greatness and courage."[42]

That radicals were granted time at the podium of the Hudson Hotel might seem to speak to the honesty of the debate curated by the organizers at AMSAC. But when the published account of the conference appeared in 1960, the only trace of Hansberry was a photograph of her among the attendees. Hers and other radicals' speeches had been erased from the commemorative booklet. Hansberry's speech, "The Negro Writer and His Roots," remained unpublished for another twenty-one years.[43]

"Propagandistic Writing"

Ten days after her keynote, on March 11, *A Raisin in the Sun* debuted at the Ethel Barrymore Theatre on Broadway. A few Black audience members came the first night, the second night more, and by the third, at least half of those watching were African American. When the play opened, Poitier was starring in the film *Porgy and Bess*. Lloyd Richards puzzled out the math: he approached an elderly Black audience member and asked her why she was willing to pay $4 for a Poitier play when she could pay 85 cents to see him in a film. She told Richards proudly that she had heard that the play dealt with "something that concerns me." He never forgot her phrasing.[44]

Opening night ended with a standing ovation and the crowd demanding that Hansberry take a bow. She hid in her seat until Poitier strode into the audience to lead her onstage. The play won the New York Drama Critics Award, completed a long run, was translated into twenty languages, and afforded Hansberry instant celebrity.[45]

Two days after the Broadway premiere, Hollywood producers approached Hansberry, who sought a wider audience for the play, but was wary, insisting, "No one is going to turn this into a minstrel show . . . And if this blocks a sale, then it just won't be sold." In the end, it didn't block a sale. Columbia optioned it. But battles over her attempts to move the drama outside the Youngers' South Side apartment and into the streets of Chicago were constant.[46]

One producer wrote that the play's "race elements" "may lessen the sympathy of the audience, [or] give the effect of propagandistic writing." Hansberry's second draft was returned with 106 numbered notes from mogul Samuel Briskin, who tried to excise what he called "jive expressions" and deleted mentions of "Africans," "revolutionaries," and more. The strategy for marketing the film in the South was to avoid letting "people know in advance that it's about Negroes," branding it instead as a *prestige* film.[47]

Briskin's Columbia partnered with Glenn E. Miller Productions, its "new arm specializing in film production for military and defense purposes."[48] Briskin himself had done film propaganda during World War II.[49] Another major studio (Paramount) was found to have a CIA-paid undercover image watchdog on salary, someone who could kill or rewrite scripts to remove critiques of the United States, often excising realistic portrayals of American segregation, poverty, or violence.[50]

But *A Raisin in the Sun*, which opened ten days after Hansberry's thirty-first birthday, was a film of which she could be proud. Though much that she meant to keep in was left on the cutting room floor, the final result won a special humanitarian honor at the Cannes Film Festival and earned Hansberry a best screenplay nomination from the Screen Actors Guild.[51]

Hearing the Thunder

In 1962, Hansberry moved from Greenwich Village, where she'd lived with Nemiroff, into her own house in Croton, New York—which was a stone's throw from Peekskill, where infamous riots broke out in 1949. In journal entries, short stories, anonymous letters, and with friends, Hansberry came out as lesbian. While she and Nemiroff remained confidantes, friends, and collaborators, the two separated before the play was finished. Her two acres in the Croton Woods—which she named Chitterling Heights—afforded her shelter from the bustle and obligations of the city. At Croton, she began work on plays about Haiti's liberator Toussaint Louverture, white supremacists, and other political subjects, but stomach pains frequently interrupted her work.

One day, James Baldwin called to invite her to a meeting with President Kennedy's brother, the attorney general. The Kennedys' initial approach to civil rights had been distant accommodation, hoping to politically manage the protests in a way that wouldn't reflect poorly on the administration during its bid for a second term. Until 1963, they remained aloof, effectively allowing violence to besiege protesters in cities across the South while the infrastructure of white supremacy maintained its hold on institutions across the North.[52]

At the meeting, a period of pleasantries preceded Jerome Smith's criticism of the administration. But one matter that was obscured in the many retellings of this meeting was Smith's urgent anti-war message, according to Perry. The Vietnam war was accelerating. As Harry Belafonte paraphrased, Smith told the attorney general: "In the midst of our oppression, you expect to find us giddily going to fight a war? It's your war, it's unjust, unfair, and so dishonorable [that] it should shame you. I wouldn't pick up a gun to fight for this country. I'd die first."[53] It was a sentiment Paul Robeson, Malcolm X and Martin Luther King also took up.

But the reflex to defend a war waged in the name of liberals running from the charge of being "soft on communism" was the impetus for Kennedy's dismissing Smith and disdainfully turning away. And this dismissal triggered Hansberry to underline Smith's words—interrupting the pleasantries to point out the violence. It was only then that the evening "imploded."[54]

After the group split up, Baldwin took a car to an interview, spotting Hansberry on Central Park South and walking toward Fifth Avenue, "her face twisted, her hands clasped before her belly, eyes darker than any eyes I had ever seen before—walking in an absolutely private place."[55] He couldn't call out to her. He was already late.

But the winds were blowing in Smith and Hansberry's direction. Less than a month later, at his brother Robert's urging, President Kennedy "gave his landmark civil rights address during which he proposed the legislation that would be known as the Civil Rights Act of 1964." In that address, the president "spoke of civil rights as not just a legal issue but also, as Lorraine suggested, a *moral* one."[56]

Perry, whose *Looking for Lorraine* is supple, wise, radical, and intimate, makes another important stipulation: we talk today of the civil rights movement as a single movement without debates about tactics. Perry makes clear that, of course, the same debates about destroyed property took place "back then" when the Black protesters on the streets of Birmingham "were considered out of control, pushing too fast and hard." Moreover, she acknowledges that "They raced beyond the authority of Martin Luther King Jr.'s Southern Christian Leadership Conference. They had their own local leaders, and they were not uniformly committed to nonviolence."[57]

This would increasingly be Hansberry's position: scoffing at the notion of going too fast, or of the utility of making only incremental, cautious change, while activists like the three who drove Hansberry's donated station wagon were being killed. She called the influence of white liberals "corrupt,"[58] and suggested the solution was to engage in dialogues that might convince them that they should become radicals,[59] adding (a year before Malcolm X would use the phrase "by any means necessary"):

> *I think then that Negroes must concern themselves with every single means of struggle: legal, illegal, passive, active, violent and non-violent. That they must harass, debate, petition, give money to court struggles, sit in, lie-down, strike, boycott, sing hymns, pray on steps, and shoot from their windows when the racists come cruising through their communities. The acceptance of our present condition is the only form of extremism which discredits us before our children.*[60]

As she rushed to do more for the movement and to complete her plays, Hansberry was struck with pancreatic cancer, which was ominously depicted in Baldwin's observation of her leaving the Kennedy meeting. She died on January 12, 1965, at the age of thirty-four.

Malcolm X attended her funeral, sitting quietly in the back. He would be murdered five weeks and five days after Hansberry's death. Martin Luther King sent a message of tribute. "Her creative ability," said King, "and her profound grasp of the deep social issues confronting the world today will remain an inspiration to generations yet unborn."[61]

1952

Nonsense of All These Years:
Graham Greene in Vietnam

or how the film version of his novel *The Quiet American* was eviscerated by the CIA

1.

When the film version of Graham Greene's novel *The Quiet American* was released in early 1958, Greene was not happy. He skipped the premieres in New York and Washington, D.C., and later called the movie "a complete travesty."[1] Greene usually liked to see his novels adapted, but not this time. What Greene was trying to say about American ignorance and arrogance in foreign affairs was turned upside down by a Cold War, McCarthy-era fear of bringing a movie to the public that might be seen as "anti-American."

There were two key figures who prevented the faithful adaptation of Greene's novel. One was the director and screenwriter Joseph Mankiewicz. Known for such mid-century blockbusters as *A Letter to Three Wives* (1949), *All About Eve* (1950), and *Guys and Dolls* (1955), Mankiewicz had a reputation as a liberal patriot. Greene was initially hopeful about the film, writing producers to suggest locations in Vietnam, which was the setting for the novel.

The other figure involved in the butchery was Edward Lansdale. Lansdale had spent time in Vietnam in the 1950s as a CIA agent with an Air Force cover. In 1956, Mankiewicz traveled to Saigon, where he met members of the American Friends of Vietnam, the so-called "Vietnam Lobby," including Lansdale. It was a fateful turn. Mankiewicz hired Lansdale as a film consultant. Of course, the CIA man had no respect for Greene, a British novelist who could not be trusted to understand American strategies to defeat communism in Vietnam.

The capitulation of a major Hollywood director to Cold War constraints, and the feud between Greene and Lansdale that ensued, may seem at first glance to be a tale from the distant world of the 1950s, when any whiff of subversive views could get a writer, musician, or actor blacklisted. But there are two stories here and both of them speak to the world that we live in today.

The primary story is the one that Greene told in his 1955 novel, which closely tracks real events in Vietnam in the early 1950s. The American reflex to develop doomed counterinsurgency strategies that Greene was warning about led to a long series of bloody conflicts, first in Vietnam and later in Central and South America, Iraq, and Afghanistan. The other story emerged later—about how and why the movie was made the way it was. We see something familiar there, too.

The readiness of liberals and conservatives to reject or suppress the truth about the dark side of American policy—indeed, of any critique of this nation's oppression, foreign or domestic—is as present as today's wave of laws clamping down on how history is taught, what kind of "subversive" criticism will not be tolerated, and what kind of novels must be blacklisted or purged from schools—especially those featuring what censors call "divisive concepts."[2]

2.

The Quiet American is a work of remarkable prescience. Greene takes the reader into the Vietnam of 1952, just as France was attempting to preserve colonial control while American diplomats and agents began to develop schemes to foil communist plots. Greene depicted scenes that later became part of the nightly news but were unknown to most Americans in the mid-1950s: a Vietnam that was a cauldron of complicated, shifting alliances among corrupt generals with private armies, nighttime raids by Vietminh guerrillas, and French bombing raids in which napalm bombs were dropped over villages. There is sex and opium; there are Saigon hotels where diplomats mix with loud, heavy-drinking journalists. And what Greene saw clearly was the American delusion that spycraft and the promotion of "democracy" could manipulate events in a country they knew only as a piece on a geopolitical chessboard.

The story is told by a jaded British journalist, Thomas Fowler, who covers Indochina's liberation war with France. In the opening scenes, a young American operative named Alden Pyle is found dead. Fowler goes on to recall the tangled experiences he'd had with Pyle, a maddening character who befriends Fowler, falls in love with Fowler's mistress, and speaks of the noble American effort to find a "Third Force" that could save Vietnam from colonialism and communism. Pyle's ideas come straight from a Harvard professor named York Harding, who could be modeled on any number of actual Ivy League Cold War theorists devoted to foreign policy "realism," red-baiting, and modernization.[3]

As the French lose battles, Pyle is part of an American strategy to reach out to other forces. He finds a former leader of Cao Dai, an armed religious sect whose teachings blend Catholicism, Buddhism, and Confucianism. (In its grand cathedral in Saigon, the sect depicts Victor Hugo as a saint.) Trained by the Japanese, the Cao Dai first fought the French alongside the communist Vietminh, then turned against the Vietminh to help the French. Pyle makes contact with a splinter group led by General Thé, who believes he can create an independent, noncommunist state. In pursuit of this Third Force, General Thé and Pyle form the novel's nexus of shadowy alliances.

For most of the novel, Fowler doesn't know quite what Pyle is up to behind the scenes—he's too caught up in the love triangle. While Fowler covers a battle in Phat Diem,

Pyle journeys there to profess his love of Phuong, Fowler's girlfriend. Fowler is injured in a firefight and Pyle saves him from dying along the side of a road. That does little to ease the pain of losing Phuong to Pyle. Fowler's hatred of him, and all things American, rankles: "I began—almost unconsciously—to run down everything that was American. My conversation was full of the poverty of American literature, the scandals of American politics, the beastliness of American children. It was as though she were being taken from me by a nation rather than by a man."[4]

Eventually Fowler learns that General Thế has plotted acts of sabotage using bicycle pumps to seed Saigon with small explosions (which actually happened). While the Americans fund Thế, the media blames the Vietminh. Fowler fails to get the true story out: "My [media] colleagues . . . knew they could only get space [in their outlets] by making fun of the [exploding bicycle] affair. . . . All of them blamed the Communists. I was the only one to write that the bombs were a demonstration on the part of General Thế, and my account was altered in the office."[5]

The story builds to a climax that was meant to show the human toll of American meddling. A bomb goes off in a crowded square, killing and maiming civilians. On the day of the bombing, Fowler visits a nearby cafe. He overhears American Legation wives recalling how they were warned not to go out. They rush off. But suddenly the cafe's mirrors explode into shards and a woman's compact lands on his lap. Running toward the square—and seeing a trishaw driver on the ground with his legs blown off—he grasps that this has been an act of terror.

He knows that Phuong normally would be at her favorite milk-bar on the square at this very hour. Stopped at the police barricade, Fowler turns to see Pyle watching.

Fowler demands they go find Phuong. She's fine, Pyle says. He'd warned her to stay home. Fowler understands that Pyle and Thé have plotted the bombing, Pyle supplying the *plastique* explosive while Thé framed the Vietminh.

It was supposed to be a military parade, Pyle mutters—only military men were supposed to be hurt. The parade was canceled, says Fowler. Pyle observes the carnage, as Fowler scolds: "This is the hour when the place is always full of women and children. . . . How many dead colonels justify a child or a trishaw driver's death, when you are building a national democratic front?"[6]

This stark reality, at odds with Washington's humanitarian rhetoric, was Greene's warning. Shortly before the bombing, Fowler had upbraided Pyle with his British skepticism: "We are the old colonial peoples, Pyle, but we've learnt a bit of reality, we've learned not to play with matches. This Third Force—it comes out of a book, that's all. General Thé's only a bandit with a few thousand men: he's not a national democracy."[7]

3.

Joseph Mankiewicz was fresh off of projects with Marlon Brando (*Julius Caesar*, 1953) and Humphrey Bogart (*The Barefoot Contessa*, 1954) when *The Quiet American* landed on the *New York Times* bestseller list. It stayed there for sixteen weeks. His older brother was Herman Mankiewicz, famous as the co-writer of *Citizen Kane* (recently the subject of the David Fincher film *Mank*). Joseph Mankiewicz secured the movie rights to *The Quiet American* in 1956. He has admitted in interviews that he was offended by the portrayal of Pyle and the novel's lack of sympathy with American anti-communist intentions. He was quoted when the movie came out explaining that "Greene's book made me so mad, I was determined to make a picture of it."[8]

He found just the man to share his ire. Edward Lansdale was a former adman who became an important figure in American counterinsurgency. In a previous posting in the Philippines he found dead civilians whom his trainees took for Huk fighters. Seeing a missed opportunity (the dead men had not been tortured for information), Lansdale had his men place two holes in one's neck and hang him upside down from a tree near the forest's edge. To exploit the villagers' fear of vampires and block them from enlisting, he ordered the trainees to drain the corpse's blood.

In Vietnam, too, optics mattered. Lansdale grew close to the corrupt US puppet, Ngo Dinh Diem, who assembled a Vietnam Lobby of conservative Catholics, liberal anti-communists, and intelligence-adjacent wonks who vowed to use nonprofit fronts to prop up an anti-communist regime whose methods included mass arrests and torture.

Mankiewicz knew before he met Lansdale that the Hollywood production code would not allow certain details from Greene's novel to reach an American film audience: for instance, Pyle would never be portrayed as working for the American government. Mankiewicz also knew from the start that he wanted a more admirable Pyle, so he cast Audie Murphy, a World War II hero and budding actor. Other cast members complained of Murphy's acting and of his menacing gunplay on set. But Lansdale relished the chance to "correct" Greene's narrative.

The key historical detail, the bombing in the Saigon square in January of 1952, was an event Greene knew about from his trips to Vietnam while reporting for *Life* magazine. The scholar Jonathan Nashel (author of *Edward Lansdale's Cold War*) found a letter to Mankiewicz from March 1956 in which Lansdale admits that the explosives were American made, adding that "General Thế claimed credit for this explosion via a broadcast over the National Resistance radio." But Lansdale advised: "let it be finally revealed [in your screenplay] that Communists did it after all, even to faking the radio broadcast (which would have been easy enough to do)." This way, it favored the American storyline.[9]

Mankiewicz sent Lansdale the final draft for approval. Lansdale's aide wrote that "Colonel Lansdale . . . wishes to convey to Mr. Mankiewicz his appreciation of the script as well as his best regards."[10] According to Nashel, the film production company Figaro, Inc. also met with CIA Director Allen Dulles before the film's release to coordinate its messaging.[11] In the book, Fowler comes to realize that many in Saigon assumed Pyle was working for the US intelligence service. "What is he? O.S.S.?" Fowler asks one source, who responds: "The initial letters are not very important. I think now they are different."[12] The reference is to the World War II-era Office of Strategic Services and its successor organization, the CIA, which was established in 1947.

In the movie, Fowler is portrayed as having fallen for communist disinformation when he concludes that Pyle and Thế were responsible for the terrorist bombing. "They have made a bloody fool of you," he is told by a French police investigator, a line that does not appear in the book, just as the OSS line does not appear in the movie.

Though unaware at the time of Lansdale's role, Greene recoiled at what Mankiewicz had produced, calling it "a propaganda piece for American policy in Vietnam."[13] He wrote later of his suspicions of a coordinated campaign to attribute the bombing to the Vietminh, adding that a *Life* magazine photograph featuring the legless trishaw driver was reproduced in propaganda magazines, including one he saw in Manila over the caption "The work of Ho Chi Minh."[14]

4.

The controversies that swirled around *The Quiet American*—both the book and film—never faded. By the 1970s, nobody could have been unaware of how central the CIA had been in Vietnam. As Viet Thanh Nguyen recalled in a 2016 interview, the same year he won a Pulitzer Prize for his novel *The Sympathizer*:

> *[My parents] were part of a great migration of about eight hundred thousand North Vietnamese Catholics who had been persuaded by their parish priests that the communists were going to massacre them or at the very least persecute them. And that idea had been promulgated by the CIA, by Colonel Edward Lansdale who became famous for helping the Philippines suppress a communist insurgency in the 1950s, and then he brought his talents to South Vietnam. And he became the inspiration—so it was rumored—for Alden Pyle in Graham Greene's* The Quiet American. *So that was the history behind why my parents had decided to flee.*[15]

It was a common assumption over the years that Greene had based the Pyle character on Lansdale. Lansdale himself encouraged such speculation while also laughing it off. Greene disavowed it. "Just for the record," he wrote in a letter to the *Sunday Telegraph* in 1966, "your correspondent . . . is completely wrong in thinking that I took General Lansdale as the model for *The Quiet American*. Pyle was a younger, more innocent and more idealistic member of the CIA. I would never have chosen Colonel Lansdale, as he then was, to represent the danger of innocence."[16]

Correcting the record in a letter to the same outlet in 1975, Greene wrote, "I grow tired of denying that there is any connection between my character Pyle in *The Quiet American* and General Lansdale, the American counterinsurgency expert whom I have never had the misfortune to meet. Pyle was an innocent and an idealist. I doubt whether your correspondent . . . would so describe General Lansdale. . . . Other journalists please note."[17]

The salient questions that linger from this matter have to do with never-ending debates over American folly, or the so-called realism associated with the likes of Lansdale. In 2020, Scott Anderson borrowed Greene's title for a biography of Lansdale and three other intelligence officers. *The Quiet Americans* offered a critical take on what his subtitle describes as "the dawn of the Cold War—a tragedy in three acts." Remarkably, former Democratic presidential candidate Pete Buttigieg, now secretary of transportation in the Biden administration, wrote his Harvard thesis on the Lansdale-Greene feud, echoing Lansdale in calling Greene anti-American for trying to report what actually happened.

Even today, neoconservatives and their centrist Democratic counterparts tout counterinsurgency as a key tool in US foreign policy. The one-time Iraq war booster, Max Boot—who wrote a Pulitzer-nominated 2018 hagiography of Lansdale, *The Road Not Taken*—has seen new possibilities for Lansdalian counterinsurgency, suggesting the Biden administration represents a "return to normalcy" in this respect. This proved prescient.

Twenty years after the novel appeared, the US failure in Vietnam turned out worse than Greene predicted. In a 1952 article for *Life* magazine (which never ran), Greene foresaw a stalemate in Vietnam institutionalized through an "armistice comparable to the arrangement in Korea." But it wasn't so much an armistice as a full US retreat. In Congressional postmortems, one general was grilled over whether he actually understood the novel's warning. Mankiewicz's obituary in *The New York Times* ignored the film, which the director had come to disavow. In 2002, Hollywood even redid the film with Michael Caine starring as Fowler. Even then, the fear of "anti-Americanism" was in the air: in the aftermath of the 9/11 attacks, the film's depiction of a terrorist bombing, according to Caine, almost caused Miramax mogul Harvey Weinstein—now in prison for rape—to shelve the movie.

Greene's critiques of Lansdale and the "innocence" of other officials still matters, as new retreats have become necessary, as multi-trillion-dollar dalliances of destruction and bloodshed in theaters like Iraq and Afghanistan pile up, and as civilian casualties continue to be written off as anti-terror successes (as I write this is happening in Gaza).[18] To these events, Greene still speaks to us. When Greene was in Vietnam, he finagled his way onto a fly-along with a pilot named Pinquet. During forty minutes of tumult, the French bomber took fourteen dives—from nine thousand to three thousand feet—with Greene's knees against the pilot's back. The experience inspired a scene in the novel.

Pinquet is renamed Captain Trouin, and a conversation between Trouin and Fowler takes place after the plane returns, with Trouin admitting "what I detest is napalm bombing . . . You see the forest catching fire. God knows what you would see from the ground." "But we are professionals," he adds: "we have to go on fighting till the politicians tell us to stop. Probably they will get together and agree to the same peace that we could have had at the beginning, making nonsense of all these years."[19]

That's the warning that Mankiewicz and Lansdale dismissed in their reinterpretation. They didn't see nonsense or waste or needless brutality; they saw a vital and noble American mission. "One could almost believe that the film was made deliberately to attack the book and its author," Greene remarked at one point. "But the book was based on a closer knowledge of the Indo-China war than the American [director] possessed and I am vain enough to believe that the book will survive a few years longer than Mr. Mankiewicz's production."[20] He was right.

1949

Wake Up, America!: Paul Robeson in Peekskill

or how a NYC suburb reenacted the violence
and slogans of Munich's Kristallnacht

An hour north of New York City on the Hudson Line, past the Peekskill train station, a golf course sprawls along its ponds and bridges. I grew up in the area, and in my youth the golf course was a drive-in movie theater, that soon grew weeds in the asphalt as it went into decay. But before that, it was a field in which the beloved actor, singer, activist, and lawyer Paul Robeson headlined a concert. A battle over that concert made Peekskill infamous, after a violent political skirmish known as the "Peekskill riots."

It was late August 1949 when Robeson arrived. The concert was a fundraiser for the Civil Rights Congress, one of many progressive organizations that fell victim to a right-liberal backlash—known in policy terms as the Truman Doctrine—against the social and economic policies of Franklin D. Roosevelt. The start of the Cold War gave power to conservatives eager to put the brakes on an early movement for civil and economic rights, whose most forceful advocates were radicals and socialists.

On the day of the riots, Robeson and his entourage saw a burning cross on the hill above the concert grounds. Racists flipped over the cars of the singer and his crew, pelting them with rocks. At first, the rioters kept the concert from happening, as the mob shouted racial epithets against Blacks, leftists, and Jews and injured a dozen attendees. Throngs of rioters who assaulted concertgoers and performers stretched all the way to Yonkers, some thirty miles south.

A week and a day later, the concert proceeded. But the damage was done: the Ku Klux Klan gloated, plastering Peekskill with slogans lifted from Germany's Kristallnacht. In the public school I attended in nearby Croton, this history was absent. We didn't study Robeson in social studies or history courses. A cultural amnesia blurred and erased these events, interrupted only by a small group of people able to draw a connection between the horrors of 1949 and the rightward surge of the present.

Larger Than Life

Paul Leroy Robeson was the son of William Drew Robeson, a runaway slave turned Presbyterian minister, who had fled from his captors to Princeton, New Jersey, in 1860 at the age of fifteen. From there he met Robeson's mother, Maria Louisa Bustil, a schoolteacher from a family of prominent anti-slavery and Jim Crow campaigners. On Sundays, Robeson watched his father's weekly sermons boil over into operatic morality tales on the importance of race pride.

Young Robeson's own membership in this educated African American milieu gave him access to the liberal corners of society. Although he would in his later years describe Princeton as still "spiritually located in Dixie,"[1] he would eventually be admitted to Rutgers University on a full scholarship. At the respected institution, Robeson would go on to be star of the university's glee club and an all-American football player.

From New Jersey, Robeson moved to Harlem and applied to Columbia Law School, where he was accepted. He landed a job at Stotesbury and Associates, a prestigious Manhattan law firm, though here he hit a wall. A racist secretary informed Robeson's colleagues that she would not take dictation from a Black man. The partner who hired him (as a favor to a mutual friend) warned that clients would not let Robeson represent them in court. He took the hint and tried his luck on the stage.

In 1923, Robeson earned the lead in Eugene O'Neill's *All God's Chillun Got Wings*, one of his first major roles.

The play depicted an interracial relationship between a white woman and her Black husband, whose success she resented so deeply that it led her to sabotage his budding law career. The resonances with Robeson's own life must have been clear to him. But the script called for the lead to kiss his co-star, Mary Blair, the wife of literary critic Edmund Wilson.

Delays in the production caused by an illness which afflicted Blair during rehearsals led to an unusually long buildup, which offered the media an opportunity to work the public into a frenzy over the kiss. Weeks before the play was due to air, the *New York American* ran a story titled, "Riots Feared From Drama," and a Long Island KKK chapter threatened to blow up the theater.[2] Although Robeson's co-stars and the play's director, Eugene O'Neill, came to his defense—dismissing the supposed controversy—right-wing groups railed against the performance.

On opening night, steelworkers close to the cast guarded the dressing rooms from possible attacks, as police fenced the theater in response to numerous threats. Fortunately, the attacks did not materialize. Though critics were generally not enthused by the play, they praised Robeson's contribution. One went so far as to write that "Caucasian superiority does suffer a little, because Paul Robeson is a far finer actor than any white member of the cast."[3]

International Solidarity

In 1928, the Robesons moved to London, where Paul starred in a production of *Show Boat*, a West End musical adapted from a best-selling book about race relations in the American South. The appearance of Robeson was the talk of the town. On one occasion he was denied entry to the Savoy Grill, a fancy London eatery, in an incident that became national news and was discussed in British Parliament. Yet even within the cosmopolitan world of the arts, Robeson felt that he struggled to reconcile his ideals with the films in which he was cast.

In 1934, the Hungarian-British filmmaker Zoltán Korda asked him to star in *Sanders of the River* alongside Kenya's future president, Jomo Kenyatta. The film depicted British colonialism, and Robeson thought it would offer a critique of the institution. But Black nationalists like Marcus Garvey later ridiculed Robeson for starring in what turned out to be another "white man's burden" narrative. Regretting his role in the film, Robeson described it as something that could have been "shown in Italy and Germany, for it shows the Negro as Fascist States desire him—savage and childish."[4]

But according to Robeson, London was where he received his true education, landing a handful of films more in line with his left-veering politics, that told stories of people's struggles. In *Song of Freedom* (1936), he played a dock worker whose rich singing voice makes him famous, and whose fame lets him discover his regal bloodline in Africa. In *Jericho* (1937), he played a heroic World War I officer who refuses an order to abandon ship and saves his men's lives. But Robeson truly hit his stride with a film based on the plight of Welsh coal workers.

His relationship with these miners began a decade earlier, when he emerged from a matinee performance of *Show Boat* in London and encountered a chanting crowd of Welsh miners. They had marched all the way from Wales to London, and were on strike, blackballed, and going hungry. After inviting them to a meal and hearing of their union efforts and their difficulties, Robeson took up their cause.

He visited Wales and brought their story to the screen in the musical *The Proud Valley* (1940), in which he plays a sympathetic American named Goliath. Without prospects in America, Goliath works in the Welsh mines, and ultimately saves his comrades from a tunnel collapse. "It was through his contact with the Welsh miners that he realized he was working class, *as well as* Black," recounts leftwing member of British Parliament Tony Benn, in the 1999 documentary, *Paul Robeson: Here I Stand*.[5]

War and Fascism

During the Great Depression, Robeson's visit to the Soviet Union highlighted the contrast between fascism and socialism. Russian film director Sergei Eisenstein had invited him, hoping to direct *Black Majesty*, a film on the Haitian Revolution, to star Robeson as the island's liberator, Toussaint Louverture. The partnership never panned out. But while he traveled by train through Nazi Germany in 1934, officials harassed Robeson for accompanying a white woman. "I could read hatred in their eyes," he recalled. "This is how lynch mobs start."

Viewing international socialism as a great equalizer and the only real solution to fascism, he was impressed by the collective farm where Eisenstein shot scenes for another of his films. And given that the Soviet constitution guaranteed full equality for all (in Article 123), Robeson praised the workers' state, saying, "Here, I walk in full human dignity."[6]

Then came a battle in the counter-revolution. In 1936, with a fascist coup overturning the elected progressive government of Spain, Robeson made the consequential decision to deepen his commitment: he would relegate his career to second place, behind the anti-fascist struggle.

"I stand before you in unalterable support of the government of Spain, freely chosen by its sons and daughters," he told European audiences. "The battlefield is everywhere. The artist must take sides. He must elect to fight for freedom or for slavery. I have made my choice."[7] Crisscrossing Spain, in hospitals or depots on their way to the front, he sang before wounded soldiers and demoralized partisans. Singing in English, Spanish, and Russian, he aimed to inspire hope in the leftist Republican forces.

But as a greater European war loomed, Robeson and his family prepared to return to the United States. After spending so much time abroad, his reputation was somewhat dimmed in his homeland. At the height of the jingoistic fervor generated by the war, Robeson took on a patriotic radio musical produced by CBS. *Ballad for Americans* was hackneyed and uninteresting—war propaganda set to soaring music mashed up with a 1940s "History for Dummies" libretto.

But it broke audience records for the network, and helped make the singer more famous in the United States than ever. Riding on this high, he went on to take the lead role in the longest running Broadway production of *Othello*. But the period linking his artistic and political good fortune would not last.

Truman

Preempting the rise of Joseph McCarthy and the House and Senate Un-American Activities Committees, President Harry Truman presided over a purging from government posts of progressives whose views he thought might make them sympathetic to Russia. It was in this tense atmosphere that Robeson helped found the American Crusade

Against Lynching (ACAL) with a launch rally in Washington on September 23, 1946.

The rally was followed by a meeting with President Truman. The president responded to the ACAL by dismissing its concerns, saying that it was not the time for such divisive issues. In his meeting with Robeson, Truman insisted that the United States and Great Britain represented "the last refuge of freedom in the world."[8]

Robeson scoffed, referring to rampant imperialism from both, adding that "if the federal government refused to defend its Black citizens against murder, Blacks would have to defend themselves." At this point, "Truman declared the interview at an end."[9] Truman tactically supported the broader backlash against progressive politics of the FDR era. With Robeson now in its sights, he was called for the first of many times before the House Un-American Activities Committee (HUAC), likely because of the Truman meeting.

As liberals realigned around anticommunism, often joining conservatives in the paranoid climate, Robeson maintained his progressive allegiances, at home and abroad. In Paris at the Partisans for Peace Congress in 1949, Robeson shared a stage with the Spanish painter Pablo Picasso and the Chilean poet Pablo Neruda. He issued an anti-war statement that warned of the horrific consequences of war with the Soviet Union.

As Robeson contrasted the valor that African Americans displayed during the war to the poor treatment they received back home, the media misreported his statements, playing up a suggestion of Black revolt and disloyalty. As the media depicted it, it was verbal treason. "Black Stalin Aim Laid to Robeson," ran a July 1949 headline in *The New York Times*.[10]

At first oblivious to the reaction back home, Robeson continued his tour, proceeding to Eastern Europe and arriving in Moscow in June of 1949. Hoping to refute rumors of antisemitic repression in the Soviet Union, Robeson asked to see his friend, the poet Itzik Feffer. It turned out Feffer was locked in Moscow's Lubyanka prison, incommunicado. Robeson had met Feffer along with Albert Einstein six years before at an event in New York for the Jewish Anti-Fascist Committee. In Moscow, the actor waited several days to see his friend, who finally appeared at Robeson's hotel. Feffer signaled that the room was bugged, and the duo exchanged small talk cautiously, while passing notes.

Where have you been? Robeson jotted.
Prison.
What can I do?
Say nothing or we prisoners are dead.[11]

Robeson followed the visit with a concert in Tchaikovsky Concert Hall. Broadcast live, with Soviet leadership in attendance, Robeson announced—"to gasps," according to his son[12]—that he had seen his friend Itzik Feffer. With little fanfare, after reminding the audience of the long-standing cultural ties between Jews in the United States and those in the Soviet Union—then asking for silence—Robeson sang the Warsaw ghetto resistance song, "Zog Nit Keynmol," as his encore. It was an extraordinary moment of defiance to Stalin.

When Robeson came home, however, he found himself in a bind. He had opposed Stalinist terror, but he did not wish to give support to a Cold War that many feared would grow into a direct war between rising nuclear powers. Unable to find a solution, he opted simply to lie.

When asked directly by a small right-wing newspaper about Stalin's persecution of Jews, he denied knowledge of the purges that afflicted Feffer, who, with twelve other Russian Jews, were executed three years after his visit.

But more than his silence over Feffer, it was his antiwar message in Paris that haunted Robeson's return to the United States. Aware that the moment was defined by a reactionary media that performed like a deputy to the security state, he watched as his plea for peace and freedom from fear was twisted into an expression of disloyalty.

The HUAC-enforced reaction even saw baseball great Jackie Robinson pulled into the debate. Robinson was allegedly strong-armed into testifying against Robeson, convinced that he wouldn't have a career if he objected, apologizing later. When Robeson arrived in Peekskill in 1949, this climate of anti-communist blacklists and purges served as the backdrop for his arrival.

It was poised to boil over into violence.

Veterans of Foreign Wars, the American Legion, and Catholic organizations had rallied the opposition in the Peekskill *Evening Star*. Knowing Robeson's three prior concerts here had been successes, the groups pitted Peekskill's traditional working-class inhabitants against a relatively new enclave of wealthy, educated, left-wing weekenders, many of them Jewish, by calling the latter communists.

Peekskill

As he drove toward the field with his sixty-five-year-old mother, the folk singer Pete Seeger rolled down his window. He told the cop he had to get through: he was here to sing. There wasn't going to be any concert, said the cop, gruffly turning away.

Helen Rosen picked up her friend, the star attraction, at the Peekskill train station. Robeson had called ahead and told her that he'd been warned of disruptions. As they approached a field known as the Lakeland Acres picnic area—a few miles from the future golf course—Rosen recalled seeing unusual traffic, hearing noise, even screaming. A gang of veterans broke through the barricades. Its members proceeded to vandalize the stage.

Seeger recalled seeing piles of stones beside the road on the way out, with rocks as large as tennis balls piled several feet high.[13] The piles must have been covered when he came in, he told an interviewer—otherwise, he surely would have seen them. Rioters turned cars on their sides and smashed windshields with rocks, injuring dozens.

In the aftermath, and with the rescheduled concert to proceed a week later, signs appeared across the town that read, "Wake up, America. Peekskill did." Supporters of the violence plastered these lines on store windows and car bumpers, Seeger recalled.

"In Europe, they were horrified," Seeger recalled. "They said those were the same signs that went up in Germany after *Kristallnacht*. Only in Germany they read: 'Wake up Germany: Munich did.' . . . As pogroms grew, they whispered, 'Throw stones at all the Jewish storekeepers,'" Seeger recalled.[14]

At the second concert, twenty thousand supporters arrived to hear Robeson, Seeger, and others, who were met by eight thousand protesters. Like two decades earlier in Provincetown, Robeson's people organized trade unionists to link themselves, arm in arm, around the stage, forming themselves into a human wall.

Though the concert was finally able to go forward, protesters shouted violent antisemitic and racist threats, chanting, "We'll kill you," and "You may get in but you won't get out."[15] The volunteer security, made up of union members and progressive veterans, flushed snipers from trees above the field. With high-powered rifles, their sights had been aimed at the stage.

After performers left under close protection—with only a verbal barrage able to reach them—a mass beating followed. Batteries of stones and blows rained down on union members; left-wing supporters of Robeson were corralled in the field that became the golf course that remains today. Until 1:30 AM, the police oversaw and did nothing to stop this beating, almost certainly egging it on. A hundred and fifty were injured.

In the days that followed, right-wing officials and media launched witch hunts. A nasty combination of racism and anti-communism came over the town. Fascists plastered posters which read "Communism is Treason, Behind Communism stands—the Jew!" on cars.[16] In neighboring Harmon, one of the few Jewish homes had its windows smashed and the American Legion requested that books written by "known communists" be removed from Peekskill's library. Robeson's friends, the Rosens, were chased out.

Faced with a backlash that grew national in scale, Robeson remained defiant. In a press conference held after the grand jury hearing into the riots, created to investigate the *victims* of the violence, he told reporters that "the Communist Party has played a magnificent role in fighting for the freedom of the American Negro."[17] Despite vitriol leveled at him from the right, he defended freedom of speech and of association as core American values, rejecting the idea, sixty-eight years before the Charlottesville riots, that violence used in Peekskill could be justified.

Divisions which the right attempted to exploit in Peekskill illustrate a broader strategy. Robeson's enemies sought to attack him as an individual, but also to attack the political culture from which his ideas emerged. In the climate of fear they whipped up, the violence was blamed on the left, as a natural consequence of its alliance with international communism. Rather than oppose this idea that Robeson was un-American, some liberals played into or preempted the logic.

As Robeson worked on the "We Charge Genocide" petition with the Civil Rights Congress in 1951, Truman's State Department wrangled Raphael Lemkin, who coined "genocide," to downplay lynching as somehow less serious than all that. It also placed an article in the NAACP's *The Crisis* magazine, chiding Robeson as a communist dupe.[18] And with his passport suspended, Robeson was unable to attend the petition's unveiling in Paris.

Though he would die—due to backlash—in relative obscurity, his income having been reduced from $104,000 to $2,000, Robeson's politics were prescient, his accomplishments legion. Sometimes called the Great Forerunner, who quipped, "The answer to injustice is not to silence the critic, but to end the injustice,"[19] his influence on the second half of the twentieth century and the early twenty-first remains impossible to measure.

As Gerald Horne notes, "Robeson pioneered the struggle against Jim Crow throughout the 1930s and 40s. It was with Robeson's fall that King and Malcolm could emerge as they did; the undermining of Robeson created a vacuum that these two leaders filled."[20]

1953

Fifty Years of Disquietude: Gabriel García Márquez in *Mundo Nuevo*

or how he found his masterpiece smuggled into a CIA magazine while he was banned on US soil

The road from the capital to Acapulco was riddled with deadly switchbacks. Navigating the sharp turns left him just enough residual focus to daydream about his novel. Gabriel García Márquez was driving his family to their first vacation after long stretches of poverty. Ad work and then films had somewhat stabilized the thirty-seven-year-old Colombian writer's finances, and some awards had come. But he'd been stalled on a novel, one he had dreamed of writing since his teens. His working title had been *The House*, conceived as a tribute to life in his family's ancestral home in the little Caribbean outpost of Aracataca. Suddenly a string of words came to him: "Many years later, as he faced the firing squad, Colonel Aureliano Buendía was to remember that distant afternoon when his father took him to discover ice." It was perfect: a first sentence which entailed the ending, a narrative loop.

What happened next is shrouded in myth. The most common version has García Márquez turning the family's white 1962 Opel around (he'd bought it with prize money from an earlier novel), returning to Mexico City, and abandoning his hard-won economic stability. He went into debt with his landlord and for a year secluded himself in his "mafia cave," as he called his smoke-filled writing studio. The book was highly anticipated: his life in Mexico City exposed him to the city's literati; he'd dramatized his writer's block as a precipice above a great discovery.[1]

The final chapters were still being written when requests came for advance excerpts. One such request came from a Uruguayan critic named Emir Rodríguez Monegal, who was editing a new literary magazine, *Mundo Nuevo*. But it wasn't just any literary magazine. According to rumors, the magazine was backed by gringo spy money. Like much of the Latin American literary world, Rodríguez Monegal heard about the novel nearly a year before it appeared. Latin American intellectuals were still bitterly divided over the Cuban Revolution, which *Mundo Nuevo*'s paymasters opposed. However willingly García Márquez was to contribute to a magazine that openly sought to publish work from both sides—as this one claimed to do—he was not interested in doing covert cultural propaganda for the gringos.

And yet, as *One Hundred Years of Solitude* was being published to immediate and universal acclaim—the literary equivalent of Beatlemania, one critic has written[2]—and as the book's author had a new empire to manage—between the foreign rights, translations, sales numbers, requests from fans, interviews, and film options—a barnacle clung to his newfound success. Newspapers were reporting that much of the cultural world had been ensnared in a CIA scheme to marshal culture for Cold War gain against the Soviets. It must have been an "oh shit" moment equal and opposite to his Acapulco epiphany: *Mundo Nuevo* was one of those magazines, and he had been stupid enough to say yes. He wrote to his editor-friend to protest his evident ensnarement in the scheme. What did it feel like? In a quietly seething letter, he wrote that he felt like a cuckold.

In Dubious Congress

As García Márquez's great novel turns fifty and panels and think pieces debate its legacy—and as the book's US boosters focus on its mechanics, its inspiration, and its influence on future writers and those who influenced it—it's high time to unravel the novel's incidental and almost invisible political weaponization in the Cold War. For decades, the story has gone that the CIA's Congress for Cultural Freedom, its covert propaganda front, was one of the best things the

CIA ever did. It never censored, and it published a string of great writers. But as one of those writers can attest—one who happens to have been the 1982 Nobel laureate—at least some of them were tricked into the scheme.

García Márquez was nothing if not a politically minded Latin American writer with a stubborn memory for historical misdeeds. As a young man coming of age near the coastal city of Barranquilla, he was inducted rudely into the manipulative foreign policy of the northern behemoth. On December 6, 1928, when he was almost two, United Fruit colluded with the Colombian Army while it massacred striking banana workers who had rallied in the town square of Ciénaga. His hometown, Aracataca, was about thirty-five miles away. Too small to remember the tragedy directly, García Márquez grew up fluent in the legend of those massacred workers. This was due to the endless retelling of the assault, including by his family. "I knew the event as if I had lived it," he wrote:

> having heard it recounted and repeated a thousand times by my grandfather from the time I had a memory, the soldier reading the decree by which the striking laborers were declared a gang of lawbreakers; the three thousand men, women, and children motionless under the savage sun after the officer gave them five minutes to evacuate the square; the order to fire, the clattering machine guns spitting in white-hot bursts, the crowd trapped by panic as it was cut down, little by little, by the methodical, insatiable scissors of the shrapnel.[3]

In García Márquez's literary recreation of the massacre and its aftermath, a plague-like pall is cast over the town.

Stories about his life tend to focus on the unique character of his inspiration, or his publishing success by the numbers (fifty million copies of *One Hundred Years of Solitude* sold worldwide), or his friendships, or his reading. These are all valid. Meanwhile, a paucity of English translations of his nonfiction means that it is easy to ignore his political convictions. When stories do focus on his politics, they tend to point to his friendship with Fidel Castro for the sole purpose of condemning it. This was a blind spot, it's euphemized. Lost from his legacy are the political events that actually mattered to García Márquez: our blind spots in the North. From this standpoint, *One Hundred Years of Solitude* was an attempt to help others see what he saw.

In 1948, for instance, he was a twenty-year-old studying law in Bogotá when Jorge Eliécer Gaitán, the Liberal candidate for president, was gunned down in broad daylight a block from García Márquez's home. A Gaitán supporter, García Márquez was preparing to eat lunch when he heard the uproar. He knew exactly what must have happened and ran a block to Seventh Street, where the killer was being kicked and beaten to death. The city burned, including García Márquez's house. A friend was stunned to find García Márquez crying. "I didn't realize you were such a devoted disciple of Gaitán," said the friend. "No, what are you talking about?" he said. "It's that my stories burned."[4]

On a stage much later, Fidel Castro, who had been in town for a youth summit, told a tongue-in-cheek story of that day of infamy and its mayhem. García Márquez sat quietly with him until the very end of the tale. "The most vocal unleashed their frustration by shouting from the street corners, garden terraces, and smoky buildings," Castro began. "One man," he continued, "vented his fury by attacking his typewriter, beating it, and then to save himself the laborious effort, he threw it up into the air, and it smashed to bits when it hit the pavement . . . As I was finishing telling my story, I knew that Gabo had been there too, and . . . I asked the question with my usual dispassionate curiosity . . ." "And what were you doing during the Bogotazo?" Castro asked him. "And he, calmly, entrenched within his vibrant, provocative, exceptional imagination, answered simply, smiling . . . 'Fidel, I was that man with the typewriter.'"[5]

The agency's director later admitted under oath that it had indeed been surveilling Gaitán.[6] And much later in life, García Márquez suspected that the CIA, which had only recently launched out of the remains of the wartime Office of Strategic Services, may have had a hand in the Gaitán killing.

Chronicle of a Shipwreck, Revised

After things quieted down, García Márquez returned to Bogotá to work at the newspaper *El Espectador*. But on June 13, 1953, there was a coup. General Gustavo Rojas Pinilla took power. His four-year rule was marked by restrictions on civil liberties across the country and by tentative US support. Though at first his junta was seen as a respite from the brutal war between the Conservative government and Liberal opposition, he increasingly packed the courts with cronies, strong-armed opponents, and censored the press.

Meanwhile, in late February 1955, after undergoing repairs in Alabama, the Colombian Naval destroyer *Caldas* lost eight crew members sailing for Cartagena. After four days, the search for survivors was called off. Rojas Pinilla's government blamed the shipwreck on a storm. Ten days after the incident, a crewman named Luis Alejandro Velasco washed ashore in Northern Colombia. Velasco had been tossed overboard and had survived on a simple raft. The media was ravenous for stories about his survival and resilience. A Naval hero's photograph splashed across the newspapers is rarely a bad thing for a military dictatorship. But this one had a secret: there hadn't been a storm.

As the attention waned and his credibility was strained under relentless self-promotion, Velasco turned up at *El Espectador*'s offices hoping to tell the full, detailed version of his story for the first time. According to Velasco, the great weight of the cargo, not a storm, had hindered the ship's maneuvering. This was what had led to the crew being thrown overboard. The ship had carried heavy goods from the United States: refrigerators, washing machines, and TVs purchased with the crew's back pay but prohibited on a military ship. The true saga of the *Caldas* afforded Colombians an all-too-vivid reminder of the human costs entailed in the dictatorship's sluggish reign of low-level corruption and high-level coverup. Rojas Pinilla's regime had endorsed the story of Velasco the hero. But when García Márquez revealed a version laced with greed, the administration denied it. *El Espectador* printed photos confirming the illegal merchandise, and García Márquez was chased from Colombia by anonymous death threats.

Truth and Consequences

By 1959, García Márquez was jobless in France, forced to resign from another job in solidarity with a friend in Venezuela rather than write lies praising US Vice President Richard Nixon. His hopes for a democratic socialist government now focused on Fidel Castro. After his revolutionary forces took Havana on New Year's Day, Castro called the world's writers to witness the changeover in a program called

Operation Truth. The CIA was even sympathetic enough to the new regime to sponsor its own junkets, in another program called Operation Amistad, which offered free flights from North America to writers and intellectuals so they could visit during the revolution's early days. Writers like George Plimpton, Kenneth Tynan, and Tennessee Williams came to see the new Cuba. But the agency's approval was short-lived.

"Operation Truth" featured trials in which functionaries of the US-backed dictator Fulgencio Batista's regime were read their records, allowed a defense, and then in some cases, eventually executed. Few were pardoned, though there was a formal means to appeal. Covering the trials for a Venezuelan outlet, García Márquez and his friend Plinio Apuleyo Mendoza were persuaded of the fairness of Operation Truth. After Castro had greeted them personally, they "immediately attended the trial of Jesús Sosa Blanco, a colonel of Batista's army, accused of murdering various locals from a small rural area known as El Oro de Guisa who had supported the rebel army. He was sentenced to death. His wife and children asked many of the journalists to sign a document requesting a revised sentence." García Márquez and Mendoza signed the appeal, but it was ignored. They nevertheless deemed the trial fair as revolutionary justice went[7]—particularly in view of the American record of supporting state-sanctioned executions of leftist dissidents. They even signed on to work at Cuba's new press conglomerate, Prensa Latina, or Prela for short.

A picture from his time at Prela's Bogotá office shows García Márquez with a thin mustache and prominent cheekbones. A tightly rolled cigarette dangles from his thin lips. His hair is greased back and he wears a fine suit. This was the young man who trained in Havana, joking later how he did nothing but work and could name only the small circle of restaurants around Prela's Havana headquarters. But it wasn't all so boring.

One day in early 1961, García Márquez's colleague Jorge Masetti "stumbled" across an encrypted telex to Washington, which he supposed could be important. Indeed, he surmised that it was for the CIA. He gave it to their colleague, Rodolfo Walsh, who spent several days in his dining room, blocks from the Prela office, until he successfully decoded it using a book on decryption. What it laid out were plans for the Bay of Pigs invasion. Masetti, García Márquez, and Walsh brought it to the Cuban government with a plan to surprise the Americans. But the three writers learned that the Cubans already knew about the invasion and had their own plan.

García Márquez would have been safer on the beaches of the Bay of Pigs, he wrote, than where he was during the invasion, in New York City. Since witnessing his colleagues decode the telex, he had been transferred to Prela's New York office. The threats he described in New York, from Cuban exiles possibly working for US intelligence, were aimed both at him and his family. As in the aftermath of his reporting on the Velasco shipwreck, the threats he faced again came from the reactionary right, from characters whom he called *gusanos*, or worms. He resigned from the Cuban press agency.[8]

Opening and Closure

In 1965, García Márquez is driving his wife, Mercedes (a dead ringer, it was said, for Sophia Loren), and two boys to the sea. Suddenly, the magical sentence and everything that comes with it announces itself as he navigates the sharp turns. This was the book he had struggled to describe to Mercedes when he spoke upon their engagement of his vision for a great Latin American novel. He pulled over the car and told her that they had to go back to the capital. He knew how to make the novel go. In addition to the great sentence about discovering ice, which would give the novel its circular form, he understood that he must use the narrative style of his grandmother, Tranquilina. She told fantastical stories, he said in an interview, but told them "with a brick face."[9]

García Márquez and Mercedes's two sons, Rodrigo and Gonzalo, were real responsibilities that he took very seriously. But when he finally conceived how to write the novel, he couldn't let the voice or the vision fade. They sold the Opel, and he secluded himself in his "mafia cave" at Calle Lomas #19 in Mexico City.[10] Once ensconced, he left the work of getting by to her while he chain-smoked (at a clip of about sixty cigarettes per day) and wrote out page after page at an incredible speed. What was coming into focus was a family saga, but also a love letter to Latin American history told through the Buendía family.

The novel's unprecedented success would change his and his family's lives. The book's anti-imperialist politics were just one element of its masterful voice and structure, embedded within its so-called magical elements. The politics were important both for Latin Americans, who often saw themselves as a common people, and for citizens elsewhere in the developing world, who recognized themselves, too, in the prismatic novel.

"I knew García Márquez's colonels and generals," wrote novelist Salman Rushdie, "or at least their Indian and Pakistani counterparts; his bishops were my mullahs; his market streets were my bazaars. His world was mine, translated into Spanish. It's little wonder I fell in love with it—not for its magic . . . but for its realism."[11] The Nicaraguan writer Gioconda Belli pronounced García Márquez the "biggest hero that Latin America has ever had. He did more for us than Bolívar, Martí, and Sandino. [He united us] in a recognizable identity."

Part of that unity involved purging the worst of US hostility, along with the region's self-inflicted misery. In one of the book's iconic depictions of political violence, García Márquez records something he may have felt watching the execution of Jesús Sosa Blanco in Cuba, the colonel in Batista's army whose trial he witnessed: "For the rest of his life he would remember the livid flash of the six simultaneous shots and the echo of the discharge as it broke against the hills and the sad smile and perplexed eyes of the man being shot, who stood erect . . . and who was still smiling even when they untied him from the post and put him in a box filled with quicklime. 'He's alive,' he thought."[12]

His first impressions of the United States (via the United Fruit massacre) also underpinned the historical urgency of the book. The segment dealing with the banana company treats the massacre in a dispassionate tone of stark, documentary horror. In its immediate aftermath, José Arcadio Segundo has been mistaken for a corpse and wakes on a train among the real corpses: "Trying to flee from the nightmare, José Arcadio Segundo dragged himself from one car to another in the direction in which the train was heading, and . . . he saw man corpses, woman corpses, child corpses who would be thrown into the sea like rejected bananas."[13] This was García Márquez purging the horrific inheritance and justified resentment he has carried with him, but with the passions muted one last time by the need to capture the terrible scene perfectly. Summarizing his obsession, he wrote: "I never could overcome the bitterness with which my grandparents had evoked their frustrated wars and the atrocious slaughters of the banana companies."[14]

But the book's success seemed foreordained on the basis of its sweeping literary vision as well as its historical restoration. "If everything is like this fragment," said future Nobel laureate Mario Vargas Llosa, "the novel must be a marvel."[15] The so-called Latin American Literary Boom had already been under way. Of the four titans—García Márquez, Julio Cortázar, Carlos Fuentes, and Vargas Llosa—García Márquez may have been the least known when the CIA launched *Mundo Nuevo*. After more than a decade and a half of CIA-sponsored literary output, *Mundo Nuevo* was the result of a new philosophy in US cultural propaganda that finally allowed what was called "an opening to the left."

Emir Rodríguez Monegal had been a brilliant critic and editor for *Marcha*, the cultural supplement to the leading newspaper in Uruguay. Prior to his recruitment to *Mundo Nuevo*, the magazine's predecessor, *Cuadernos*, had failed to draw intellectuals and leftists toward its hard-line anti-communism. Even prominent anti-communist liberals from the region, such as the Mexican poet Octavio Paz, had largely avoided *Cuadernos* for its overt North American bias. The Congress for Cultural Freedom, based in Paris, had launched in 1950. Its American offshoot, the American Committee for Cultural Freedom, preceded the Paris headquarters by a decade but its frequent red-baiting made it anachronistic. The new organization took a somewhat softer tone in its own array of publications, which numbered more than two dozen, with at least half a dozen for Latin America and Spanish speakers alone. The CCF also sent writers and artists abroad for junkets and exhibitions in Europe, Asia, and elsewhere. Acting out of a palpable fear of the Soviets penetrating cultural organizations, the CIA's leaders made sure that writers and activists in its employ preemptively penetrated the same organizations: student and labor unions, refugee relief organizations, the media, the municipal symphony orchestra.

The Cuban Revolution and decades of Yankee imperialism made hardline anti-communism untenable in the region as in its magazines; and in the latter it failed to lure the people who mattered into the conversations that mattered. It was in recognition of this shift that *Mundo Nuevo* was born. Today we'd call the García Márquez of 1966 an emerging voice in the literary mainstream. He was an important contributor to *Mundo Nuevo*, not just for the cultural legitimacy that came with his latest novel or the award he'd received for the last one. He was also one of the influential Latin American leftists actively courted by the magazine's brain trust. Bringing on au courant writers like García Márquez would perfectly fulfill the magazine's new posture. He was temperamentally inclined against the Soviet Union and the imposition of its clunky system onto the Eastern Bloc countries. But thanks to US meddling in the region, he was favorably disposed toward the Cuban experiment.

Just Too Left Enough

Involving García Márquez through his fiction meant that the CCF's embrace didn't automatically translate into an endorsement of the writer's leftist politics. In fact, publishing García Márquez's fiction in *Mundo Nuevo* meant that there were no explicit politics. The chapters chosen for excerpt would, by the magazine's internal logic of self-censorship, have omitted mention of the United Fruit–sponsored massacre. And so the thinking went that an esteemed leftist writer could land on the cover of *Mundo Nuevo* in recognition of his creative output—while also telegraphing the journal's apparent openness to leftist political views. But when readers proceeded to purchase *Mundo Nuevo* and inspect its contents, they encountered a steady barrage of pro-American and anti-Communist arguments. The head of CCF called it Fidelismo sin Fidel, or revolution without dictatorship.

This was the case not only for García Márquez, but also for leftist poet Pablo Neruda, another writer whose poems about Paris—published in an early issue of *Mundo Nuevo*—were hardly an assault on the Soviet Union. Nor were the works published by left-leaning writers in *Mundo Nuevo* a direct attack on imperialism, which would be anathema to the magazine's secret Cold War mission. After reading the draft of his new novel in February 1966 before it was finished, Rodríguez Monegal wrote to García Márquez ecstatically, hoping *Mundo Nuevo* might participate in its release. García Márquez suggested that the second chapter might be the best for excerpting, since it was the "most rounded."[16] A year later, he would regret offering it to *Mundo Nuevo*.

This was partly because revelations of CIA support for the Congress for Cultural Freedom were timed with another *Mundo Nuevo* excerpt about Macondo's chronic insomnia that became chapter 9 in the novel. So while Latin Americans debated the Congress for Cultural Freedom's depth of penetration, the latest issue of its Latin American magazine had García Márquez's name on the cover.

But his regret was more than just a matter of personal embarrassment: having come of age in the shadow of United Fruit's Colombian henchmen, he knew what such support entailed in broader intellectual and political terms. In its short life, the magazine ran political scientist Robert

Nisbet's defense of a US/CIA attempt to infiltrate Chile's intellectuals. The plan, Project Camelot, fanned out into Chilean universities, with CIA and US military agents posing as social scientists, offering outwardly harmless questionnaires in the service of a plan to study what could be done to fortify a country's institutions against revolutionary unrest. Project Camelot took on an especially ominous cast when seven years later General Augusto Pinochet mounted a successful coup against the democratically elected socialist president of Chile, Salvador Allende, with the backing of the CIA and several major American corporations.

But even without that grim legacy, Camelot itself was creepy enough on its own terms. The Congress for Cultural Freedom, its sibling university project the National Student Association, and organizations such as Michigan State University's Vietnam Project all engaged in a similar pattern of sponsoring benign scholarly activity that doubled as a cover for CIA nation building, spying, and other repressions. These efforts operated alongside a concerted bid to stack US media outlets and organizations with agents provocateurs, as in Operation Chaos, which was only exposed in the mid-seventies but was already widely suspected by leftists to be an ongoing function of government in the United States.

These momentous revelations, appearing in the leftist glossy *Ramparts* and *The New York Times*—and translated in *Marcha*, the Uruguayan cultural supplement where Rodríguez Monegal had worked prior to taking charge of *Mundo Nuevo*—grew to discredit the covert funding of culture, just as the outed conspirators were tasked with defending their benevolent acts of patronage as coming, they insisted loudly, with no strings attached.

Keith Botsford opted not to comment publicly, so the record of his dissent has sat for fifty years in archives, winding up most recently in Rodríguez Monegal's papers at Princeton. Botsford was a *Mundo Nuevo* contributor and a CCF operative in Latin America who had brought poet Robert Lowell to South America on an infamous junket. *Cuadernos* had been a "fink magazine"—its readers the "paralytic wing of the liberal reaction" and its editor himself a "fink"—Botsford complained. Claiming he hadn't known about the CIA sponsorship of the Congress for Cultural Freedom, he alleged to CCF ally Daniel Bell that constant pressure from its Paris headquarters amounted to severe censorship during Botsford's time in Latin America.

In a remarkable seven-page letter, Botsford set out to prove methodically, point by point, that Bell's defense of the CIA's "no strings attached" reputation was untenable. Echoing criticisms of the exposed program in Chile, Botsford used a revealing analogy to illustrate the compromised position of the CCF's unwitting operatives—people such as García Márquez. He compared them to legitimate scientists who have been working for the advancement of science, but who find out that secretly their work was financed by the Department of Defense. In the wake of this revelation, Botsford noted, the "possibility has been introduced" that there were other purposes for their work "of which [the scientist] has no cognizance, over which he has no control, and of which he may not approve."[17]

No One Writes for the Generals

If the Congress for Cultural Freedom defended its record by pointing to its now-discredited no-strings patronage, it also hailed the roster of great writers it published. As a mere list of names, this was an irrefutable record of achievement. But many had no say in their being used this way, and this lack of choice explained the seething dissent from the likes of García Márquez—a dissent that has sat in that same Princeton archive all these years.

"When you invited me to contribute to *Mundo Nuevo*," he wrote Rodríguez Monegal, "many friends with less political sense of humor . . . warned me . . . that the Congress for Cultural Freedom had certain extramarital ties to the US Central Intelligence Agency. I didn't worry that those suspicions might be well founded, because I . . . believe that when you write for a magazine it is you who influence it, not the other way around." Still, he described the covert funding as "symptoms of a supreme idiocy."

"Around it all," he expanded, "there was a certain humor in the fact that part of the budget for North American spying was used to promulgate the work of this writer, who was not permitted to enter the United States as a tribute to his dangerous politics." In the end, though, news of the CIA's funding for the magazine "scandalously surpasses the limits of humor," he wrote, "and crosses into the slippery and unforeseeable terrain of fantasy literature. In these conditions, Mister Editor, [you will] understand that I will not continue to collaborate with *Mundo Nuevo*, not while that magazine maintains any ties with the organization that has brought you and me together . . . in this oppressive state of cuckolds."[18]

The secret funding of figures like Neruda and García Márquez through editorial fees while they were still legally banned from entering the United States—alongside the revulsion many Latin Americans felt toward the more hard-core interventions of the American covert state, from the coup on Guatemala in 1954 to Vietnam to the toppling of

Allende in 1973—paints the Congress for Cultural Freedom's legacy in a similar light to the disastrous 1961 invasion of the Bay of Pigs. What the United States and its shadow corps of spooks and foreign contract workers had done in each case suffered greatly from the studied misrepresentation of the true aims of the architects of the American Cold War. True, on the surface, the longer-term consequences of the CCF debacle were not nearly as momentous as those of a botched foreign invasion. It did, however, create its own species of cultural blowback, costing in this case the good will of one of the greatest writers of the twentieth century.

But America's blind spots ran deeper than this. As a result of the exposure of the CCF and the covert agendas of other fronts in the late 1960s and early '70s, the CIA chose to pursue a still-deeper plan of undercover media penetration to avoid such embarrassments in the future. As was subsequently recounted in exposés in *Rolling Stone* by Carl Bernstein and in *The New York Times* by John Crewdson and others, the CIA proceeded to place operatives at the largest newspapers and news networks in the country and foreign papers around the world, in a new campaign called—without any evident trace of irony—Mockingbird. The same cycle of exposure and blowback was once more set in motion. Any residual credibility that American sympathizers could claim in the Latin American cultural scene—or anywhere else in the non-aligned world—was destroyed once and for all.

It was, as García Márquez prophesied, an act of supreme idiocy indeed.

1950

**Indestructible: George and Mary
Oppen in Mexico City**

or how Fascist Black Shirts and the FBI seeded
ground for his long poem on the US in Vietnam

1.

During the mad rush of leaving, they had to find homes for 60 animals, a menagerie of horses, snakes, turtles, and other creatures. Only two made the cut to tag along with them: their blue budgie parakeet, Bird, who went eerily still as they crossed the Sonoran Desert, and their Doberman, Kinch, who panted in the scorching heat.

Traveling with their 10-year-old daughter Linda and their friend Raf in a red Dodge, George and Mary Oppen fled Redondo Beach, California, on June 11, 1950. They were in flight from the FBI. Special agents had visited their house days earlier to ask about their relief work during the Depression, and about a former roommate suspected of "espionage." Nationally, it was a tense time. North and South Korea would clash two weeks later, launching a war. Dissent was unpatriotic; a person's past could send them to prison. Blacklisted after he testified before the House Un-American Activities Committee, the Oppens' friend Dalton Trumbo, a screenwriter, spent most of that year in a Kentucky prison for contempt of Congress. Having worked with the Communist Party during the Depression, the Oppens knew that they were considered enemies of the state. They headed for Tucson, and the border beyond. Calling themselves political refugees, they spent a decade in Mexico City under constant surveillance.

George famously stopped writing during this period. His silence lasted 25 years. He didn't want his work to become what Mary derided as a shallow version of writing—which merely encompassed the "day-to-day ideology" of their times rather than a deeper vision.

In 2017, after Donald Trump was inaugurated, I walked through New York City listening to a 10-minute recording of Oppen reading the first half of his long poem "Of Being Numerous." George's gentle, softly hoarse voice struck me as the antidote to insincerity. His poem was the antithesis to the abuse of language rampant in American politics. The poem exists at the other end of a continuum that includes T. S. Eliot's "The Waste Land." Beneath its modernist machinery thrums a haunting melody about shipwreck and Robinson Crusoe, and a response to the essential, if paradoxical, solitude of urban life: "the shuffling of the crowd is nothing . . . . nothing but the many that we are." Listening to George's wounded voice, I wondered what lay behind the poem. What inspired the Oppens, like many other American leftists of their time, to make that treacherous desert crossing?

Having read Mary's memoir *Meaning a Life: An Autobiography* (1978), which mentions the security visits, I petitioned the FBI, CIA, and the National Archives under the Freedom of Information Act for files related to the Oppens. I wanted to know what the couple did during the period Mary refers to as "the violent years"—years that bridged a long literary silence encompassing the Depression and the war. Other biographers and scholars have sought (and received versions of) these files, yet much in them is still misunderstood. The Oppens themselves often obscured the facts. In *Meaning a Life*, Mary depicts her and George working with the Communist Party only during the Depression, stating that their ties to the Hollywood refugees in Mexico were social, not political.

But if the FBI files are to be believed, the Oppens were immersed in a network of activists affiliated with the Communist Party who were engaged in campaigns to end the lynching of Black Americans and stop the US coup in Guatemala. In one FBI memo, George, who went on to win the 1969 Pulitzer Prize for Poetry, describes himself as an enemy of the US government and as one of the leaders of US communists in Mexico. In the end, the Oppens' homesickness, and George's famous dream of his poetry practice "rusting," finally brought them back to the United States, and effectively ended their Communist Party ties, more than a decade later than has been typically understood.

But the Oppens' repudiation of US policy only deepened alongside George's modernist aesthetic. As war raged in Vietnam in the 1960s, he began drafting "Of Being Numerous," one of the twentieth century's most haunting anti-war poems. To understand the full story of how Oppen's radical activism converged with an avant-garde aesthetic, I needed the FBI files. One day, almost two years after applying for them, they came in a modest package in the mail.

2.

George and Mary met in a poetry class at Oregon State University in 1926. After hearing Carl Sandburg read "Fog" on campus, they embraced poetry themselves. They stayed out all night, were expelled, and soon got married without their parents' approval. George used an alias on the marriage certificate—David Verdi—that later appeared in his FBI file.

In 1929, the Oppens embarked from San Francisco to Europe, on a month-long voyage at sea. As recounted in *Meaning a Life*, they spent the night in Le Havre, a port town in northern France, then proceeded to Paris by horse and cart. They traveled through small villages on Pom-Pon, a docile half-Arabian, half-English gelding who only disobeyed when in pursuit of bananas, which its prior owner imported. Mary studied the hard labor of the village women as she traveled; she records in her memoir that she and George happily "now lived out of doors."[1]

Arriving in Paris with Conrad Aiken's *An Anthology of Modern American Poetry* (1927) among their few possessions, they reveled in the city's "wealth of art."[2] Such abundance of museums and galleries was found nowhere in the United States, a country the Oppens considered disdainful of artists. Near Marseilles, they rented an empty house in a vineyard in the village of Le Beausset. As in the north, they were welcomed here; the local butcher boasted of his support for Tom Mooney, a socialist labor hero from San Francisco who was in prison for a bombing that he surely did not commit.

From France, the Oppens launched TO Publishers, in collaboration with the US-based poets Louis Zukofsky and Charles Reznikoff. They printed books by Ezra Pound (*How to Read*) and William Carlos Williams (*A Novelette and Other Prose*), and formalized their loose movement, Objectivism, which had been the focus of a special issue of *Poetry* magazine in February 1931. *An "Objectivist" Anthology* (1932), edited by Zukofsky, featured work by Reznikoff, Pound, Kenneth Rexroth, Basil Bunting, and others. George defined Objectivism as "the sense of the poet's self among things,"[3] or the objectification of the poem itself. Pound's "In a Station of the Metro" is an example of the earlier movement known as Imagism.

The Oppens had mixed feelings toward Pound, whom they visited in Rapallo, the small town on the Italian Riviera coastline where he'd lived since 1924. Despite their more than 20-year age difference, Pound and the Oppens admired each other's poetics and shared an interest in Europe's avant-garde. But as the Great Depression worsened, Pound deconstructed capitalism from the far right, gesturing to the chestnuts he gathered in the hills and declaring them beyond capital. He offered TO Publishers a second book on the ABCs of economics. The Oppens demurred. Their political differences only intensified. When Pound spoke of Benito Mussolini as "the Boss" (il Duce), Mary interpreted this with shock as "the sudden intrusion of a madness."[4]

Meanwhile, wandering in the Piazza San Marco in Venice, she wrote

> *we were suddenly surrounded by Black Shirts pouring into the [square] . . . so fast that we could not escape. We were pinned against the monument at the center of the Piazza by the press of the crowd, crying "Il Duce—pericolo del morte" . . . and we were trapped in this sudden, impressive demonstration. We saw no differences of expression on the faces of the young men, only of blind fanaticism, in ecstasy and worship of Il Duce.*[5]

3.

The Oppens' publishing venture fell into limbo, due to mismanagement on the US side. Books shipped from France to Zukofsky's apartment in New York often sat undistributed. The Oppens returned to the US in 1932. Driving from Philadelphia to New York, they were shaken by the sight of otherwise dignified men in tattered clothes—"our fathers," Mary called them—who asked for a nickel to wipe their windshield with a rag.[6]

In 1934, George's first book, *Discrete Series*, was published. To help sell it, he and Mary visited the few bookstores willing to carry an unknown poet during such dire economic times. "In German neighborhoods in New York City and New Jersey," Mary wrote,

> *right-wing organizations were drilling in fascist military style. Father [Charles] Coughlin was using the radio as it had not been used before; every Sunday, especially in working class neighborhoods, the windows were thrown open, radios were turned up full blast, and the voice of . . . the Radio Priest blared divisive, vituperative anti-Semitic fascist propaganda.*[7]

Nationally, it was a bleak time. President Hoover left office in 1933 with an emptied treasury. Welfare organizations, mostly philanthropic, were out of money. In New York, the Oppens saw "families sleeping on their household goods, piled on the sidewalks."[8]

In the summer of 1935, the couple heeded the seventh World Congress of the Communist Parties' appeal to intellectuals to join together to defeat fascism. Theirs was a firm decision. "We decided to work with the communist party, not as artist or writer because we did not find honesty or sincerity in the so-called arts of the left," Mary wrote. They told each other, "Let's work with the unemployed and leave our other interest in the arts for a later time."[9] Thus began American poetry's longest and most mythologized case of politically motivated writer's block. George did not publish another book until 1962, nearly 30 years after *Discrete Series*. Mary did not publish her memoir until 1978. Activism was foremost on their minds.

The couple wanted to help the unemployed, and found that "the Communist and the Socialist Parties were the only [entities] . . . organizing the unemployed to do something themselves about their predicament," she wrote.[10] They met Doretta Tarmon of the Communist Party's Workers Alliance of America, who "came to New York where the Movement was her breath, her sustenance, her life." Mary recalled,

> [Doretta] had intense black eyes behind thick lenses which flashed as she tossed her head in impassioned speech. She . . . wore a leather jacket and a hat with a long red feather; having come recently from Paris, I was bare-legged and bare-headed, wearing a Paris dress. Doretta cautioned me, "You don't want to be sectarian, comrade."[11]

In 1928, a writer named William Dudley Pelley transformed himself from a spiritualist to a rabidly anti-Semitic, Hitler-boosting, anti-communist who worked through a fascist college he founded in North Carolina, a printing press, several newsletters and newspapers, and a recruiting organization called the Silver Legion of America. Doretta dodged milk bottles thrown by these and other fascists. But, as the Oppens noted, the Italians to whom Doretta appealed nevertheless quietly sought her out, as they wanted "the Relief" from rent penalties and eviction, and also money for food.[12]

George later trained to bring these relief efforts to the Borough Hall section of Brooklyn, where the Alliance blocked evictions and fostered worker solidarity. Stretching from Atlantic and Flatbush Avenues "to the waterfront and from Brooklyn Bridge to the Manhattan Bridge, with all the slums that crowded under the El," the neighborhood blended Filipino, Puerto Rican, and Syrian-Lebanese families. Whole neighborhoods in Brooklyn seemed to be out of work. If the tenant was denied "the Relief," the threat of eviction culminated with the arrival of "the city marshal, who with several assistants put the furniture in the street and put a lock on the door."[13] This triggered the all-seeing, all-hearing "Petra Roja, who called a crowd together by leaning out her tenement window and beating on her dishpan."[14] The Alliance members and neighbors crowded into the apartment and did everything possible to block the marshal. When all else failed, the neighbors sat on the furniture in its place on the sidewalk to prevent the Sanitation Department from hauling it away.

Mary worked in a Black neighborhood around Nostrand Avenue. The chapter office was built up by Black women, many of whom were denied relief for having migrated recently from the South, a residency requirement being just one test that blocked aid otherwise available to whites. The Alliance's success in organizing around the principle that government can easily solve these issues with progressive policies led to intensified attempts by police and business interests to break the Alliance.[15] They sent in thugs to intimidate and assault the leadership, police arrested them, and trials involving the organization's leaders were strung along for years. George and Mary endured such a trial in the late 1930s. Given the thugs and the trials, it became too difficult in the city. The couple transferred upstate, working to unite small dairy farmers against exploitative conglomerates.

As war loomed, George sought skills that could be useful in the antifascist effort. The couple returned to New York City, where George trained as a machinist to make aircrafts for Grumman. With the bombing of Pearl Harbor in December 1941, he changed jobs for a higher machinist rating, knowing that this transfer exposed him to the draft. "De facto" enlistment, an interviewer called it. "We agreed that the war must be fought," Mary wrote, "that the lives of all Jews were endangered by fascism . . . and not to fight in the war was to ask of others what we would not do for ourselves." When George left for Europe, however, she insisted: "You must come back alive, do not throw yourself away in any moment's heroism. I want you to return."[16]

4.

In the Vosges Mountains on Germany's border with France, in a forest just south of where the Battle of the Bulge later occurred, George's unit was bogged down on the front lines. For six weeks no replacements came after they had relieved a regiment of Black soldiers that had taken heavy casualties. George froze through that bitter winter, unable to change clothes or bathe for over a month. "We came down through the Vosges mountains into a town leveled by artillery fire," he wrote Mary, "and which had only a cellar remaining; into it my company crowded—not a good position to be in."[17]

His French reassured the villagers, who provided soup and milk to the Allies. Victory Day was close when German fire pelted George's unit as it moved south near Urach, between Ulm and Stuttgart. He and the other convoy drivers jumped from their vehicles, desperate for cover. George dove into a hole left by the fresh blast of an 8mm shell. Another soldier also took cover there, then a third soldier fell onto them. One man was killed immediately when a shell exploded. "The shrapnel from the explosion passed through the other soldier and into Oppen," writes Eric Hoffman in his biography *Oppen: A Narrative* (2018):

> Oppen considered taking him to safety, but very soon realized that, given the shelling, to do so would amount to suicide, and that, given the nature of the other soldier's wounds, he was probably not going to survive anyway.

> *Instead, Oppen pulled the mortally wounded soldier's body over his own, and used him as a human shield. It became apparent to the other soldier that Oppen was not going to help him, and he began to protest.*[18]

Confused and immobile, George—two days from his 37th birthday—lay in the hole for 10 hours, awaiting nightfall. To pass the time until it was safe to leave, he recited poems by Reznikoff and Thomas Wyatt's "They Flee from Me." George convalesced in a hospital in Nancy, France. "Following his recovery," Hoffman writes,

> *he went to collect his belongings, his flak jacket among them. The attendant who gave him back his jacket was convinced that the serial number must be incorrect, that it was simply impossible for someone to survive such a barrage of shrapnel.*[19]

Mary sent a letter commanding, "You are to come home alive, no matter what the scars."[20] Spending much of that year in the hospital, long enough to learn that his division liberated the Landsberg concentration camp, George returned to New York City in 1946, decorated with numerous medals and deaf in one ear. Lingering guilt over his act of self-preservation troubled him for years. Soon after his homecoming, his trauma—PTSD, yet unnamed as such—required that he be left alone in silent, dark rooms. This was his habit throughout Linda's childhood. George remained irritable and depressed with his wartime firearm at hand, unwilling to sit with his back to the door or window. In late 1946, the Oppens moved to Southern California. Shortly after, with George's nerves already frayed, they began to notice dark cars outside the house.

5.

The FBI's repeated visits to the Oppens' Redondo Beach home turned an otherwise placid neighborhood suspicious, even hostile. "Do you visit those people often?" agents asked the Oppens' neighbors. "Whose car is that in [their] driveway?" The persecution-by-investigation—which made the Oppens outcasts—was visited upon "every friend, every neighbor, every person who had signed a petition, every trade unionist, every supporter of [former Vice President] Henry Wallace," Mary wrote.[21]

On one visit, she and George "decided to give no answers to [the FBI's] questions, although their insinuation was: give information, tell all, expose your neighbors, friends, comrades—that is the only way to be safe. One young man did the questioning, the other took out his notebook. When I walked around in back of the one who was writing, he looked up and asked, 'Are you going to watch to see what I write?'" "I am going to do just that," she replied.

According to the FBI files,[22] the topic of discussion that day was Whittaker Chambers, the former Communist Party member turned conservative anti-communist. Testifying before the House Un-American Activities Committee in 1948, Chambers named members of the so-called Ware Group of communist organizers, including Alger Hiss. As a result, Hiss was convicted of perjury around claims that he engaged in espionage while in the State Department. He served more than three years in prison but maintained his innocence until his death. All that was proven was that Hiss, like the Oppens, had been a member of the Communist Party before and during the war, which was not an especially dramatic revelation given that the Soviet Union was fighting as an Allied Power. The party was only (effectively) outlawed after the war.

Hiss and Chambers were on the minds of the agents who visited the Oppens on May 13, 1949. After calling ahead, Special Agents Arthur Wittenburg and Harold F. Dodge interviewed the Oppens "relative to their association with David Vernon Zimmerman." The agents believed that Zimmerman lived with the Oppens in the 1940s in Long Island, when George was remaking himself as a machinist to build war planes. "Zimmerman was a photographer for Whittaker Chambers," the agent noted, who worked "in a Soviet espionage apparatus operated on the East Coast in the 1930s." When asked about Zimmerman, the agents wrote:

> *Oppen stated that he knew that Zimmerman had never engaged in any espionage activity, but . . . that so far as Communist activity is concerned, he would not answer the question, because . . . the United States Government has no authority to ask questions concerning political beliefs. When asked additional questions, Oppen refused to answer . . . and did not even state whether the Oppens were acquainted with Zimmerman.*

The agent realized that George had made an accidental confession:

> *When it was pointed out that Mr. Oppen had already stated that he knew that Zimmerman was not engaged in espionage activities, from which statement it could reasonably be assumed that he [knew] Zimmerman, Oppen replied that he would withdraw this answer . . . and that he and his wife would answer no*

> *further questions. Throughout the interview . . . Mr. and Mrs. Oppen maintained an antagonistic attitude.*

Another memo elaborated on George's "antagonistic attitude," paraphrasing him as saying:

> *if the FBI has authority to ask questions concerning political beliefs of Communists, then tomorrow they will have authority to investigate a person because he is a Republican or Democrat. Oppen then went into a tirade concerning reports that telephone lines of private citizens are being tapped and civil rights are being infringed upon. Mary Oppen expressed the same views as did her husband.*

FBI recaps of the visit, alternately dated both May 13 and June 24, reveal that Mary was already on the FBI's Security Index, a list of leftists collected for use in possible mass arrests and political imprisonment. How threatening was this? Less than a decade earlier the government arrested Americans of Japanese and German descent and held them in internment camps for the duration of World War II. The Japanese got the worst of it, thanks to anti-Asian racism. Meanwhile, some German internees were Jewish (like George) and therefore unlikely to be conspiring with Hitler's regime. In an early form of rendition, the FBI rounded them up using its B and C Teams in Latin America.

Tensions flared after China's communist victory in 1949 and during the leadup to the Korean War in June of 1950. The Hiss case was mentioned during Congress's push to pass the McCarran Internal Security Act in 1950, which nearly failed but which was ultimately ratified in September of 1950. In practice, this law made some leftist politics of the past—such as working with United Front groups to stop evictions—retroactively illegal. President Truman vetoed the bill, calling it "a mockery of the Bill of Rights."[23] Congress overrode him. In this way, progressive activism during the Depression was recast as subversion and espionage. This was the impetus for the Oppens and their friends in the film industry to flee south. George was terrified of arrest.

6.

In Mexico City, Mary wrote, "we got in touch with a family whose name had been given to us by our movie writer friend." Once settled in a large house in the San Angel neighborhood where Diego Rivera kept a studio, she wrote that the Oppens were "prepared to receive political refugees, sure that many . . . would be coming. A Hollywood family arrived and moved in with us in our convent apartment, and I began looking for a larger place." Jean Rouverol, an actress friend of the Oppens, described the couple as "true Bohemians":

> Their apartment, off a stairway next to the San Angel post office, was a rambling series of rooms . . . strung together one flight up from a small back courtyard where one of the neighbors kept chickens . . . Their front door, off the landing, opened into George's woodworking shop, a confusion of worktables and a lathe and tools and bits of raw lumber and . . . several half-finished portrait carvings of his friends in bas-relief.[24]

Mary's own workspace "tended to be in whichever room could currently accommodate her easel and painting supplies and elderly sewing machine and photography equipment."[25] Rouverol describes being "entranced" by the Oppens during a dinner that she and her husband attended. "George's lean Old World face, with his dark eyes and his shaggy mustache and his thin forehead and aquiline nose," looked almost "hawk-like," while Mary was "his antithesis . . . with clear blue eyes, blond hair done up in a careless bun . . . I had the fleeting feeling that when I grew up I wanted to look just like her."[26]

But the all-seeing eye of US surveillance followed the Oppens across the border, with "two men hanging around our house day after day," Mary recalled.[27] One of the agents who questioned them "had the same dossier, with all the same background that the FBI men had had back in California and all the same errors, but these were Mexican men, supplied with dossiers that the CIA and FBI had compiled."[28] George, whose PTSD confined him to bed for days, was distressed by the visits. So was Mary.

The Oppens complained to their lawyer, Carmen Otero Gama. The sister-in-law of leftist labor leader Vicente Lombardo Toledano, Otero Gama was "a key contact in the Mexican government for left-wing radicals," wrote the Oppens' surveillant. She chased down files and found that the men monitoring the Oppens were attached to the presidential security detail. Otero Gama confronted the men after the Oppens identified them on the steps of a government building. She scolded them for "ugly" behavior, insisting that from now on they come to her with questions.[29] Remarkably, the Oppens never saw the men again. But the surveillance didn't end, even if George and Mary no longer noticed. It simply moved deeper into their circle.

According to FBI files, the Oppens' political activism continued in Mexico, though Mary downplays this in her memoir. They attended parties with the blacklisted filmmaker Trumbo, who wrote Oscar-winning screenplays (*Roman Holiday*, *The Brave One*) under pseudonyms during his Mexican exile. The surveillance files, which also contain errors, nevertheless record extraordinary details logged by informants who penetrated the Oppens' social life, suggesting that the couple's activism with the Communist Party continued for perhaps five years or more, into the mid-1950s. While the first surveillants may have been reassigned after the confrontation with the Oppens' lawyer, files show that those agents became moot after the Hollywood group was penetrated with paid and unpaid undercover informants.

Special Agent George Munro arranged to have his informant attend a December 1952 party at the home of Waldeen (von) Falkenstein Brooke de Zatz, a pioneering choreographer who was Mary and George's dance instructor. At this going-away party for the Polish communist Gitta Sten, an informant created a detailed list of attendees, with the makes, models, and license plate numbers of their cars, and he zeroed in on the rumored appearance of an unnamed but very important alleged communist who might stay with the Oppens. The memos don't disclose who the communist was.

In addition to Trumbo, the screenwriter Albert Maltz, another member of the blacklisted Hollywood Ten, was also present. At one point, the informant noted that an unknown couple from Guatemala was also there, and the "Unknown Male told George Oppen that he had a message from 'your friend Rupert' . . . Oppen, the unknown male and Albert Maltz immediately thereafter conferred in private. Both Oppen and Maltz were observed taking notes during the ensuing private conversation."

In a memo to J. Edgar Hoover, the informant concludes that this party "consisted of the largest gathering of known American Communists ever assembled in one place in Mexico City." At the end of the 12-page memo, the agent recommends that George—given his absence from the United States—be labeled in the "Unavailable Section of the Security Index."

By 1954, the FBI's Los Angeles field office had written to the State Department and to the Legal Attaché in Mexico requesting information that either agency may have about the Oppens. When George told one secret informant that he personally knew artists Diego Rivera and David Alfaro Siqueiros—in addition to knowing labor leader Vicente Lombardo Toledano—the statement was added to his file. Rivera was one of the art world's most famous communists and Siqueiros had been involved in the attempted murder of Leon Trotsky in 1940. Mary was overheard arguing that even if Rivera had once been a Trotskyite, she still found him charming and admirable.

Another informant overheard a rumor that Oppen "considered himself to be the 'titular head of the Communist Party, USA in Mexico.'" The Oppens agreed to attend a fundraiser for the "official newspaper organ of the Mexican Communist Party" but were unable to go due to heavy rains. "Having failed to attend the party," the memo says, "Oppen sent his personal check . . . in the amount of 150 pesos, which was added to the collection." This and other FBI memos reveal that the bureau was either directly opening the Oppens' mail, or one of their informants worked for the Mexican postal service and was doing so there.

Other fundraising initiatives included George's campaign to get the Civil Rights Congress's pamphlet "[We Charge] Genocide" translated into Spanish. This report for the United Nations, printed as a booklet in 1951, charged the United States with atrocities against Black Americans. The Civil Rights Congress hoped to make lynching and other acts of murderous racism illegal and subject to prosecution. While the FBI treated the Civil Rights Congress as a communist front, the scholar Gerald Horne has analyzed how the CRC's procedural understanding of rights, its legal defense of alleged communists, and its focus on attacking racism years before *Brown v. Board of Education* made it far more (and something less) than a communist front. It was a template for the better known Civil Rights Movement of the late 1950s and early '60s. Though Robeson supported it in Peekskill, it was effectively disbanded after the McCarran and Smith Acts forced it to register as subversive.[30]

According to FBI files, George wanted to coordinate the communist groups in Mexico. When questioned at the border while crossing into Guatemala to renew his tourist visa, he allegedly described himself as "an enemy of the North American Government" who could not enter the United States. Other "subversive" activities involved a letter to President Eisenhower suggesting clemency for Ethel and Julius Rosenberg, the American couple convicted of spying for the Soviet Union. Informants also confirmed that George had been an important Party leader in Southern California and would remain so wherever he went. Mary was quoted as saying that she and a friend had been members of the same communist "cell" in New York, that "the two of them had frequently lunched with Communist Party National Committeewoman, Elizabeth Gurley Flynn."

In a section of the FBI files labeled "Statements by Subjects," Mary told an unnamed informant in March of 1953 that it was "unfortunate that Stalin could not have outlived Eisenhower." She also predicted that, having lost most of its allies, the United States would be "rudely surprised if there were another war, 'when they lost it.'" In June, 1954, during the US coup on Guatemala, she told friends how to contribute to the Guatemala Relief Committee and "commented that in addition to receiving contributions [her contacts] were preparing a list of persons who would be willing to go to Guatemala to assist in the 'Red Cause.'"

Even in the mid-1950s, the Oppens' criticism of the Soviet Union and of the Communist Party USA was recorded in their file by an agency whose very methodology was paranoia. George was overheard criticizing anti-Semitic statements and attitudes made by Albert Maltz, whom George criticized "for his low characterizations of Jewish people in his books." George also expressed disappointment with leftists who blindly accepted Soviet and Marxist art as the paragon of culture. "After all," an informant quoted him, "there are good points in the cultural system in the United States." He criticized the Soviet Union directly, for example, after Khrushchev's unfair treatment of Lavrentiy Beria, the former secret police chief and deputy premier who was executed in 1953. George did not consider Beria "a capitalist traitor and spy," his surveillant wrote, as the Soviet regime did.

Other entries show the Oppens asking US officials how they might get their names cleared of subversion and obtain a passport to return home. That goal informed their time in Mexico, writes Mary, and led to the Oppens distancing themselves from friends there. While George and Mary drifted from the so-called American Communist Group in Mexico, their FBI files indicate years of committed leftism interspersed with ambivalence. The Oppens are even reported to have been kicked out of the Party for desertion when they crossed the Mexican border without notifying the Party's Los Angeles chapter.

Even as they begged officials to help clear their record so they could come home, they insisted that their political views—leftist, communist, or otherwise—were none of the government's business. The informants heard the Oppens criticize the USSR and watched them take notes among people from communist-controlled countries, but they also witnessed the Oppens thinking freely, denouncing US policy where it was fascist and Soviet policies where they were violent or abusive, and praising US culture when it seemed attractive. The Oppens were coming to their own judgments even as spies encircled them. Every conversation was layered with paranoia and suspicion.

7.

By 1958, the Oppens were estranged from their friends in Mexico. Linda was nearing college age. The family still didn't have passports and couldn't return to the United States. "We needed to be freely in our own country, to have time to assimilate the violent years before turning them into thought and poetry," Mary wrote.[31] She was anxious and found it difficult to cope with George's depression. She began therapy with a progressive, feminist psychiatrist who asked about her dreams, one of which featured a small man eating peanuts from a paper bag while Mary stood before an abyss that she couldn't bear to look into. Noting her anxiety, the psychiatrist said, "But no one is preventing you; you are free to move forward, to become whatever it is you decide to become." Even so, Mary felt stuck in "the frustration of only being a wife and mother."[32]

The following year, Linda was accepted to Sarah Lawrence College in Bronxville, New York, not far from where George was born. But the State Department had been denying

Americans passports since the early 1950s. When the family sent their passports for renewal, the documents were destroyed, George was labeled a "premature antifascist"—opposing Hitler too soon for the government's taste—and no new passports were sent. A parallel case of passport denial—that of the artist Rockwell Kent—made its way to the Supreme Court in 1958 and was decided in favor of political dissidents. With the Oppens' passports restored after the Kent ruling, Linda went to New York for school that September. Though the ruling meant that George and Mary could visit her, Mary's anxiety persisted: the psychiatrist asked to meet George and Linda, in order to interpret their dreams.

Before his session, George had his famous dream that his father died. He and his sister were "going through his father's papers. . . . In a file marked 'miscellaneous' was a paper entitled 'How to Prevent Rust in Copper.'" George thought, "My old man was a little frivolous perhaps, but he certainly knows copper doesn't rust."[33] Mary woke to George shaking in bed with laughter. She didn't find it funny. When he laughed off the dream in front of the psychiatrist, the doctor said, "You were dreaming that you don't want to rust."[34]

"On the way home," Mary wrote, "George stopped and bought a pad of paper and some pencils and started to write *The Materials*."[35] The question that produced the most anxiety was how to write about his life, including his political struggles, without falling into the trap that Mary described in her memoir of art without sincerity. "It is possible to say anything in abstract prose," George wrote in the early 1960s, "but a great many things one believes . . . or thinks he believes will not substantiate themselves in the concrete materials of the poem."[36]

"Blood from the Stone," the first poem George wrote after his 25-year hiatus, follows an image of Mary carrying bundles ("Everything I am / is us"). He draws street scenes from the days of Doretta Tarmon and the Workers Alliance:

> The Thirties. And
>
> A spectre
>
> In every street,
> In all explicable crowds, what they did then
> Is still their lives.
>
> As thirty in a group—
> To Home Relief—the unemployed—
> Within the city's intricacies
> Are these lives. Belief?
> What do we believe
> To live with? Answer.
> Not invent—just answer—all
> That verse attempts.
> That we can somehow add each to each other?
>
> —Still our lives.

George juxtaposed poetry and activism, but he worried about being obvious:

> And war.
>
> More than we felt or saw.
> There is a simple ego in a lyric,
> A strange one in war.
> To a body anything can happen,

Like a brick. Too obvious to say.
But all horror came from it.

He recounted trooping through French villages in boots and helmet, struggling to see around every impediment to spot danger, and then feeling sudden joy at the scent of wood smoke and the hope of life continuing. He recorded his current age in 1958 (he was 50), adding, "Among them we were lucky—strangest word / . . . because we find the others / Deserted like ourselves and therefore brothers. Yet // So we lived / And chose to live. // These were our times."

The stylistic innovations and metaphysical concerns that later made up "Of Being Numerous" are evident in *The Materials*: bricks and ordinary objects signal the constructions of time and history; the vicissitudes of the body are evident; the experience of city life among crowds is vividly rendered, as is the cherishing of family. Both books limn the horror of war (and the search to reconcile oneself to the solitude that this horror generates). There is also the notion of being stranded ("deserted" or "shipwrecked") and the solidarity emanating from seeing that all are also stranded ("therefore brothers").

George published *The Materials* in 1962. It featured "Blood from the Stone" and other poems set in New York, Central America, and Mexico. Petra Roja appears in the poems, as do the Silver Shirts. By the early '60s, with their passports restored, the Oppens returned to the United States and settled near Brooklyn Heights. They returned with their car and a 25-foot boat that George built. A package filled with his papers, including new poems, got lost. Nevertheless, George's third book, *This in Which*, appeared in 1965. The book's centerpiece is "A Language of New York," a prototype for George's later 40-section "Of Being Numerous."

The poem captures New Yorkers in their routines: "They are shoppers, / Choosers, judges; . . . And here the brutal / is without issue, a dead end." So estranged is his gaze on New York life, though, that George veered into a meditation on baseball: "baseball's their game / because baseball is not a game / but an argument and difference of opinion / makes the horse races." He broaches the war: "I cannot even now / Altogether disengage myself / From those men // With whom I stood in emplacements, in mess tents, / In hospitals and sheds and hid in the gullies / Of blasted roads in a ruined country."

George wrote to several friends about his struggle to finish reworking "A Language of New York." New snippets of the poem emerged in these letters. In fact, friends recall him driven to write five hours a day in the 1960s and '70s, presumably to make up for 25 years of silence. (Remarkably, he always planned to return to poetry; one colleague teased George that it took him 25 years to write his second book.) To further immerse himself in the objects of New York, and to protect his writing time, George rented a room under the Brooklyn Bridge. Soon the sight of it entered the poem that he wrestled to finish.

> The great stone
> Above the river
> In the pylon of the bridge
>
> '1875'
>
> Frozen in the moonlight
> In the frozen air over the footpath, consciousness

Which has nothing to gain, which awaits nothing,
Which loves itself

But while George toiled to construct his most ambitious poem, he was stuck. First, he was stuck foraging through metaphysical and philosophical texts by Heidegger, Kierkegaard, Wittgenstein, Kant, and Yves Bonnefoy. He had to find a proper image for solitude—the void, he called it in a letter to Linda. The solitude he experienced in war returned frequently in his bouts of depression. In a different writer's hands, this impulse would feel like protest writing. George's fear of dying alone in France, away from his family, made him want to risk his pristine, apolitical modernism and test its accommodation of a political and moral message against killing. But as a realist-objectivist, he refused to go beyond what he observed directly. Constantly reworking language that contained his observations and experiences, he found that poetry could accommodate his anxiety over this tension.

To solve the first problem, he had to contrast his vision of solitude with scenes of crowds:

"The shuffling of a crowd is nothing—well, nothing but the many that we are, but nothing."

As an image for solitude, George envisioned Robinson Crusoe. The idea may have come from Mexico. One of his Hollywood friends, Rouverol's husband, Hugo Butler, wrote a film adaptation of Daniel Defoe's *The Adventures of Robinson Crusoe*. Directed by the celebrated Spanish-Mexican director Luis Buñuel—and filmed on location in Mexico—the film was released in 1954. Biographers[37] indicate a possible connection between Buñuel's Crusoe film and the use of Crusoe imagery in "Of Being Numerous." But the image could have cropped up naturally from George and Mary's love of sailing through the fog and using maps and a compass to find small islands and harbors off the coast of Maine.

> We are pressed, pressed on each other,
> We will be told at once
> Of anything that happens
>
> And the discovery of fact bursts
> In a paroxysm of emotion
> Now as always. Crusoe
>
> We say was
> 'Rescued'.
> So we have chosen.
>
> *
>
> Obsessed, bewildered
>
> By the shipwreck
> Of the singular
>
> We have chosen the meaning
> Of being numerous.

While George expanded "A Language of New York"—first from his room under the bridge, then from San Francisco, and finally from Deer Island, Maine—he read, heard, and thought about the US involvement in Vietnam. "I'm finding it difficult to write poetry," he complained to his niece in 1965. "An eerie feeling writing poetry with the war going on. I don't know if I can." He complained not just of his own conflicting emotions, but of public distrust in leadership. "A lot of resistance, a lot of doubt, too much as things stand to induce people to throw away a few million lives of young men." Six million Southeast Asians were killed in the conflict, roughly the number of Jews killed in Hitler's camps.[38] Reflecting on the power of the antiwar protests, he wrote, "People have never been so close to a refusal, the American Legion 'patriotism' has never been so near to the disreputable." He shifted to the use of napalm, writing in a meandering stream:

> *Meanwhile burning gasoline; it is "eerie" also to talk about "politics." We sit in this little room—it's really like a light-house. . . . I know it has roots in our whole history and in the talk on the streets as far back as I can remember. . . . Impossible not to wonder if a disgruntled CIA high command asked a vice president how he'd like to be president. . . . It is a thing like that, a kind of mad clown, nothing that was even respectable intended this, there's obviously insane talk about dominoes and [saving] face. . . . I don't think it can be continued, I think it will be stopped. But I don't even KNOW how many people have been burned alive, how many half-burned children.*[39]

The same anti-communist impulses that chased the Oppens from Redondo Beach spilled countless gallons of napalm on Vietnamese children; the logic of anti-communism, like the logic of lynching Black Americans, went beyond the platitudes of political debate. George's dreams began to play tricks on him. Hunting for philosophical quotations for "Of Being Numerous," George dreamed he plagiarized Heidegger in an early poem. Upon waking he realized he made it up himself: the last word in the line he feared he plagiarized was "incalculable." But he could not find the word in Heidegger.[40]

In February 1966, the Oppens attended a large rally of veterans against the war in Washington, D.C. But they demurred from marching, worried they wouldn't have the energy to last the whole route. After viewing the march, and after reading about the war, George finally found words to link his experience of war with the creeping evil of the US presence in Vietnam. To express his disgust, he invoked an image of suicide:

> It is the air of atrocity,
> An event as ordinary
> As a President.
>
> A plume of smoke, visible at a distance
> In which people burn.
>
> [. . .]
>
> Now in the helicopters the casual will
> Is atrocious
>
> Insanity in high places,
> If it is true we must do these things
> We must cut our throats
>
> The fly in the bottle
>
> Insane, the insane fly
>
> Which, over the city
> Is the bright light of shipwreck

8.

Of Being Numerous was published on March 31, 1968, just days before Martin Luther King denounced the American war on Vietnam in a speech describing the United States as the "greatest purveyor of violence in the world today." Like George, King was influenced by the suffering of children, and was particularly moved by photos in *Ramparts* that documented the effects of napalm on Vietnamese children. George's previous collections received mixed reviews. But several critics recognized the modernist power that marks *Of Being Numerous*.

Writing in the *New York Times Book Review*, the poet Louis Simpson perceived in the book "all that has been excluded by a very discriminating mind in order to arrive at significant life. The mind, moving toward clarity, sheds those matters that are, as Gatsby said, 'just personal.' As it begins to know itself, the mind moves, and thought is felt as movement, along the line. We experience the life of the mind in its physical reality, the movement of Verse."[41]

As a member of the Pulitzer Prize jury, Simpson lobbied the other jurors to honor *Of Being Numerous* with the award that year. It was the only collection that the three white male jurors could agree upon. Simpson added in his juror's citation that the poetry had "some startling things in it; it's true, and intelligent, and experimental."[42]

But George's response to his victory was less than elated. Calling the award "a questionable compliment,"[43] he had mixed feelings when the choice was announced in May of 1969. Vaguely sensing that even a little fame could convert his private process into a public performance, he canceled the tour of poetry readings arranged by his publisher and friends and over the next few years tried to step out from the shadow of the book's success.

In letters, he discussed the difficulty of getting past the long poem at the book's heart, asking poet and friend Harvey Shapiro, "You think *Numerous* is as far as I'll get?"[44] But he also admitted to needing the prize, needing it because it was "gauche" to be a 61-year-old "self-confident unknown" at parties.[45]

In a letter to his son-in-law, Alex Mourelatos, George added that the poem's success was causing him to imitate himself. Defending the poem's material as realism to his sister June Oppen, he credited his winning the Pulitzer to "Celebrating a victory (possibly temporary) over surrealists and symbolists I had thought were dead."[46] Yet of the poem's antiwar section—which begins with the aforementioned "It is the air of atrocity"—George admitted that it "might be felt to be over-clever," or even

> *appear somewhat as an outburst, an outburst of horror . . . [or that] the flat drop to the line / "Is atrocious" / might carry the sense of arbitrariness . . . the need to make a stance somewhere*[47]

In the Vietnam War era, however, George insisted it was mere reportage, though it "Reports not a proof but a vision," staying "close to that realistic point" that "the atrocious is the atrocious." This range from observation to a vision of horror pointed to the value of poetry, which offered glimpses, George wrote, into "the size of reality."[48]

9.

A decade later, in 1978, Mary Oppen published *Meaning a Life*. The book is direct, amusing, comprehensive, and wry, filled with her and George's love of animals, their bond to each other, and their discipline of practicing life as an art. But it downplays their political activism in Mexico, therefore somewhat obscuring the obsession that at least George felt for merging his poetry with activism. The book's dedication, "To George, whose life and mine are intertwined," echoes the dedication of George's 1975 *Collected Poems*: "For Mary, whose words in this book are tangled inextricably among my own."

The echo stretches further. The same publisher, Black Sparrow Press, printed both the autobiography and George's final book of poems, *Primitive*. When George's Alzheimer's worsened, he asked Mary to finish preparing *Primitive*. The two books were reviewed together in *The New York Times*. While "Of Being Numerous" struggles to convey his innermost thoughts on trauma, solitude, and war, it also points to Mary, using his old image of the brick:

> In a brick wall
> The eye picks
>
> So quiet of a Sunday
> Here is the brick, it was waiting
> Here when you were born
>
> Mary-Anne.

The Oppens weren't unique as writers harassed and surveilled by the FBI. The American Nobel laureate Ernest Hemingway was hounded by the Bureau in a way that likely hastened his suicide. Like the CIA, the FBI also created a mechanism to censor books from the left that challenged their image or ideology: J. Edgar Hoover recruited publishing insiders to send him controversial manuscripts for his political appraisal.[49]

But the section on atrocities in *Of Being Numerous*, with its image of the fly in the bottle, is a powerful if insufficient response to the harassment the Oppens underwent. Especially given that George's mother committed suicide when he was small—and that his will to live was tested during World War II—his suggestion that Americans in the Vietnam era "must cut our throats" is unlike anything that came before it in American poetry. In the same letter to George's son-in-law cited above, his musings make clear he thought hard about that line.

As Mourelatos himself had provided the "fly in the bottle" image, George wrote to thank him. He described the image as depicting "the vision of the insane, poisonous Johnsonian flies" who were engaged in mass killings in Vietnam. Of those Democratic Party-affiliated tendencies George likened to flies, agents working for the administration kept tabs on the Oppens, via FBI's security updates, through much of Johnson's presidency and until the spring of 1966, whether George and Mary knew of this continued domestic surveillance or not.

Those poisonous flies, George wrote, "are not us. Not the four of us." Somehow writing the poem momentarily put George and his family outside of those atrocities. "Whatever our differences," he wrote, "we are not those insane flies. I have no way to say how grateful I am, or how fortunate I feel."[50]

II

"Throughout most of our political history the intellectual has been for the most part either an outsider, a servant or a scapegoat."
—Richard Hofstadter

1999

Silver Spoons: Frances Stonor Saunders in Kansas

or how reporting on CIA censorship got her work censored

1.

If her editor had gotten his way, Frances Stonor Saunders's history of literary spooks may have remained a casualty of censorship. Her book, *The Cultural Cold War: The CIA and the World of Arts and Letters* examined the CIA's meddling in literature, magazines, and media. But in a late draft, her editor insisted she praise the CIA as with the angels. Her refusal almost tanked the US edition.

It's worth celebrating Saunders's investigative triumph—one that's spurred ongoing debate, helping launch an academic cottage industry that has been dubbed cultural Cold War studies. Scholar Edward Said called *The Cultural Cold War* "a major work of investigative history" adding that "the dispiriting truth it reveals, or confirms, is that few of 'our' major intellectual and cultural figures resisted the blandishments of the C.I.A." But as *The Cultural Cold War* reaches its twenty-fifth anniversary, many misrepresent what the cultural Cold War actually was, suggesting that the program was an unmitigated success, helping "win" the Cold War, or that vast swaths of the rebel left are "synthetic," still—that is, counterfeit, as if the left were created out of whole, fake cloth by the state.

When I meet her for lunch on a rainy September day on Grove Street, she is still livid, twenty-five years later. I place a transcript of my 2016 interview with her on the table, and she orders smoked salmon and eggs with creme fraiche and capers. She makes small notes in the margins, amplifying or augmenting the original story she told me of wanting to tell the story of the Congress for Cultural Freedom properly.

"If I'm going to do this," she vowed, "I'm going to be absolutely clear with anyone I'm talking to; I'm not doing anything off the record," lest she continue "repeating some of the errors of the whole program."[1] After interviewing a key player in the Congress for Cultural Freedom, she grew demoralized, an obstacle course of sorts having spread before her. And yet, after wringing the truth from those who were expecting more praise and whitewash, she was most taken aback when her own editor nearly tanked the book before it could be published.

2.

One of the Congress's sentinels, Irving Kristol browbeat her with a disingenuous warning. "It's an *old* story," he said. "Everybody *knows* this. . . . Why are you doing this *now*?" Growing nervous, she "almost fell for it." "Oh, God," she recalls thinking, "there's a whole library out here on this stuff and" it was already mossy. To protect the secret program's crown jewels, this old saw that it was an "old story" was honed. (The Censor's Mantra today, rhyme and all, goes: *What's New is Not True and What's True is Not New*.) Saunders's favorite childhood rhyme countered: "Truth, truth, nobody's daughter, jumped out of the boat and into the water."

Overshadowed by Vietnam, the CCF scandal erupted in *The New York Times* eleven days after Saunders was born. Born in London, Saunders studied English at St. Anne's College, Oxford. On her mother's side, she hails from a blue-blood pedigree that occasionally embarrassed itself correcting for extremism. (In a much-discussed memoir, her mother exposed her grandmother's Nazi sympathies). On her father's side were Jews exiled to England during the war. The mashup spawns a twin persona—the dispassionate proceduralism of a well-heeled Oxbridge barrister colliding with the radical cussing of a Vivienne Westwood

Aries. Dressed in preppy but understated layers, she dons glasses with red frames and simple pearl earrings.

The phrase she has done most to popularize was used in 1968 by the historian Christopher Lasch, who described the same New York Intellectuals like Kristol—who formed the American CCF, and later neoconservatism—as a clique of "high-level McCarthyites" who sometimes supported McCarthy explicitly.[1] Critics like Lasch went ignored in the debate that followed revelations of the CIA's subsidies to intellectuals. It is only for this reason that those who further his critique—like Saunders—can be called "revisionists."[2]

In this light, Saunders felt it to be "a story that hadn't been told *fully*. I just felt like" Kristol's "was a strategy and he was trying to put me off. He was calling all his friends, saying, 'Don't talk to this woman.'" So when the cohort insisted "You're fifty years too late," she started to realize, *They don't want me to do this.* It "was clearly an incentive." One claim was, "Yes, it was a necessary evil" to use CIA funds, "but none of us did or said or wrote anything that we wouldn't have otherwise, and freedom of expression was in no way curtailed. It was, instead, *advanced* by this [program].' That was the Gloria Steinem line. We still hear it all the time."[3]

She found it contradictory. "What a peculiar defense of the organization built covertly for the theft of culture—saying it didn't matter because they were going to do it anyway." On the other hand, some of those she interviewed were bluntly honest. "The ones I have more respect for said, 'You know, it was a question of exigency, and we did it and we're glad we did it.'" "But the number of people trying to keep every level of their involvement secret, it just made me think that these two things don't sit together."

Digging into the archive, she read the former operatives' letters. But the old secrecy kicked back in. A few of the guardians of free speech blocked her with threats over copyright. It staggered the mind. "You can't on one hand say *It was necessary and worth it, I'm proud I was associated with it*, and at the same time say *I don't want any of the details of this to come out, and I'm not going to give you copyright to print my letters* . . ."

Met with sneakiness, Saunders adopted a savvy counteroffensive, showing up to interviews with her notebook hidden, hoping to establish trust. In one case she met a former CIA officer in a bar, as he drank himself silly on cheap wine. Her patience yielded if not a "smoking gun," then an opening.

After Thomas Braden worked directly for CIA Director Allen Dulles (under the pseudonym Homer D. Hoskins), in his post-CIA life he was co-host of *Crossfire* and creator of *My Three Sons*. But sitting with Saunders, he let slip "that the CIA had a power of veto" over its editors and writers—a euphemism for censorship. She convinced him to admit this by guessing, asserting it with conviction, watching him calculate, then agree.

Initially, it stunned her. "Ok, that's interesting," she recalls thinking.

But again the narrative defaulted to stonewalling; and her doubts returned. "For a long time, I believed pretty much what I'd been told, that it was really theoretical, that" the veto "was never used, and it didn't need to be, because everybody was seeing it from the same" script. As the cover stories knocked her off the scent, she came to view the uniformity as "interesting in itself. Because people were agreeing" on what to publish. "Who was it who called them 'a herd of independent minds'?"[4]

By uncovering the agency's veto, she wielded new leverage in interviews. As she read *Encounter's* editorial letters, she knew what to look for, and found "at least 20 or 30 instances of direct intervention stroke censorship stroke the CIA acting as executive editors." ("Stroke" in the Queen's English is like "slash" in the colonies.)

After our first interview, she emails me a list of fifty entries. Referenced by date and subject, each letter records CIA officers invoking the need to censor its authors—exercising this infamous "veto" over its editors' judgements. In one letter, CCF executive Nicolas Nabokov reminds his editors of a rule from the magazine's founding: that anything politically controversial must be ok'ed at Paris headquarters. The letter proves that Agency censorship was explicit and structural. When enforced, it warned editors away from controversy or criticism of US policy—especially foreign policy—in advance of doing it again.[5]

For three decades, CCF veterans had maintained Three Holy Tenets: 1.) they never censored 2.) the CIA never meddled and 3.) they published great writers. With the Nabokov letter and the larger batch, Saunders killed the first two tenets. (Gabriel García Márquez caveated the third, when he wrote his editor, "I will never write for you again."). But the CCF would not relinquish its story readily, and she considered how to frame it against an anticipated chorus of denial.

For the examples of censorship she found, she imagined "many, many more. But I would still say that it's a small percentage of the total output, in all media, of what the Congress for Cultural Freedom, and these other CIA fronts, were doing. It would be wrong to say that they had a department in the CIA that was frantically trying to keep this riotous lot in order."

But if the CIA embarrassed its editors by making them undo an acceptance—as happened in the 1950s—the editors' embarrassment was itself instructive. Saunders came to view it as "a very cleverly developed and maintained consensus that was funded and delivered unto the world as a defense of *liberalism*, and all the cherished liberal principles of free democracy, where freedom of expression is paramount." Yet "if you weren't within those orthodoxies and were receiving CIA dollars—there was a lot of heterodox opinion—it just didn't get heard. It did not get as much airtime for that brief period of what? . . . seventeen years or whatever. Because it wasn't in the fold of the CIA, MI6, CCF family."

As evidence in other genres, she recalls figurative—or social realist—painters who couldn't get exhibitions during abstract expressionism's secretly subsidized reign. (I read of Black social realist artists Charles White and Elizabeth Catlett, who at the dawn of the Cold War lit out for Mexico City.[6] It got—and stayed—so bad, Catlett never came back.)

After the Bay of Pigs and the rise of the New Left, the subsidized editors got even more effective at camouflaging their sponsorship. At the BBC, they called insertions included to mask their bias "credibility items"[7]—an acceptable critique meant to gain uptake among particular audiences. A counterfeit progressivism, yes—but used by non-progressives in the interest of fooling and discrediting very *real* progressives.

3.

With enough to start writing, Saunders returned to England. She likes to write in "a shed under a chestnut tree. The falling chestnuts hitting the roof in autumn keep me awake." Her coverage proved broad, spanning laws that gave birth to the CIA, how it was funded; how funds from the Marshall Plan were used, sub rosa, to beat the Soviets in cultural funding; how the CIA and MI6 used taxpayers' funds to sponsor classical music tours, to organize abstract expressionist exhibits in Europe, and to launch magazines.

Her most troubling findings traced the overlapping personnel who created *Encounter* with those who were launching international crimes like the overthrow of Iran's elected prime minister, Mossadegh. Which gave us the Shah. Which gave us the Ayatollah. Who gave Rushdie hell, and who helped elect Reagan.[8] CCF anti-communist talking points spread from dozens of small-circulation intellectual magazines like *Encounter*, where Kristol was editor, into other magazines, finding their way ultimately into mass media. Since the CIA was banned in its charter from operating at home, this flow was a crime. And this influence was rampant, resulting in Congressional hearings.

Saunders revealed moles in Hollywood, whose connivance kept American poverty and racism out of the industry's films. One mole got multiple films stalled for depicting the US in an unflattering light—poverty and racism washed out, foreshadowing the age of Zero Dark collaboration and the Marvel Spectacle that we live in today. In the most ironic revelations, *The Cultural Cold War* examines operatives at publishing houses like Praeger, who could get your book killed if it failed to celebrate the "West."

As she stitched together archives in the US and UK, she lifted the veil of occlusion. "The most effective kind of propaganda," she quotes one of her subjects,[9] "is defined as the kind where the subject moves in the direction you desire for reasons which he believes to be his own."

At Faber, the book was approved, intact. But at Free Press, a large independent New York house that was dissolved after Simon and Schuster swallowed it, her editor suggested a surprising disclaimer. She saw her Free Press editor as an odd fit. When "offered to every publisher in

New York, no one took it except for the Free Press." But the press published at odds with her viewpoint.

Founded in 1947, the Free Press took a new approach under neoconservative Edwin Glikes's leadership in the Reagan era. It published Robert Bork's *The Tempting of America* and Allan Bloom's *The Closing of the American Mind*. Under Adam Bellow's leadership it grew worse, publishing Dinesh D'Souza's *Illiberal Education*, David Brock's *The Real Anita Hill*, and Charles Murray's racist classic *The Bell Curve*. In 1989, it crowned its canon with *The Liberal Conspiracy*, the book she hoped to correct for its whitewash, and which praised the CIA for the CCF scandal.

Saunders asked her agent, "'Why would they take it? I mean, they publish half the people I'm going to be writing about, and not very favorably." When the deal went through, Saunders met her editor in New York. "Are we absolutely clear that if I find any prima facie evidence that is not necessarily entirely flattering to do with any of your authors that this is not going to be a problem?" she asked. "Don't worry," he said. As long as it wasn't ad hominem, "I can handle it." Faber and the Free Press agreed "that the same manuscript would be used for both books, and that meant [the US editor] would play second fiddle to my editor here."

But while her US editor "initially was really pleased and loved it," he asked during the first edit to make "adjustments." He suggested a Trojan horse disclaimer, reversing her argument. "All I needed to do," she says, still livid twenty-five years later, "was to say that the CIA were *on the side of the angels*, I quote, and that America's was a good cause. I was like, 'No, I don't think so. I'm not going to change the polemic. I mean, what are we talking about here?'" After faxes seeking clarity went unanswered, "they dumped the book."

But falling victim to corporate censorship wasn't the worst of it. For failing to tell a more useful story of the

American century, The Free Press then billed her. "They said I owed them the $15,000 they had paid me as the first advance. And it was an incredibly distressing time, because I had no money and I'd spent what little money I had just getting flights to the States and paying for a month's motel in Abilene, Kansas, and all that shit. It was really, really, really kind of crazy." Stepping back, it suggests that by never being held to account, a batch of shady "centrists" who penetrated publishing and media in the 1950s were active and spawning, there to "veto" critiques like hers quietly.

Finally, socialist author and New Press publisher André Schiffrin "came to the rescue." Her experience had been so unpleasant that Saunders tried to fall on her sword. "I don't think, legally, I can give you this contract," she said. "Don't worry," he said. "We'll sort it out." He brought in "a lawyer who did a lot of work for the ACLU," saving her book.

Some reviewers, like Joseph Joffe in *The New York Times*, quoted her selectively, suggesting a native inability to hear criticism of the West on its merits. Implying that Saunders was anti-Semitic—despite her father's background—Joffe demanded more on "Communist manipulation" in a book explicitly about the capitalist kind. A magazine man, Joffe would found *The American Interest* after Nixonites ate *The National Interest*.* Climaxing to a chorus of "moral equivalence," he wrote—using 90s lingo for "wokeism": "Echoing the conventional multiculturalist critique, Saunders relentlessly equates the sub rosa subsidies of the West with Moscow's heavy-handed propaganda efforts." Except she didn't.

---

*   Itself founded by Irving Kristol, who wangled yet more CIA funds to launch *The Public Interest*; these were instruments of future frauds like the Iraq War and pushing private and charter schools as a response to Brown v. Board of Education.

The book was shortlisted for the *Guardian's* first book award and won the Royal Historical Society's William Gladstone Memorial Prize. In 2018, she was elected as a Royal Society of Literature Fellow. As Diego Rivera's biographer recalled of his abandoning Cubism, to read Saunders is "like watching [someone] focusing [their] eyes after an extended period of blurred vision."

After my own book comes out and is met with selectively dishonest readings by one or two of its (conflicted) reviewers, I email Saunders to bitch and moan. She writes, "I understand why you're unhappy with the review you've sent me, and I'll only say that I had to put up a fight before, during and after the publication of my book, and it was exhausting. Was it Thomas Mann or Goethe who said you should never answer a critic unless he accuses you of stealing twelve silver spoons?"

1965

Infiltrated: Malcolm X at the Audubon

or how he received mouth-to-mouth from an informant,
with eight other informants in the room

The only time Malcolm X met Martin Luther King, Jr.—in the Capitol Building in March 1964—he told King, "Now you're going to get investigated."[1] By then, King had fought for and gained a place in America's conscience at the same time that Malcolm had just fallen out with his teacher and the Nation of Islam. Malcolm hoped to forge a united front of Black liberation groups that included a rapprochement with King. The meeting took place a year before Malcolm's death, during a time of intense travel and speeches, landmark civil rights legislation, and rampant government surveillance of both figures.

But while Malcolm joked about this surveillance to King, the degree to which various agencies were spying on the Nation of Islam's most famous apostate escaped even him. In his final months, Malcolm softened his antagonism to King's nonviolent approach, while speaking openly to friends of the near-constant death threats. A series released in 2020 on Netflix suggests that the role US law enforcement officials played in Malcolm's murder has been understated—and gets closer than ever to laying the blame at the feet of the US government.

Who Killed Malcolm X?[2] features Abdur-Rahman Muhammad, a journalist who, over six episodes, guides the viewer through his investigatory labyrinth to reveal that two of the three men convicted for Malcolm's murder were innocent. He goes on to show that the FBI knew this but did not submit evidence to exonerate the men. During a key episode, he meditates on why. Taking his questions to Nation of Islam veterans and Pulitzer Prize–winning and in-house FBI historians, Muhammad finally establishes that this oversight could not have been accidental. As a protagonist and guide through the annals of Malcolm X revisionism,

Muhammad is so convincing that Malcolm's murder case was reopened shortly after the series aired.

Timed with the fifty-fifth anniversary of the murder, the series includes among its experts the scholar Peniel Joseph, whose *The Sword and the Shield*, a side-by-side biography of Malcolm and Martin Luther King, Jr., came out in April 2020. While the Netflix series emphasizes the important relationship with Nation of Islam leader Elijah Muhammad, Joseph provides context around that other important relationship—with King—that should have been allowed to ripen further. Though it was frequently antagonistic, the relationship bore features of an unspoken collaboration that made each figure a better analyst of history and a more effective activist.

The relationship also kept FBI director J. Edgar Hoover up at night. He worried enough about a single charismatic figure, let alone two Black radicals working together.

Denying Respectability

Abdur-Rahman Muhammad is a journalist and a proud working man who leads tours of lower Manhattan. On camera, he looks like a business-casual-clad bureaucrat with an affable face, a wry smile, and a warm, steady voice. As a teen, he was targeted by police for being out with a white girlfriend. Police forcibly took him on a ride around the city, mocked and threatened him. It made him distrustful of police and an admirer of Malcolm X. "I became a Black militant activist . . . who wasn't going to take this shit anymore."[3]

When Malcolm was killed, he never believed the official story. Much later, he started to dig. Soon his work was featured in *A Life of Reinvention*, a 2011 biography of Malcolm by the late Manning Marable. "No one alive has done more to solve Malcolm's killing than Abdur-Raman," says Pulitzer Prize-winning historian David Garrow.

The official story of Malcolm X's killing is that he and his teacher, the spiritual leader of the Nation of Islam, Elijah Muhammad—sometimes known as the Messenger—had a falling out. The inciting incident was a remark Malcolm made after the Kennedy assassination. Muhammad had asked him not to weigh in or criticize the slain president, as he was growing increasingly wary of Malcolm's political punditry. At the end of a speech a week after the assassination, someone in the audience asked Malcolm's opinion and Malcolm famously said that the assassination was like "chickens coming home to roost," referring to the violence perpetrated by the Kennedy administration all over the world.

Recognizing Kennedy's popularity, Elijah Muhammad "muzzled" Malcolm for ninety days. Nation of Islam (NOI) members started to take sides. The feud escalated with Elijah Muhammad and Malcolm engaged in a war of words, including threats from the Messenger often coded in religious imagery.

On February 21, 1965, Malcolm was shot at close range at New York City's Audubon Ballroom, in front of his wife, Betty Shabazz, and his children. Although multiple assailants fired at him, the wounds from a sawed-off shotgun (used by a man in a long coat who appeared from the front row) were ruled to be the cause of death. Another man with a gun, Talmadge Hayer, from the Newark, New Jersey mosque known to NOI followers as Mosque No. 25, was apprehended at the crime scene. After he was shot in the leg and caught in a melee, police pulled him from the crowd, and he confessed to being one of the co-conspirators.

Two other men, Norman 3X Butler and Thomas 15X Johnson, were arrested. Both maintained their innocence.

Police had no physical evidence against them, but their weaker cases were bundled together with Hayer's, and they were convicted. All three were given twenty years to life. Through a series of files debunking the thin case against Johnson and Butler, Abdur-Raman Muhammad alleges these men were telling the truth; two were innocent, and only Hayer, who confessed, was guilty.

However, the popular story of Malcolm X's murder is untrue, Abdur-Raman Muhammad asserts in the first episode of *Who Killed Malcolm X?* Muhammad's revisionist version starts with J. Edgar Hoover terrified of a "Black Messiah," insisting that

> there must be a goal of preventing a coalition of militant black nationalist groups, prevent[ing] the rise of a [figure who] can unify and electrify the black nationalist movement, along with preventing militant black nationalist groups and leaders from gaining respectability, by discrediting them to the community.

To the same end, an internal FBI memo asked what could be done to "stop Malcolm X."[4]

The Sawed-Off Shotgun

The New York Police Department (NYPD) knew about the threats on Malcolm's life. But it didn't have a security detail checking for weapons at the door of the Audubon Ballroom the night Malcolm would speak. No uniformed police officers came inside the venue to guard the famed leader during his talk. Instead, the NYPD stationed cops on the roof and on the sidewalk in front of the building. The lackadaisical attitude didn't end there.

When police arrived to investigate the scene, they reportedly sauntered through the ballroom, as if on a Sunday stroll. After Hayer's capture, eyewitness accounts corroborated that there were five gunmen, one of whom, according to the series, may have slipped away in the melee. Somehow, after they captured Hayer, then Johnson, and then Butler, the police arbitrarily reduced the number of suspects from five to three—a decision they never explained. Aside from taking photographs of bullet holes in the podium and in the chest and chin of Malcolm, police barely secured the room or its evidence. That night, they even allowed the owners to hold a dance.[5]

After the rift over Malcolm's Kennedy comments, Malcolm had written apologetically to his teacher but got no answer. The series asserts that the FBI had been exploiting the schism in the months leading up to the killing. They fed stories to the media about the rift and they may have used informants to spread rumors about each figure's animosity toward the other.

The sheer number of informants known to have penetrated the Nation of Islam created paranoia— one of the explicit goals of the FBI's COINTELPRO, or Counterintelligence Program, which spied on progressives, pitting them against each other. John Ali, the national secretary based in the organization's Chicago mansion, has been frequently accused of having been an informant, as well as helping stoke hatred between the former collaborators. He responds to the filmmakers' questions about these accusations with odd phrases like, "I *could* have," while insisting the bureau didn't accept him as an informant.

Other interviews feature the affable Abdur-Raman Muhammad asking witnesses questions, nodding along, raising his brow before a follow-up. After casually befriending witnesses who tell him they saw it as a closed case, he asks, "But how could justice be done if two innocent Black men served time?" Series co-director Rachel Dretzin conducts another kind of interview. Both interviewers are virtuosic at drawing out their subjects, but Dretzin's interviews are filmed more like police interrogations, with the camera on the subject directly, while Muhammad's feel like eavesdropping on a conversation. Her interview of Cory Booker, who has an eerie, incidental tie to the presumptive killer through a campaign video, is gripping.

When files must be examined, Muhammad either examines them with another historian or archivist, or points to key sentences that loom onscreen. We learn that Johnson was arrested as the trigger man, for instance, despite not matching the description of the real killer in an FBI file. Episode One ends with Abdur-Rahman Muhammad finding a file describing the shotgun shooter as stocky, dark-skinned, and coming from the Newark mosque—none of which characterized Johnson, who was light-skinned and from Malcolm's Harlem mosque.

Why did police miss this?

Kennedy Attacked Islam, a Religion

From there, the series turns into a meditation on FBI surveillance and COINTELPRO. Garrow tells viewers how thoroughly the bureau infiltrated the Nation of Islam, citing "multiple high-ranking paid human informants in the leadership . . . Could it have been that FBI paid informants were involved in Malcolm X's murder?" he asks in a bookish drawl. "Almost certainly."[6]

The Nation of Islam's need for revenge, the series posits, may have been the cover for members who joined as informants, or who—thanks to money offered after they joined—turned dirty while rising in the leadership. Soon we see that the need for revenge itself may have been manipulated. Who egged on whom?

While the FBI surveilled Malcolm, the NYPD sent the Bureau of Special Services and Investigations—known as BOSSI, or the Red Squad—to his rallies and to record his phone calls. BOSSI was effectively a police unit made over as a spy ring. One of its agents boasts how he knew Malcolm's habits so well that they switched on their wiretap on the second ring, when Malcolm would always pick up, so he wouldn't hear the click. Tony Bouza, one of the more wryly unapologetic BOSSI officers in the series confesses, "I don't think he understood that we were tapping his wire and listening to the tapes . . . Did we intrude into privacy? Yes. But I was alright with it."[7] If Malcolm spoke before a broader audience, then FBI agents (all white) could attend. If not, they found Black men in the streets, and met them in movie theaters to arrange the surveillance or to trade information.

A series like this—or Erroll Morris's *Wormwood* (2018, also on Netflix)—convinces you that paranoia, as a mode, isn't so quaint or *paranoid*, after all. So it was for Malcolm, who began opening his addresses with "Mister Moderator, friends . . . uh, enemies . . ." While the audience looked around at each other and laughed uneasily, Malcolm would continue, "*Everyone* is here."[8] In *The Sword and the Shield*, Joseph quotes Malcolm admitting that, when "speaking publicly, I'd guess which were FBI faces in the audience or other types of agents."[9]

A 1962 FBI memo shows that the FBI knew about Elijah Muhammad's multiple extramarital affairs, often with underage girls, including several with whom he conceived children. Agents schemed to send "anonymous letters to [his wife] Clara Muhammad."[10] This was stirred into the cauldron to poison the two men's relationship. To encounter his teacher's rampant hypocrisy would have offended the happily married father of four, especially as he bristled at the muzzle against his own outspokenness.

One event during the Kennedy administration offers a window into the growing conflict. In 1962, Malcolm's friend, a Nation of Islam member named Ronald Stokes, was shot and killed by Los Angeles police officers. The incident marked the only time that his wife, Betty Shabazz, recalls seeing Malcolm cry. Footage from a speech Malcolm made in the aftermath of the killing shows the activist with blown-up photographs of the scene, one featuring the back of Stokes's head with a bullet hole in it. An FBI memo describes his full-throated denunciation, which compared the LAPD's actions to gestapo-like tactics:

> *Subject's opening statement was that ". . . Seven innocent unarmed black men were shot down in cold blood by Police Chief WILLIAM J. PARKER'S Los Angeles City Police." The . . . subject referred to the incident as "one of the most ferocious, inhuman atrocities ever inflicted in a so-called 'democratic' and 'civilized' society" and subject referred to Stokes' murder as "a brutal and cold-blooded murder by PARKER'S well-armed storm troopers."*[11]

When Muhammad cautioned Malcolm to de-escalate, Malcolm reportedly felt shame that the Nation of Islam wouldn't stand up to defend its own members. Part of why Muhammad wanted to keep Malcolm from going too far, however, was because the Nation of Islam had lucrative commercial interests in Los Angeles. These funded its ministerial work and enriched Elijah Muhammad and his family, and a war with the LAPD would jeopardize business.

The series is good on this and other details. But Joseph gives broader context about the questions around Malcolm's political outspokenness and Muhammad's affairs. Malcolm had always been outspoken politically, and it helped boost the organization's members, spurring publicity and filling seats. For that, Muhammad would have been grateful. Malcolm was often booked to speak with Elijah Muhammad—the genius orator and acolyte warming up, as it were, for the Messenger himself as the main event. But Muhammad had a lung condition and as the 1960s progressed, Muhammad missed events due to illness.

In his many appearances before the media or a live audience, Malcolm was often tasked with explaining how the Nation of Islam's policy of separatism was distinct from segregation. Pundits expected to discredit Malcolm and the Nation by likening this separatism to reverse racism. Segregation was the control of Black people, Malcolm said, while the Nation's separatism "was the voluntary promotion of self-determination for a Black community in search of its own place in the world."[12] To Malcolm, King's gospel of nonviolence was bargaining from a position of weakness, akin to asking white people's permission for freedom rather than taking it. Malcolm saw King's bids for integration as "admitting [King's] inferiority, because he is also admitting that he wants to become part of a 'superior society.'"[13]

Well before his comments on Kennedy, but especially after his falling out with the Nation, Malcolm circled around the idea of a broader coalition. He interspersed invitations to work alongside King with a steady barrage of critiques of nonviolence as ineffectual. Perhaps this was why King tended to decline, or not answer, Malcolm's invitations—as with his 1961 Harlem Freedom Rally. Nevertheless, the two leaders engaged in a fascinating, indirect conversation, which Joseph draws out well in a tandem biography. A virtuoso at articulating the undercurrents of Black Power, including in his equally meticulous biography of Stokely Carmichael (*Stokely: A Life*, 2014), Joseph adroitly places the two leaders in contrast to each other as in a contrapuntal duet. This duet demonstrates the awful silence we would feel with just one of their voices missing, as was exemplified by Malcolm's death three years before King's, let alone with both of them gone after 1968.

The most fascinating part of their joint performance was how Malcolm was constantly using his rhetoric to amplify the terms in which King could work, and vice versa. If one fought for Black citizenship, and the other for Black dignity, their disagreement over nonviolence was a disagreement merely over tactics, Malcolm said in a period of softening toward King. In their socially distant partnership, something small might echo from one to the other. First Malcolm, as around the 1962 Ronald Stokes killing, and then King (as in Birmingham) might take turns calling police methods Gestapo-like.[14] Malcolm obviously followed King's movements and speeches (and vice versa; King sometimes responded to Malcolm's speech the very same day).

Malcolm would at times even debate King through a proxy, like Bayard Rustin, one of the lead organizers of the March on Washington. The two would joust ruthlessly on stage, but they enjoyed themselves so much that they soon agreed to take their routine on the road. Their first debate, at Howard University, impressed students, like the young Carmichael, and faculty alike. Rustin accused the Muslims of having "no political, social, or economic program," but Malcolm's

> talk of racial pride, political self-determination and Black solidarity motivated a generation of young activists to imbibe large quantities of Black history, to investigate the significance of African decolonization, and reimagine the meaning of African American identity within Western culture.[15]

Much of their mutual curiosity, or at least Malcolm's, circled around Kennedy. When commissioner of public safety Bull Connor was beating up civil rights activists like Jerome Smith in Birmingham, Alabama—siccing dogs on small children and their mothers and blasting them with fire hoses—Malcolm grew incensed. But aside from complaining privately that the pictures of such police brutality "made [him] sick,"[16] Kennedy himself did nothing. This "earned him the permanent enmity of Malcolm X, who criticized the president for authorizing force only when white property and lives, rather than that of Black women and children, hung in the balance."[17]

As for King and Kennedy, King had been waiting for a meeting for the first seven months of Kennedy's term.[18] Whether King saw it or not, Malcolm's criticism of Kennedy gave King cover for his own. Malcolm also knew that the original vision for the March on Washington—which A. Philip Randolph imagined decades earlier, in the 1940s—was more radical and was focused on shutting down the capital. Malcolm complained that when the president saw that he couldn't stop it, he joined it. Once it had Kennedy's blessing, Malcolm felt it became too timid, focused less on stopping traffic, stopping work, and flexing Black Power, and instead concerning itself with providing places to urinate and faint.

Before a gathering of newspaper editors, Kennedy denigrated Muslims as extremists. "Instead of attacking the Ku Klux Klan and the White Citizens' Council," said Malcolm, "Kennedy attacked Islam, a religion."[19] And did Malcolm also blame Kennedy for the assassination of Congolese leader Patrice Lumumba, who was killed just days before Kennedy's inauguration? Or for the Bay of Pigs invasion of Cuba, in April of Kennedy's first year? Regardless, Malcolm's quip about Kennedy and violence had more behind it than the random act of cruelty it was portrayed as.

Courteous but Not Too Cooperative

According to the docuseries, John Ali, Elijah Muhammad's secretary, called Chicago and reported Malcolm to the Messenger after he made the chickens roosting comment. Newspapers and TV networks distorted the quip—which was only made in ironic indignation over the United States' hypocrisy—framing it as if Malcolm had expressed joy over Kennedy's death. Malcolm worked hard to make peace with Muhammad. But his letters of humility and regret to Muhammad were either intercepted by the Messenger's children (heirs to his empire) or others who would have been threatened by Malcolm. His suspension was indefinite.

In the aftermath of the incident, the press continued to refer to Malcolm as Muhammad's "heir apparent." This annoyed Malcolm, who knew it would only heighten the animosity of the actual heirs. Worried about the loss of his livelihood through an organization he had built and expanded like no one else, Malcolm spent the winter correcting interviewers, saying he was never the heir apparent, emphasizing that he was suspended over his own actions and that the Honorable Elijah Muhammad had taught him everything he knew. It was a moment of real humility for the firebrand activist and preacher, who was also trying to survive.[20]

Two months into the rift, the FBI visited Malcolm at his home. He welcomed them in. In an exploratory interview, they offered to pay him to inform on the Nation of Islam. They spoke, in tentative tones, of records he may have access to. They were there to test the psychology of Malcolm during the rift—a rift that these agents had quietly curated. Denying he had such access, Malcolm secretly recorded the two agents, one of whom was named Fulton, who speaks to Dretzin but refuses to show his face on camera.

"Money brings out the information," Fulton told Malcolm, instantly realizing he'd erred. "You insult my intelligence," Malcolm objected. "In fact, you insult your own [that] you wouldn't know in advance what I'm going to say." He emphasized that he was no Quisling or fink, that "no government agency should *ever* expect information from me." One of the agents described Malcolm during the visit as "nice and courteous, but not too cooperative."[21]

Benching the Slugger

To cool him down, Malcolm's cohort took him to Miami, where Nation of Islam member Sam Saxon introduced Malcolm to Cassius Clay. The two quickly became friends. Malcolm converted Clay, who was on the verge of becoming heavyweight champion in his fight against Sonny Liston. Malcolm hoped that by recruiting the boxing star, he would help restore to Black Americans a "racial pride"—part of Malcolm's program of Black dignity. Still looking to return to the fold, Malcolm also hoped to offer the champion as a peace offering to Elijah Muhammad.

But Elijah Muhammad outmaneuvered Malcolm. After Clay's championship win, Muhammad held a public reception, praised Clay, and gave him his Muslim name, Muhammad Ali. Joseph tells the filmmakers that Malcolm wasn't as good at power politics as Muhammad. "Elijah Muhammad was playing chess, and Malcolm was playing checkers."[22]

Celebrated New York literary socialite George Plimpton caught Malcolm for an interview in Miami. At the time Plimpton was writing about Ali for *Sports Illustrated* (and his book *Shadow Box*). Depicting Malcolm as hopeful that in five days "he was going to be unmuzzled," Plimpton blames Malcolm's subsequent death on the rift between the two and goes on to lightly ridicule most of Malcolm's indignation over brutal historical injustices. Plimpton highlights the way Malcolm popped peppermints into his mouth, and finally implies that an undercurrent of antisemitism tainted the work of the Nation of Islam.

But after the fight, Malcolm knew he wouldn't be reinstated. BOSSI agent Tony Bouza delighted in this: "I thought it great. I thought it wonderful. Elijah Muhammad was divesting himself of his greatest asset and weakening his organization. It's like a baseball team depriving itself of its greatest slugger. How much better does it get than that?"[23]

On March 8, with no peace brokered with the Messenger, Malcolm announced the permanent split. It was also the final year of Malcolm's life. He was both active and hounded. He launched his own fledgling Nation of Islam (which he called Muslim Mosque, Inc.), reinventing himself as a roving ambassador—some called him the president—of Black America. Touring Africa and the Middle East, he founded the Organization of Afro-American Unity (OAAU). The OAAU linked a Black minority in the United States with a great worldwide constituency.

Malcolm had made a kind of tactical shift, reframing civil rights as global human rights in his search for a broader moral and historical constituency, which brought nationalist and anti-colonialist movements in Africa into solidarity with American liberation movements. From the United States' standpoint, this was an attempt to embarrass the US globally by holding up its actual treatment of Black Americans to its image of itself as the seat of freedom.

Hype Talk or Death Threats?

Malcolm and the Nation of Islam began a battle over his small Queens house. Muhammad tried to evict him, and the case went to court. Malcolm had spent twelve years of his life expanding the membership of the Nation of Islam, and was justified in feeling that, given his effective organizing work, he was indispensable in building the movement. To squabble in court over his family's modest place of shelter, while Elijah Muhammad resided in mansions in Chicago and Phoenix, further embittered Malcolm. How Malcolm learned of his teacher's affairs, and whether the FBI played a role in this, isn't said explicitly in the documentary. But footage shows him seething outside the courthouse after losing the fight over his home, denouncing Muhammad for having "eight children by six teenage girls who were his private secretaries."[24]

To many Muslims, such as James Shabazz who was the minister at the group's Newark Mosque No. 25, this was an unforgivable betrayal of the man who guided Malcolm to straighten out his life after prison and gave him a vocation.

A CBS TV interviewer asked Shabazz, featured in archival footage, if he wouldn't "put it past" some of his followers who might want to "get" Malcolm. "I wouldn't put it past a Christian," Shabazz responded, "to punch somebody out for talking about Jesus."[25]

Other members of the mosque said, "it never even entered my mind that Malcolm was right," that it felt "like a man turning on his father." Footage shows Malcolm, on the verge of homelessness, escalating the feud further, saying "Elijah Muhammad has gone insane, absolutely out of his mind. Besides, you can't be seventy years old and surround yourself by a bunch of sixteen, seventeen, or eighteen-year-old girls and keep your right mind. You can't do it." The crowd laughs. Malcolm believed Elijah Muhammad was behind the threats against him, telling an interviewer, "Elijah Muhammad has given the order to his followers to see that I am crippled or killed."[26]

Since Elijah Muhammad was the most wiretapped target of the FBI's COINTELPRO program—which spied on civilians illegally during this time—Abdur-Rahman Muhammad searches in the government record for a coded or explicit order to have Malcolm killed. "Elijah stated that with these hypocrites, when you find them, cut their heads off," reads one FBI memo from 1964, from a wiretap of Muhammad's Phoenix home. As a Muslim, he decodes this for Garrow, explaining that the phrase "cut their heads off" refers to the teachings of the Nation of Islam founder Wallace Fard Muhammad, who said that whoever takes the heads off four devils will go to Mecca. A subsequent reference to Moses in another memo could be another coded death threat against Malcolm. "It's very clear what he's calling for. He wouldn't have to say it."[27]

The Fruit of Islam was Elijah Muhammad's security force. But they could be seen, too, as his enforcers, about whom authorities worried since they could be converted into a paramilitary force. Historian Zak A. Kondo explains that they might say, "We want you to bless him," but it might mean taking him into the park and beating him up. The leadership of the Nation of Islam were "basically saying things that gave people the notion that [they] wanted Malcolm X dead."[28]

One of the Nation's newspapers featured a cartoon of Malcolm's disembodied head rolling down the street, his horns growing with each bounce. A whisper campaign intensified, suggestions like, "Man, if you knew what Malcolm was saying about the leader, you would kill him yourself." Talmadge Hayer, the only confessed killer convicted of his murder, felt that he had to correct Malcolm's slander, but he stated that he did not need a direct order. [29]

Norman Butler—later known as Muhammad A. Aziz—remembers Elijah Muhammad's son, known to many simply as "Junior," telling an audience, "'You should cut out [Malcolm's] tongue, and I'll stamp it APPROVED, and send it to my father,' words to that effect."

But he took this to be "hype talk."[30]

Chasing William X, Breaking News to Cory Booker

After he was found guilty of killing Malcolm, Butler hired William Kunstler, who publicized Hayer's signed affidavit on television. The document's purpose was to exonerate the innocent Butler and Johnson. In the affidavit, Hayer names four men from the Newark mosque who conspired with him. In details about how the crime was planned and executed, Hayer writes that it was "William" who "had the shotgun"—the weapon that had killed Malcolm. "If you want to answer the question of who killed Malcolm," summarizes Abdur-Rahman Muhammad, "it was the man who fired the shotgun. According to Hayer, that man's name was William X."[31]

When the courts denied Kunstler's request to reopen the case, Kunstler petitioned Congress, but to no avail. In his affidavit, Hayer described William X as twenty-seven years old, of stocky build, around 5'10", with a dark complexion and short, cropped hair. A member of both the Newark mosque and the Fruit of Islam, his last name was Bradley.

Muhammad declares that if Bradley is the killer, he wants to confront him face to face. But first he needs to find his adopted Muslim name. In an informal discussion, he gets lucky. Someone tells him offhand: Al-Mustafa Shabazz. He travels to Newark and meets a clutch of Newark old timers who tell him not to stir up ghosts. It turns out that Shabazz's involvement was an open secret. The rumor itself, plus the fact that he was never convicted, leads to the suspicion that he had some type of immunity. This brand of impunity led Shabazz on, under the name Bradley, to wield a long and violent rap sheet: terrorist threats, sexual assault, armed robbery.

"Leave him alone, leave him alone, leave him alone," says one community member. "Because he's probably being protected by the state." Many in Newark knew who Shabazz was and what he is said to have done in 1965. In fact, he was so well enmeshed in the Newark community that he was featured in Cory Booker's 2010 mayoral reelection campaign video.[32]

The video opens with Booker telling Newark voters that "Violent crime in our city was getting worse. But together, Newark, we took action, adding 300 police to our streets." Then Bradley, aka Shabazz, shakes hands with a cop in the video. The directors freeze it and zoom in on the burly, grinning Shabazz. "This is the first time that the world has seen the face of the man who took the life of Malcolm X," declares Abdur-Raman Muhammad. Booker's campaign voiceover continues, "We are making Newark safer and stronger. And together, Newark, we are taking back our city."[33]

In the next scene, Dretzin is in Booker's office. There are many awkward interviews in the docuseries and they make for addictive viewing. This is easily the most awkward of all.

> Dretzin: Are you familiar with . . . William Bradley, or Al-Mustafa Shabazz?
> Booker: In Newark, from Newark?
> Dretzin: Yeah.
> Booker: Yeah.
> Dretzin: Do you know that he . . .
> Booker: [gleaming eyes wondering where this is going]
> Dretzin: . . . appeared in your reelection campaign video of 2010?
> Booker: [looks down and to the left]
> Dretzin: . . . And that he is one of the people who allegedly murdered Malcolm X?
> Booker: [eyes going very wide, head tilting up, slight smirk] That connection I was not aware of. No.
> Dretzin: You weren't aware of that?
> Booker: You are breaking news, to me. He's one of the people that is alleged by whom?
> [Dretzin tells him that Hayer named him.]
> Booker: I was not aware of that.[34]

Dretzin asks Booker if he wants to see the video. Booker (whose face says no) asks, "Do you have it with you right now?" The laptop lands on Booker's lap; his eyes are bright with anger, his mouth is smiling—his scheduler's head is going to roll. The video plays, and Dretzin indicates Shabazz. "Yeah," says Booker, "I know him well. I know him well." Soon, they go back and forth, Booker saying vaguely that we should get to the truth. When Dretzin uses the word "assassin," or "potential assassin," Booker flinches, moves out of the shot, and adds, "Please keep saying 'potential.'"[35]

A Father in Name Only

In the final episode, Muhammad wonders aloud why the FBI's narrative around the killing differed from the official case. If both Hayer and Butler insist Butler was innocent, why was he allowed to languish in prison for two decades? Muhammad's research on Al-Mustafa Shabazz/Bradley finds that multiple descriptions, including his status as a lieutenant in the Newark Mosque, match the eyewitness descriptions that the FBI had on file. Then he examines an FBI internal memo warning that Shabazz/Bradley's fitting the description of the trigger man "should not be furnished to the NYCPD without first receiving Bureau authority."[36] Strange.

Norman 3X Johnson, a light-skinned man from a different mosque, had already been arrested as the trigger man. "Why wouldn't the FBI immediately notify the New York City Police Department?" Muhammad asks. Yet another file provides a possible answer. It said that "a lieutenant from Newark may have been involved in the slaying of Malcolm [X]," and that the New York Police Department "had . . .

not . . . been advised of the identity of this [lieutenant] for use in the [Malcolm X] case."[37]

While a jury considered the innocence or guilt of these two men—men who didn't match the FBI's description of the person with the shotgun or others at the Audubon Ballroom that afternoon and for whom there was no physical evidence—the FBI just watched. Once these innocent men were convicted, they closed their own file concluding that it was Bradley. They did so without offering to correct the case and made sure anyone attempting to correct the record would notify them first. After two decades in prison, Johnson died in 2009 without clearing his name. "It just makes you wonder," says Muhammad, "could Bradley have been an informant working for the FBI?"[38]

Meanwhile, Muhammad prepares to confront him, hoping to "look the man eye to eye, man to man [and ask him,] 'How could you do that, how could you do that, how could you do that to our people?'" But he learns during production that Bradley has died. When this news comes, he admits to feeling depressed.[39]

The final segment does the most to personalize Muhammad. We meet his son. We watch the son recite poetry and then point to the Marable biography where his father's important work appears. We learn from Muhammad in voiceover that much of his scholarship has "come out of my own pocket."[40] Stories like this, time and again, are too hot to report, the real story unsayable, protected like Shabazz and other collaborating men.

The final episode also does the most to personalize Butler. Bearded, acerbic, and afraid to hope for much, he tells interviewers that—thanks to his two decades in prison—"I don't know my grandchildren, my great-grandchildren, or my great-great-grandchildren." Caught between narratives, that of an ex-con who is expected to repent and look optimistically forward and that of a framed man, he can engage only in "filler talk" with his children, and feels like "a father in name only." The segment shows him looking up his family members on Facebook: "I think this is my granddaughter."[41]

Muhammad, sitting next to him on a bench outside, promises to file a wrongful conviction report for him. Butler—now Aziz—is hesitant to reignite hope. His hesitancy is moving. Malcolm's own quest for Black dignity, and Black self-determination, was of course violated and disfigured by his death, meant as an indiscriminate warning to men and their families alike.

Malcolm's Lungs

On Valentine's Day, the week before Malcolm was to give his fateful talk at the Audubon Ballroom, his house was firebombed. While he was able to evacuate his wife and children before the house was consumed by flames, it took nearly an hour for the police to arrive. "I stood in my underwear in my driveway with a gun for 45 minutes," he complained. In need of money, without clothes or insurance and now effectively homeless, he continued his busy schedule of paid speaking appearances.

The night before his Audubon speech, he stayed at the Statler-Hilton across the street from Penn Station. His security team, led by his personal bodyguard, Eugene Roberts, would have kept his location under tight wraps. At 3:00 a.m., Malcolm's hotel phone rang. When he picked up: silence. Were his whereabouts known to those behind the death threats? Everyone else on the roster to speak that day made last-minute cancellations.

When he was shot, his bodyguard, Roberts, smashed a chair over the back of one of the assailants, probably Bradley, leapt onto the stage, and gave Malcolm mouth-to-mouth resuscitation. The series cuts to Bouza frowning, calling Malcolm a "thug," suggesting it was inappropriate for Roberts to try to help Malcolm. Why? Because Roberts was a paid NYPD informant, working undercover for BOSSI. The goal had been to penetrate Malcolm's security and make himself useful to the activist. He was chosen partly because he had no family ties to NYPD. For Roberts to leap onstage and perform mouth-to-mouth was in violation of police-spy protocol, Bouza suggests. Nevertheless, for several minutes, Roberts kept breathing air into Malcolm's lungs, trying to save him. Eventually he realized Malcolm had no pulse and couldn't be saved.[42]

While Malcolm's wife continued to try to save his life, police were busy with the one person they caught who actually *was* involved in the conspiracy to murder Malcolm X: Hayer. Though they had stood down when they should have been guarding the entrance—and the speaker—they couldn't have avoided nabbing Hayer if they wanted to, because of the brawl underway after Malcolm admirers saw Hayer with a gun. But while police wrestled with those attacking Hayer, footage shows a ringer for Al-Mustafa Shabazz, Malcolm's presumptive killer, skirting the melee.

At least nine informants crowded into the Audubon Ballroom that Sunday afternoon. Did Malcolm play his game that day, trying to guess which ones were the informants? "I don't think he understood that his closest associate was working for us," Bouza boasts in deadpan.[43]

The Grace of Betty Shabazz

An extraordinary record of its subject matter, *Who Killed Malcolm X?* features a grueling clip of Betty Shabazz being interviewed after her husband's murder. She is dazed, freshly traumatized, looking down. Off camera, in milder tones, a battery of journalists—all men—fire a barrage of leading questions at her.

The questions are restatements of Malcolm X's alleged feelings of racial superiority, some with an insinuation that he brought this violence on himself. The questions are uttered gently, almost whispered, but there are violent, baiting (almost gloating) undertones. Unmoved to respond, Shabazz appears unwilling even to gesture at an answer. Did she remember her husband, who had rejected police protection after the firebombing, saying,

> *The policemen in this country are the ones who are responsible for the brutality, the policemen themselves have become guilty of violating the rights of the people . . . So what are the people to do? Call upon the same ones who are victimizing them to protect them? No, they have to protect themselves.*[44]

She blinks, her mouth parts briefly.

One of the newsmen asks if she was about to answer, but she stays quiet a little longer. Her husband also said at the dawn of the Vietnam war: "If violence is wrong in America, violence is wrong abroad. If it is wrong to be violent defending Black women and Black children and Black babies and Black men, then it is wrong for America to draft us and make us violent abroad in defense of her. And if it is right for America to draft us, and teach us how to be violent in defense of her, then it is right for you and me to do whatever is necessary to defend our own people right here in this country."[45]

Picture that February meeting with Malcolm, after his main source of income—his ministerial work with the Nation of Islam—is lost. The FBI knocks on his door. Where is Betty when her husband welcomes them into their house and they invite him to snitch? Now picture that same meeting taking place with one of Elijah Muhammad's surrogates, someone in line to inherit what Malcolm helped the Messenger build. Picture that surrogate admitting that his curiosity is piqued, conceding that by helping keep Malcolm out of the Nation of Islam, both the FBI and Muhammad will achieve their goals together.

Now picture Eugene Roberts, who goes secretly into the precinct only when absolutely necessary (like the morning after Malcolm's murder), being handed a file about Elijah Muhammad's extramarital affairs. Doesn't he hand it to Malcolm? Isn't that his job? Malcolm starts to ask questions, to interview these women and girls, just as the Messenger is telling him not to be too hard on the LAPD who killed his friend Ronald Stokes. Does this complicate the idea that "the rift" grew up naturally between them, and led to Malcolm's murder?

The winds of the surveillance state—of COINTELPRO and the CIA's tandem Operation CHAOS—blew poison into rifts like these in an effort to deny these men respectability, dignity, livelihoods, and lives. "If the NYPD had an agent in the Audubon that day, close enough to give him mouth-to-mouth, it makes me wonder who else law enforcement had on the inside that nobody knows about," Abdur-Raman Muhammad concludes.[46]

As the barrage of hostile questions continues, the newly widowed Betty Shabazz looks down in silence until something flashes, like she has suddenly remembered something. Looking up, she softly utters her first phrase in this new phase of life, a life of preserving a brilliant legacy and carrying it forward: "I think he accomplished more than can be realized at this moment."[47]

1968

Ars Politica: Octavio Paz at 100

or what the events of October 2, 1968
teach us about his mind

1.

In 1968, when protest movements spread through cities around the world, Octavio Paz looked upon these "great youth rebellions," he wrote, "from afar, with astonishment and with hope."[1] As Mexico's ambassador to India, he had escaped the summer heat of New Delhi into the foothills of the Himalayas, but he followed the global protests on the radio. Soon, he learned that students in Mexico, whose leaders were preparing to host the Olympics in October, had also joined the rebellions.

As the protests grew entrenched, and as students threatened to disrupt the games, government repression intensified. On October 2, hundreds of student protesters were killed at Mexico City's Tlatelolco Plaza. Hearing news of the killings, Ambassador Paz's response was a swift vote of no confidence, a letter of unambiguous dissent. It was, as he described the rebellions themselves, the merging of poetry and action, a merger he constantly craved.

Paz was poetry's great universalist. Winner of the 1990 Nobel Prize in Literature, he absorbed many of the great movements of the twentieth century: Marxism, surrealism, the European avant garde. Early in the Spanish Civil War, he tried his hand at social realism, and he admired North American poetry, especially Whitman, Pound, Eliot, and Williams. His ambassadorship to India in the 1960s introduced him to the pillars of Hindu and Buddhist thought.

In 2012, in anticipation of the fifteenth anniversary of his death, New Directions brought out *The Poems of Octavio Paz*. All but ignored since publication, *The Poems* deserve attention, because—in addition to being frequently masterful, and impressively translated into English—they represent hybridity, universality, and an aesthetic and political middle way. Upon Paz's 100th birthday at the time of this writing, it's worth looking again at the life and work of a man unfairly maligned as an apologist for the right during the final decade of the Cold War.

2.

Born in 1914, Paz was raised in Mixcoac, today a part of Mexico City. He grew up in a house he described as disintegrating:

> *Our family had been impoverished by the revolution and the civil war. Our house, full of antique furniture, books, and other objects, was gradually crumbling to bits. As rooms collapsed we moved the furniture into another. I remember that for a long time I lived in a spacious room with part of one of the walls missing. Some magnificent screens protected me inadequately from the wind and rain.*[2]

At seventeen, he published his first poem, "Game." Two years later came his first book, *Luna Silvestre*. Also at a young age, he witnessed the first incident in what became one of his lifelong obsessions: political repression. It was late in the Mexican Revolution, when Paz and his mother were traveling to meet his father, a political journalist and lawyer for Emiliano Zapata. They were traveling by train, under armed protection, to visit the elder Paz, who was exiled in San Antonio, Texas, when suddenly Paz's mother covered his eyes. This had the ironic effect of waking him, while failing to shield him from the grim sight outside the train. "I saw an elongated shadow hanging from a pole."[3] He was six.

At the invitation of Pablo Neruda, Paz traveled to Valencia, Spain in 1937 to join the Second International Congress of Anti-Fascist Writers. He spent a year there before going to Paris, where he advocated for the Spanish Republic. He met poets W.H. Auden, Stephen Spender, Antonio Machado, Tristan Tzara, and of course Neruda. The civil war steered his poetry into a short-lived social realist mode, perhaps his first attempt to join words and action.

"Elegy for a Friend Dead at the Front in Aragon" and "Ode to Spain" stand out as examples of this effort; the former addresses Paz's "comrade" and finds brief moments of felicity in the psychology of grief and loss, asking, "What fields will grow that you won't harvest? / What blood will run without your heirs? / What word will we say that doesn't say / your name, your silence, / the quiet pain of not having you?" Paz also became known for "No Pasarán," or "They Will Not Pass," a call to arms in verse that caused a minor sensation.

Upon his return to Mexico City, he launched a magazine of new Mexican poetry named *Taller* (Workshop). Ambivalent about the European avant-garde, Paz's opening manifesto cited copiously the Spanish perspectivist philosopher José Ortega y Gasset, declaring that the purpose of the magazine was "to be not the place where a generation is erased but the place where the Mexican is being made and is rescued from injustice, from a lack of culture, from frivolity and death."[4]

During the Second World War, Mexico became a haven for displaced Europeans. Amid the capital's newfound cosmopolitanism, Paz met refugees like Victor Serge, the Russian writer who "opened [Paz's] eyes to the realities of life in the Soviet Union," according to Joseph Roman.[5] He also edited a massive anthology that brought together

Spanish-language writers in a controversial way: he allowed political opponents to sit alongside one another in its pages. What his most important translator, Eliot Weinberger, calls his "first substantial collection" of poems, *On the Bank of the World*, appeared in 1942;[6] in one poem in the book, he wrote, "He wanted to sing, to sing / to forget / his true life of lies / and to remember / his lying life of truths."

After the war Paz took a low-level post in the Mexican foreign service in Paris, where he met Andre Breton and Albert Camus. There he fell in love with the streets, and his encounter with surrealism deepened. Paz's lifelong meditation on poetry and words *doing* something led him to abandon realism in favor of more experimental verse. "I should say that I write as if in a silent dialogue with Breton," Paz once admitted. In an introduction to his work, Michael Schmidt amplifies this sentiment: "Under Breton's influence, Paz tried automatic writing and produced his great prose-poems. But it's interesting that in his valedictory essay on Breton, Paz quotes none of his master's poetry, only his critical statements."[7]

Being abroad also helped clarify his understanding of his native Mexico. "Solitude is the profoundest fact of the human condition," he wrote in *Labyrinth of Solitude,* his book-length essay deciphering the Mexican character.[8] By denying one part of their identity, that of the Indigenous (which Paz inherited from his father), Mexicans had become stuck in a world of solitude, he wrote. Paz's time outside the country allowed him a rare outsider's perspective, something afforded to his father before him by his times in exile.

Paz loved writing and wandering in Paris, but politics again intruded and sent him into a second exile. In the summer of 1951, he attended a fifteenth anniversary commemoration of the start of the Spanish Civil War. The director general of UNESCO, also a poet, thought this improper and suggested Paz be transferred to South Asia. Paz was apoplectic. "Knowing that I was being sent to India consoled me a little," he wrote, "rituals, temples, cities whose names evoked strange tales, motley and multicolored crowds, women with feline grace . . . "[9] He traveled by boat from Europe to Cairo, to Aden, and onto Bombay. Aboard the Polish ship *Batory*, he met Auden's brother and the writer Santha Rama Rau, who wrote the film adaptation for *A Passage to India*. A little more than a week after arriving in Bombay, he took the train to Delhi; for Paz, those tracks that evoked images of post-partition sectarian riots also recalled his early exile to San Antonio. Paz's stay in India was to be short-lived; having hardly arrived, he was transferred to Tokyo.

Paz continued writing throughout this period; he considered one long poem he produced during this time, "Sunstone," published as a chapbook in 1957 (and later in *Violent Season*), to be the hinge from his earlier to later work. Along with *The Labyrinth of Solitude*, "Sunstone" also propelled Paz's international reputation, notes Weinberger. A poem of Mexico, Europe, and New York, of war and love, a meditation as if in one long exhalation across dozens of pages, it sports a trope Paz would keep polishing for the rest of his life: a return to origins through an unself-conscious love amid history and ruin: "in the Plaza del Angel the women were sewing / and singing along with their children, / then; the sirens' wail, and the screaming, houses brought to their knees in the dust, / towers cracked, facades spat out / and the hurricane drone of the engines: / the two took off their clothes and made love / to protect our share of all that's eternal, / to defend our ration of paradise and time . . . "

The 1960s marked the publication of the collections *Salamander* and *East Slope*, among others, and his marriage to Marie-José Tramini. He also studied Indian art and philosophy during that decade, organizing the first exhibition of Tantric art in the West. Paz continued to publish other works as well: he printed book-length studies of Claude Levi-Strauss and Marcel Duchamp. Some of that work took on a meditative tone, for example "Stillness," published in *East Slope*:

> Stillness
> >not on the branch
> in the air
> >Not in the air
> in the moment
> >hummingbird

3.

In 1968 Paz found himself in the Himalayan town of Kasauli, "an old summer retreat for the British," as he followed the youth rebellions taking place around the globe.[10] Initially he found the Paris rebellion "the most inspired," as "the words and acts of those young people seemed to me the legacy of some of the great modern poets who were both rebels and prophets: Blake, Hugo, Whitman."[11] As protests intensified, he and Marie-José listened for updates on a short-wave radio. The protests joined his other obsessions: "Poetry, heir of the great spiritual traditions of the West, had become action."[12] Although Paz changed his mind about the rebellions' significance several times, his mood was consistently electric.

"Perhaps Marx had not been wrong," he thought, wandering the foothills, "the revolution would explode in an advanced country, with an established proletariat educated in democratic traditions. That revolution would spread throughout the developed world, and would mark the end of capitalism and of the totalitarian regimes that had usurped the name of socialism in Russia, China, Cuba and other places." When, back in New Delhi, Paz heard that Mexico City, too, was embroiled in the rebellions, he felt their weight. The rebellions in Mexico, he felt, "lacked the poetic and orgiastic anarchism of the Parisian rebels," but they did have one concrete demand shared by much of the country: democracy.[13]

In late September, Paz wrote a memo attempting "to justify the positions of the students, insofar as they were concerned with democratic reform. Above all, I recommended that force not be used and that a political solution be found to the conflict."[14] He was told that his memo had been read with great interest and shown to the president. He slept well for ten or twelve days, "until," he writes, "on the morning of October 3, I learned of the bloody repression of the previous day. I decided I could no longer represent a government that was operating in a manner so clearly opposite to my way of thinking."[15]

Paz spent the next few years teaching at Cambridge University, the University of Texas, and Harvard. He recorded the shock of his 1971 return to Mexico after ten years' absence in a new book of poems called *Vuelta*. He also launched a magazine of the same name that would last the twenty-two years until his death, a magazine that Weinberger and others count among "the leading intellectual magazines in Latin America of their time, unmatched in [its] range of concerns and international contributors."[16]

In his remaining decades he published autobiographical poetry in *A Draft of Shadows*; *The Monkey Grammarian*, at once an essay, prose poem, and novel; a collection of translations from six languages; a book-length study of poet Xavier Villaurrutia; his Harvard lectures on romanticism and the avant garde, *Children of the Mire*; and four books of essays. During the 1980s, his work on *Vuelta* magazine—among interviews, lecture tours, and controversies over his punditry—would result in what Weinberger describes as "his anti-authoritarian European-style socialism . . . considered right-wing by the Latin American left."[17]

4.

Nearly thirty years after Paz's resignation as ambassador, I called him up in Mexico City. I had spent two years in Costa Rica, writing, teaching, and learning Spanish, and I was heading home for Christmas. I crossed Nicaragua, Honduras, El Salvador, Guatemala, Belize, and Mexico's Yucatan peninsula by bus, then flew to Mexico City, where I had a few days before returning to New York City.

I had found Paz for the first time (on the page) in a used bookstore and cafe in Peekskill, forty-five miles up the Hudson from midtown Manhattan, just before embarking on those two years overseas. It was a small, yellowing collection among the unkempt shelves: *Early Poems (1935 to 1955)*. My courses on "Hispanic literature" rarely went past the Spanish Civil War. Paz was likely the first writer I picked up by chance, having heard nothing about him.

Late at night in the weeks before leaving the United States, I read of the ruins I would see, and of Paz's walks through Paris and Mexico City. The poems taught me to listen differently; even in translation I could hear the listening present in Paz's work, and the perpetual noon landscape, under a burning sun that was present time: "Time doesn't blink, / time empties out its minutes, / a bird has stopped dead in the air. // . . . The air is transparent: / if the bird is invisible, / see the color of its song."

My response to the ruins we visited that winter, in El Salvador, at Tulúm, Uxmal, and north of Mexico City at the Temple of the Sun and Moon, often came in Paz's voice. At Chichén Itzá in the Yucatán, I recalled Paz's "In Uxmal": "The light crashes, / the columns awake and, / without moving, dance. // . . . In the sun the wall breathes, throbs, undulates . . . And above so much life the snake / with a head between its jaws: / gods drink blood, they eat men." At Teotihuacán, I flipped pages until I found Paz's "Hymn Among the Ruins": "To see, to touch each day's lovely forms. / The buzzing of light, darts and wings. / The winestain on the tablecloth smells of blood. / Like coral branches in the water / I stretch my senses into the living hour. . . ."

Back in Mexico City, I didn't get him on the phone. I found several entries for Octavio, or O., Paz in the phone book at my hotel; I narrowed them down by looking for Marie-Jose's name, which was listed with his. A woman who didn't identify herself told me he would be back later. Was it really his number? I never called back.

Instead, I carried with me Paz's hypno-realism, his vertiginously clear jumbling of the senses. The later Paz would develop what he called a politics and poetics of the now, the perpetual present; early Paz believed in history as an aberration. Jose Manuel Zamorano Meza traces to Heidegger "Paz's romantic assessment of Western history as an error that should be corrected by returning to the origin."[18]

5.

The fall before I left for Latin America, I took a poetry workshop. Just before it ended, the professor, a Columbia poet, saw my desk piled with Paz's books and commented dismissively on his politics, in an attempt, perhaps, to excise Paz from my pantheon. I'd felt perplexed by it; I'd already read essays from such collections as *The Other Voice* and had seen that Paz's soaring love of freedom transcended nationalism and was clear in its denunciation of repression. What did my professor mean? Was he spreading hearsay?

Because Paz denounced Stalin's atrocities, he distinguished himself (often explicitly) from Pablo Neruda, who in 1953 was famously awarded the Stalin Peace Prize, as Ilan Stavans notes in a new collection of Neruda's odes (*All the Odes*). But Paz distinguished himself, too, from poets and intellectuals enlisted as cultural cold warriors, like Robert Lowell, Emir Rodríguez Monegal, and Stephen Spender. While Paz represented the kind of Latin American liberal the interventionist cold warriors liked to champion and fund—figures referred to collectively as the non-communist left—Paz's positions often started with assumptions surrounding the history of the damage, destruction, and dangers of American imperialism; his anti-communist views appear to have been un-coerced and predated the quiet funding channels that came to Latin America starting in the early 1950s, in the form of at least seven magazines: *Examen*, published in Mexico; *Combate*, published in Costa Rica; and *Cuadernos de la libertad cultural*, *Cadernos brasileiros*, *Temas*, *Aportes*, and *Mundo Nuevo*, published in Paris.

Encounter, the flagship CIA magazine published in England from 1953 until 1991 and edited by Spender, also had an edition in Spanish. These magazines were funded by the CIA's propaganda outfit, the Congress for Cultural Freedom, in some cases funneled through a Latin American think tank or a nonprofit like the Ford Foundation. They ran in tandem with campaigns that included CIA-embedded poetry tours (Lowell in South America) and the campaign (by CIA man John Hunt) to deny Neruda the Nobel Prize in the early 1960s. (He would win this prize in 1971.)

Peter Coleman writes that the Congress for Cultural Freedom–affiliated *Cuadernos* ought to have had "natural allies" in Paz, Carlos Fuentes, and others associated with *Revista Mexicana de Literatura*, "but they disliked *Cuadernos* so much"—as Keith Botsford told the directorate—"that they refused to publish an advertisement for it."[19] American adventures, including the 1954 CIA overthrow of the democratically elected Jacobo Arbenz in Guatemala and the Bay of Pigs invasion, somehow failed to endear Latin American leftists to the American proposition, whatever fond or fawning interest their magazine launches may have shown many of these writers.

Paz did appear in the CIA's *Mundo Nuevo*. But this is likely because it was better-disguised propaganda than the quasi-McCarthyite *Cuadernos*. *Mundo Nuevo* also published leftists like Neruda and Gabriel García Márquez, who would have had nothing to do with a magazine known to be funded by the CIA. In *Our Men in Paris?* Russell Cobb writes that "[Carlos] Fuentes and Octavio Paz had little respect for the CCF (Congress for Cultural Freedom); the fact that *Mundo Nuevo* was able to attract both figures to contribute to the magazine is illustrative of its significant break with the organization's anti-Communist politics."[20]

Why, when others were failing to take up the middle ground, was Paz able to position himself this way—namely, remaining critical of both American imperialism, on one hand, and the Soviet betrayal of socialist principles on the other, and noting, too, the betrayal's taint on the Latin American left? It was in part because Mexico was a haven for refugees like Serge.

Paz wrote:

> When I consider Aragon, Eluard, Neruda and other famous Stalinist writers and poets, I feel the gooseflesh that I get from reading certain passages in the Inferno. No doubt they began in good faith. How could they have shut their eyes to the horrors of capitalism and the disasters of imperialism in Asia, Africa, and our part of America? They experienced a generous surge of indignation and solidarity with the victims. But insensibly, commitment by commitment, they saw themselves become tangled in a mesh of lies, falsehoods, deceits and perjuries until they lost their souls.[21]

Their souls? He is similarly unsparing in his indictment of other beloved figures of the left, such as fellow Mexican artists Diego Rivera and Frida Kahlo:

> Diego and Frida ought not to be subjects of beatification but objects of study—and of repentance . . . the weaknesses, taints, and defects that show up in the works of Diego and Frida are moral in origin. The two of them betrayed their great gifts, and this can be seen in their painting. An artist may commit political errors and even common crimes, but the truly great artists—Villon or Pound, Caravaggio or Goya—pay for their mistakes and thereby redeem their art and their honor.[22]

Was he conciliatory? Certainly not. Was this the problem with Paz? Almost two decades later, I emailed my former professor to see which veritable crimes on Paz's part so stuck in his craw, even with the Cold War long over. It turns out it was Paz's critiques of Nicaragua's Sandinistas, and his alleged apologia for the right. I asked Eliot Weinberger, too, what ignited the Latin American left's disdain for Paz. Weinberger writes, "Because of his criticisms of the Sandinistas, [the Latin American left] thought he was supporting Reagan in the Contra war, and had a demonstration where his effigy was burned."[23]

So, what did Paz actually say? As he accepted the 1984 Prize of the Association of German Editors and Booksellers in Frankfurt, Paz defended an author he had published in *Vuelta*. Gabriel Zaid had argued that it was time to submit "the Sandinista government to a popular vote in Nicaragua," as Enrique Krauze recounts in *Redeemers*. The article was well received internationally, including in the *New York Review of Books*, "but [was] strongly attacked by many Mexican publications."[24]

On stage to receive the award, perhaps feeling partly responsible for the uproar, Paz defended his author (though not by name). First he traced "the history of the Somoza 'hereditary dictatorship,'" which had "grown up in Washington." He continued,

> *Shortly after the [Sandinista] triumph, the case of Cuba was repeated: the revolution was confiscated by an elite of revolutionary leaders . . . From the beginning the Sandinista leaders sought inspiration in Cuba. They have received military and technical aid from the Soviet Union and its allies. The actions of the Sandinista regime show its will to install a military-bureaucratic dictatorship in Nicaragua according to the model of Havana. They have thus denaturalized the original meaning of the revolutionary movement.*[25]

Did any of this substantiate the allegation that Paz served as apologist for the right? In addition to the line above about Washington supporting the reviled Somoza dictatorship, and his repeated acknowledgments of the left's legitimate grievances against American imperialism, Paz added that "technical and military aid to the anti-Sandinista Contras was encountering growing criticism from the US Senate and American opinion."[26] Presumably, if the rationale for the Sandinistas accepting Soviet funding via Cuba had been American funding of the Contras, that would soon go away. As indeed it did.

Paz had written that "the United States has been one of the principal obstacles we have encountered in our efforts to modernize ourselves."[27] That's hardly Reaganite claptrap. Was Paz being read selectively by a left that, up against the wall of anti-communist incursions, required lockstep obedience rather than open discussion or frank criticism of its own side? A few years later, in "Poetry, Myth and Revolution," he wrote, "The critics of revolution have been those nostalgic for the old order [conservatives], and liberals ... The liberal criticism has been more effective than the reactionary criticism."[28]

Paz saw the real conversation at the time of the Berlin Wall's crumbling as one between the liberal and the socialist strains of thought. ("We must rethink our tradition, renovate it, and seek to reconcile the two great political traditions of modernity: liberalism and socialism.")[29] Liberalism's issue was that it left too many questions unanswered and placed a distance between fraternity and liberty. Socialism created the temptation of a meta-history, false scientism, and, at its worst, collapsed the balance altogether, allowing the pretense of fraternity to erode liberty—and then dissipate into atrocity.

Scholar Maarten van Delden has recounted how at the time of the Frankfurt kerfuffle, Paz understood Nicaragua's anti-Americanism, and merely asked why it should lead the Sandinistas to align with the Soviet Union. Paz cited Chateaubriand: "The Revolution would have carried me along . . . but I saw the first head paraded on the end of a pike, and I recoiled. I shall never look on murder as an argument in favor of liberty. I know of nothing more servile, more cowardly, more obtuse than a terrorist. Did I not find, later on, that entire race of Brutuses in the service of Caesar and his police?"[30] Paz also wrote a "lengthy analysis of the Central American crisis," Van Delden adds, "published in *Vuelta* in October 1987, [in which he] stated firmly that his defense of democracy should not be confused with 'the defense of North American imperialism, nor with that of Latin America's conservative military regimes.'"[31]

Compare this with Borges's "ringing endorsement of Gen. Pinochet's activities in Chile," as Clive James once described it at Slate. "There was a torture center within walking distance of [Borges's] house [in Buenos Aires], and he had always been a great walker," wrote James. "He could still hear, even if he couldn't see. There was a lot of private talk that must have been hard to miss; a cocked ear would have heard the screams."[32] It would seem to make Borges a better target than Paz for Latin American apologist for the right, but he has never received the level of venom directed at Paz.

So was his Frankfurt speech taken out of context? Was it merely a betrayal of the shibboleth that the enemy (the USSR) of my enemy (the USA) is my friend? Krauze recounts Paz's reaction to the row that followed the Frankfurt speech:

> My first reaction was an incredulous laugh. How was it possible that a rather moderate speech unleashed such violence? Then a certain melancholy satisfaction. If they attack me it's because [what I said] hurts

them. But—I confess to you—it also hurt me. I felt (and I still feel it . . .) that I was the victim of an injustice and a misunderstanding. In the first place . . . it was an action conceived and directed by a group with the intention of intimidating all those who think as I do and dare say it.[33]

What "attack" so hurt Paz, just five years before the Ayatollah's fatwa on Salman Rushdie? Krauze describes it vividly: "A large crowd marched in front of the American embassy on Paseo de la Reforma (a short distance from Paz's apartment) carrying effigies of President Ronald Reagan and Octavio Paz. Some of them chanted 'Rapacious Reagan, your friend is Octavio Paz' ('*Reagan rapaz, tu amigo es Octavio Paz!*'). Someone lit a match and the effigy of Paz went up in flames."[34]

6.

Despite Paz's failing health, the 1990s saw the publication of eight more books of his prose, including a massive study on the Mexican poet Sor Juana Inez de la Cruz; three more books of essays; a survey of contemporary international politics, titled *One Earth, Four or Five Worlds*; a survey of love and eroticism; an accounting of his politics from early Marxism onward; and a survey of Indian art and culture embedded with recollections of his time there. He also released another book of poems, *A Tree Within*; won the first Nobel Prize in Literature awarded after the fall of the Berlin Wall; and published a massive fifteen-volume edition of his complete works.

As the title of his first published poem suggests, Paz was a poet obsessed with process; and like Cortázar and Borges, he loved games. His poems about times of day, interstices between coming and going, petrification, and the annihilation of time often read like exercises. Paz confessed to Chilean novelist (and recent ambassador to France) Jorge Edwards that having dismissed Neruda for his politics, he had reread his entire oeuvre in the decades after Neruda's death and begrudgingly admitted that Neruda was that generation's finest poet.

Still, their poems reflect a drastically different worldview, aesthetic as well as political. A pair of socks in Neruda was, first, a pair of socks, suggesting the worlds, rooms, and lives of real people behind them. Objects in Paz's work, on the other hand, read as transmutations, state changes—attempts to effect in words the canvasses of Joan Miró, the theories and games of John Cage. Paz is the Poet Laureate of synesthesia. Nothing—senses, self, time—is stable, as he conveys in "The Street":

> It's a long and silent street.
> I walk in the dark and trip and fall
> and get up and step blindly
> on the mute stones and dry leaves
> and someone behind me is also walking:
> if I stop, he stops;
> if I run, he runs. I turn around: no one.
> Everything is black, there is no exit,
> and I turn and turn corners
> that always lead to the street
> where no one waits for me, no one follows,
> where I follow a man who trips
> and gets up and says when he sees me: no one.

Compare this with "Borges and I," which appeared more than a decade later, and the famously cerebral Borges's disquisition on the self almost reads as sentimental.

Even when the lowercase, everyday self appears in Paz's work, its bodily and even psychological craving is overwhelmed by the spiritual pursuit of redemption through literature. Craving nicotine, Paz writes in "The Poet's Work," "I turned toward a nearby cafe where I was sure to find a little warmth, some music and, above all, cigarettes . . . I walked two more blocks, shivering, when suddenly I felt—no, I didn't feel it: it suddenly went by: the Word. The unexpectedness of the encounter paralyzed me . . ."

Paz's shorter, process-laden poems—like architecture with its structure exposed—at times feel austere. His longer poems are more capacious and Whitmanesque, filling themselves with ordinary objects in a steady stream, buffeted along by the sorcery of chiasmus. His long autobiographical poem, *A Draft of Shadows*, bowls you over with a rhythmic onslaught of his ambling, riverine veering, until family and childhood details finally start to peek out from middle-length lines, like a startling—if startlingly casual—confession that the self may, in fact, have a history, despite its instability.

His rare poems addressing a "you" perhaps best of all unite word and deed, focusing his intricate and austere alchemy, and serving as a stand-in for the reader.

In one of these, he commands:

> listen to me as one listens to the rain,
> without listening, hear what I say
> with eyes open inward, asleep
> with all five senses awake,
> it's raining, light footsteps, a murmur of syllables,
> air and water, words with no weight:
> what we were and are,
> the days and years, this moment . . .

Paz is most intelligible and affecting as a love poet, when the third person abstractions ("Time," say) are softened by an I and you. Take "January 1," one poem sorely missing from the otherwise judiciously curated new collection:

> Time, with no help from us,
> had placed
> in exactly the same order as yesterday
> houses in the empty street,
> snow on the houses,
> silence on the snow.
>
> You were beside me,
> still asleep.
> The day had invented you
> but you hadn't yet accepted
> being invented by the day.
> —Nor possibly my being invented, either.
> You were in another day.
>
> You were beside me
> and I saw you, like the snow,
> asleep among the appearances.
> Time, with no help from us,
> invents houses, streets,
> trees, and sleeping women.

While it's true that all the theoretical speculation sometimes makes for a rhetorical voice even in Paz's love poems ("being invented by the day"), I have often found this part of the pleasure of reading him; Paz makes poetry out of all the century's isms and uncertainties, and from that poetry sometimes comes a calm certitude about love and wonder.

It may be as complete, consistent, and universal an ontological statement as one finds in poetry in Spanish. Even if he depicts the self and linear time as unstable, this poetry posits that—whatever we are, however temporary, however jumbled our senses—love may save us from the world of illusions that hands us over, finally, to something mysterious, eternal, and ineffable.

Perhaps to address both those who admired him and those who burned his effigy, Paz held a public farewell in Mexico City. He would die a slow death from spinal cancer, his library having burned in an apartment fire—reminding him perhaps of his crumbling house during the civil war. As Krauze recounts:

> *He repeated his favorite metaphor of Mexico as "a country of the sun" but then immediately reminded the audience about the darkness of our history, our "luminous and cruel" duality that already reigned within the cosmogony of the Aztec gods and had been an obsession for him since childhood. He wished that some Socrates might appear who could free his people of the darker side, of all the destructive passions . . . And suddenly he looked up toward the cloudy sky, as if he wanted to touch it with his hand. "Up there," he said, "there are clouds and sun. Clouds and sun are related words. Let us be worthy of the clouds of the Valley of Mexico. Let us be worthy of the sun of the Valley of Mexico." For an instant the sky cleared, leaving only the sun, and then Octavio Paz said, "The Valley of Mexico, that phrase lit up my childhood, my maturity, and my old age."*[35]

7.

He had offered another sort of valedictory during the Cold War, this time in Spain, a nation recently emerged from fascism. It was the fiftieth anniversary of the Second International Congress of Anti-Fascist Writers. He recalled the controversy that was caused by Andre Gide's 1937 report on the abuses and corruptions of power that had occurred under Stalin. The report made Gide a pariah on the literary left.

When members of the Congress of Anti-Fascist Writers moved to censure Gide, Paz voted against it, but he didn't speak out. At the fiftieth anniversary commemoration, Paz felt the need to confess. Though the censure was eventually vetoed by Andre Malraux, and Paz had been courageous to vote against it in the minority, he nevertheless regretted his behavior as a failure of the principle of fraternity. "Although many of us were convinced of the injustice of those attacks and we admired Gide, we kept silent," he said. "And so we contributed to the petrification of the revolution."[36]

My favorite poem in all of Paz's oeuvre comes from that period of public repentance. One of his shortest, the poem indicates an awe in the face of our impotence, our smallness, our certain annihilation. It's called "Brotherhood":

> I am a man: little do I last
> and the night is enormous.
> But I look up:
> The stars write.
> Unknowing I understand:
> I too am written,
> and at this very moment
> someone spells me out.

1940

For All Mankind:
Diego Rivera in San Francisco and Detroit

or how the anti-Stalinist crusades against him
never let up despite his flight from Stalin

Diego Rivera painted his largest single work in an airplane hangar, accompanied by an armed guard. Shortly before he commenced work on *Pan American Unity* for the 1940 San Francisco World's Fair, his wife—the artist Frida Kahlo—and Leon Trotsky began an affair. Though Rivera remained an admirer of the hero of the October Revolution, he expelled Trotsky from his home in Mexico. The security budget to protect the former military leader had already been putting a strain on the household's finances. This was the last straw.

Pan American Unity features no image of Trotsky. Stalin appears on the mural's fourth panel as one set of a triad of ghouls cloaked in gray ether, alongside Hitler and Mussolini. They are surrounded by portraits of actors, chief among them Charlie Chaplin, who assumes a number of his satirical personas. A single arm, tattooed with a swastika and holding a dagger tightly, emerges from the ether, but is held at bay by another, much larger arm draped in an American flag and flanked by bombers and paratroopers: Rivera's ode to anti-fascist Hollywood.

Since July, *Pan American Unity* has been on display as the star attraction of the San Francisco MOMA's *Diego Rivera's America*. The exhibit offers canvas paintings from the 1920s and '30s alongside murals, including two earlier ones completed in San Francisco, and a handful created in Mexico, which are projected as videos on the galleries' walls. Evinced in *Pan American Unity* is Rivera's attempt to forge a hybrid art of the Americas alongside a post-Stalinist political unity.

On the tenth anniversary of the October Revolution the artist had visited the Soviet Union with hope, but some criticism, too. In the end, his window into Stalin's

Russia turned him off; he began taking commissions from wealthy patrons in the West. In place of Stalinist doctrine, the mural portrays a carnivalesque unity between North and South American innovation, held together by the culture of the pre-Columbian civilizations in the Valley of Mexico.

Palaces and Temples

Rivera was born in 1886 to a middle-class family in Guanajuato, a city in central Mexico. His twin brother died before his second birthday. Fascinated by military strategy, trains, and technology, Rivera painted from a young age. But his embrace of modernity was alloyed to an equally fervent embrace of Indigenous culture. For him, the Indigenous culture of Mexico was one in which art permeated all levels of society:

> In the pre-Hispanic world everything in the life of the people was artistic, from the palaces and temples which remain monumental works of sculpture—with their magnificent frescoes that amaze everyone peering at them in the jungle—down to the humblest everyday pots, the children's toys, and the stones used to grind grain.[1]

As a teen, Rivera studied at the San Carlos Academy of Fine Arts, winning a bursary to travel to Spain. There he painted landscapes and still lifes, deepened his love for Velázquez, and imitated El Greco. Between the travel scholarship and his first fresco commissions in Mexico, Rivera was a product of the public funding of art: his first taste, then, of a collective art.

Collective

In Europe he honed his technique. After his bursary ran out during World War I, he lived in Montparnasse, in the south of Paris. He learned pointillism and Cubism among the leading lights of twentieth-century modernism. On one occasion, Rivera accused Pablo Picasso of stealing one of his Cubist motifs; the maestro concurred silently by painting over the offending canvas. But even in this vibrant milieu, Rivera grew dissatisfied with what he felt to be its stifling ideas about art. In particular, two decades before Picasso had completed his *Guernica* painting, Rivera bristled at what he saw as the Cubists' hostility toward forms of representation that could accommodate narrative. Butting heads with Picasso's wing of the movement, he attempted to carve out a path for himself that could express the tumultuous history being made around him.

One night at dinner, a debate between rival artistic factions grew violent. An argument started in a restaurant on the Quai des Grands Augustins and spilled over into the apartment of Rivera's comrade, André Lhote. It escalated further when a young poet, spewing the main group's orthodoxies against "literary Cubism," called Rivera and Lhote's work derivative. Rivera slapped him and a fight ensued, during which the poet threw himself at Rivera and pulled his hair. After *l'affaire Rivera*, as this incident came to be known, the Mexican artist drifted out of the trendy cafe circles and came to view Cubism as a cult of personality.[2]

Aesthetically untethered, he moved toward Cézanne's methodical painting, which could accommodate the storytelling necessary for Rivera's future frescos. It was not Cezanne that led him to Cubism, as his biographer Patrick Marnham, notes, but Cubism that led him to Cezanne.

And his return to realism, this biographer added, was "like watching a man focusing his eyes after an extended period of blurred vision."[3] Under the influence of art historian Élie Faure, Rivera considered art movements as swinging between individual and collective epochs. Though neither Faure nor Rivera was religious, the former spoke of medieval churches as the grand achievement of the last period of collective art. European cathedrals were not merely houses of worship, he argued, but public markets, meeting places, the Greek agora—a dance floor and a place of ceremony.

Foreseeing the rise of steel buildings, Faure encouraged Rivera to explore fresco as an artform capable of accommodating this massive expansion of the built environment's scale. Faure saw in this transformation of the skyline a model of modernity that could improve the lives of everyday people. These words stayed with Rivera on his pilgrimage to Florence, where—before returning to his homeland to forge a truly Mexican art, and before his famous commissions in the north—he set out to examine the great Italian frescoes.

The 1930s: San Francisco and Detroit

While painting the *Allegory of California* on an upper floor of the San Francisco Stock Exchange, now the City Club (the mural is projected as part of SFMOMA's video exhibition), Rivera was struck by the beauty of the city, the generosity of its inhabitants. He made friends, presented solo shows in San Francisco, Los Angeles, and San Diego. By February 1931, he'd finished the cheerful mural with an enormous, mythic, blue-eyed earth mother at its heart, modeled on tennis champion Helen Wills Moody, with whom Rivera had a fling. The figure bears a cornucopia of California fruit in her left hand; with her right, she lifts the earth's cover to show soot-covered miners in dank conditions, clamoring for California gold and other metals. During this time the couple raced around the city in Moody's two-seater Cadillac, with the six-foot Rivera crammed in the tiny dicky seats in the car's trunk.

Throughout their 1930s stay in California, Rivera and Kahlo lived on Montgomery Street in San Francisco, near North Beach. They befriended the Depression-era photographer Dorothea Lange and were swarmed by fans. "The poor guy can't even go to the bathroom in peace because they're bugging him all day," Kahlo recalled.[4] They also met art historian Wilhelm Valentiner of the Detroit Institute of Arts. From their endless conversations on technology emerged another brilliant grand-scale US commission: the Detroit Industry Murals.

In preparation, Rivera spent months studying the Ford Motor Company's assembly lines on the city's Rouge River. "Marx made theory . . . Lenin applied it with his sense of large-scale social organization . . . And Henry Ford made the work of the socialist state possible," he remarked with admiration.[5] Even though he saw the socialist uses to which Fordism could be put, he also saw its limitations. In the real Ford factory, he found predominantly white male workers. But on his canvas, Rivera integrated the factory floor, depicting Black and Latino workers alongside the white ones, and he devoted a panel to the women who sewed upholstery in the factory, as well.

At the time, Ford manufactured planes, and in a tally of the pluses and minuses of modernization, Rivera depicted aircraft on one panel being used humanely to transport mankind and spark industry. On another panel, in contrast, he painted war planes with pilots in protective suits dropping bombs and gasses on innocent bystanders. The trick is repeated in another scene in the fresco. On one panel, a factory line produces cures; on another, the alien-like workers in protective masks fabricate mustard gas and organisms for warfare.

Easily one of Rivera's finest works, the mural features machines morphing (if you squint) into an Aztec goddess. At the heart of Rivera's image is a mechanical object equal parts Ford-factory assembly line machine and Coatlicue, the Aztec earth goddess. Its muted colors suit the Motor City's palette—grays, silvers, and gleaming blues drawing the eye across metals and crowds. Apart from a sign added later, deploring Rivera's "reprehensible politics," in Detroit the artist was allowed to paint as he pleased. New York was another story.

Man, Controller of the Universe

For Rockefeller Center's RCA building, patriarch John D. Rockefeller Jr. chose a theme that was comically grandiose: "Man at the Crossroads Looking with Hope and High Vision to the Choosing of a New and Better Future." Rockefeller wanted viewers to reflect on the state of the world as they walked past the mural, which was intended for the lobby of a building that he was also trying to fill with Depression-era renters. Rivera was not the Rockefellers' first choice, but neither Matisse nor Picasso was free. Rivera managed to earn the commission by charming the family during long, friendly dinners in which he admitted that he planned to contrast capitalism and socialism. But he also obscured a detail in the blueprints, a portrait of Lenin. When Rivera's assistant Lucienne Bloch worried the mural was veering too far left, Kahlo calmed her. Every night, she said, Abby Rockefeller (John Jr.'s wife, and Rivera's patron) climbed the scaffolding, nodding her approval.

But as its unveiling neared, Rivera snuck in the offending face, who links the hands of Black and white workers. John Jr.'s son Nelson wrote ever so diplomatically to Rivera, pleading for an alteration: "I noticed that. . . you had included a portrait of Lenin. This piece is beautifully painted but it seems to me that his . . . appearing . . . *might very easily seriously offend* a great many people."[6] After politely refusing to remove Lenin, Rivera was paid his fee of $21,000 (around $450,000 today) and escorted from the lobby. "All art is propaganda," Rivera quipped. "The only difference is the kind." The Rockefeller family, whose fortunes had been made over the dead bodies of striking workers out west, knew this, but thought they could purchase Rivera's vision. "Since art is essential for human life, it can't just belong to the few. Art is the universal language, and it belongs to all mankind . . . I want to use my art as a weapon."[7]

In the end, the Rockefellers veiled, then painted over the fresco with a more patriotic American allegory, effectively destroying Rivera's work. The great loss to New York City art was Mexico's gain. From photographs his assistant surreptitiously took, Rivera recreated the mural in 1934, renaming the Mexican version *Man, Controller of the Universe*. In the Palace of Bellas Artes, throngs of chattering tourists admire the mural from opening to closing. As revenge for the cancellation—and to the amusement of these imagined audiences—Rivera depicted Rockefeller, a notorious teetotaler, with a cocktail. For good measure, the artist gave the millionaire a case of syphilis.

San Francisco Sequel

In creating *Pan American Unity* six years later, Rivera proclaimed that he was in search of "a real American art . . . From the South comes the Plumed Serpent, from the

North . . . the conveyor belt."[8] But before starting on the commission, Rivera busied himself helping Trotsky apply for asylum from the Mexican government. Having made preparations for Trotsky's arrival, Rivera fell ill and left it to Kahlo to pick up Trotsky and his wife Natalia Sedova. When the revolutionaries landed, Rivera and Kahlo put them up in their home, Casa Azul. Soon mutual admiration bloomed into an affair between Kahlo and Trotsky. The revolutionary passed notes to Kahlo in books he lent her, "sometimes under Rivera's nose."[9] But when Rivera discovered the affair, he presented Trotsky with a large skull made of sugar and bearing Stalin's name. Though unamused, Trotsky failed to draw the connection between the artist's symbolism and the affair. This latest infidelity (Kahlo's revenge for Rivera's unforgivable affair with her sister) led Rivera and Kahlo to divorce.

By the time Ramón Mercader buried an ice pick in Trotsky's skull in August 1940, Rivera was on a San Francisco scaffolding painting his single largest mural. Fearing Stalin's cruelty more than ever, Rivera painted under armed protection before an audience for four months, reveling in the limelight. Soon the couple reconciled; Kahlo joined him in San Francisco, where they remarried (a doctor told her it would do her health some good). While she convalesced from hip and spine treatments, hundreds of thousands of Californians came to see his mural.

Unveiled in a special SFMOMA gallery with no fee for entry, the mural features dizzying panoramas of burnt sienna matching the Golden Gate Bridge, as it stretches beside prolific commissioning-architect Timothy Pflueger's prominent skyscrapers in the city's skyline; jade-blue and turquoise swaths of the San Francisco Bay and the Pacific; Mount Shasta; and the deserts of the Valley of Mexico. On the leftmost panel, Olmec, Toltec, and Aztec pyramids sprawl above a blue-caped Nezahualcoyotl, who was a philosopher, scholar and poet-king of fifteenth-century Texcoco, the Athens of pre-Columbian America. According to legend—long before the Wright Brothers—Nezahualcoyotl invented a flying machine.

The second panel mirrors the fourth, which depicts the trio of Hitler, Mussolini, and Stalin painted with the aim of lobbying the United States to join the war effort. (Rivera was hardly the Stalinist stooge characterized by Paz, at least by the late 1930s.) But rather than criminals, as in the fourth, this second panel depicts a revolutionary tradition led by Thomas Jefferson, Abraham Lincoln, liberators Simón Bolívar, Miguel Hidalgo, José María Morelos, and abolitionist John Brown. At the centermost panel is the Ford machine/Coatlicue from the Detroit mural, now fleshed out as a goddess on the left side and a metallic machine on the right.

Rivera is suggesting Mexico and California are one land, one people, which was literally true before European "discovery" and US annexation in the 1840s. Underneath are Kahlo, Rivera, and their San Francisco friend, the actress Paulette Godard, planting a ceiba tree, symbolizing "closer pan-Americanism."[10]

At his best, Rivera embodies a stupendous modernist vernacular that sits between the instruction manual and the Old Masters, the propaganda poster and the Sistine Chapel. The intricacy of *Pan American Unity*'s colors alone makes the fresco's nearly two decades in cold storage a true shame—another of the Cold War's petty crimes against culture. It was stored with the hope that the war's end might produce funds to mount it. But when the mural's patron, architect Pflueger, died in 1946, it wasn't mounted in City College San Francisco until 1961, twenty years after Rivera completed it.

Its detractors included some who called for its destruction or disappearance. But as Rivera's largest single work, its scale alone is a marvel, never mind its diplomatic and political ambition. On the canvas, Rivera succeeded in reframing the civilization of the American West and Mexico, linking together progressive political movements and artistic innovations—from Mexican independence to US abolition of slavery to anti-fascist Hollywood—by creating a mythological origin for them in Texcoco and the Aztec people.

1970

Embodiment of the Enemy: Angela Davis in California

or how the Nixon administration tried to depict the college professor as a terrorist

In December 2022, the activist, intellectual, and educator Angela Davis took the podium at Pilgrim Baptist Church in Nyack, New York. The church was not the planners' first choice but scurrilous red baiting campaigns led two venues to cancel. Waiting for the 500-strong standing ovation to quiet down, the former Communist Party member and political prisoner told her audience that "I think every day about the fact that I am associated with a people who refuse to give up, after centuries and centuries. Not only that, but who have created beauty in the process of struggling."[1]

As interviewer Amy Goodman noted on *Democracy Now!*, it was "a reprise" of what happened two years before in Davis's hometown of Birmingham, Alabama. Emphasizing words to underline her subject's heroism, Goodman recalled an award that was canceled and reinstated after the granting organization was shamed for wavering. "You ended up doing an event outside the place you were actually invited, and *so many more* people turned up." Davis admitted being stunned by the ways people misrepresent her. But more important, she told Goodman, "I'm concerned about the misrepresentation of movements against racism. Against gender inequality. For freedom."[2]

Indeed, misrepresentation followed Davis around throughout her public career. It was why she went on the lam in 1970, after a gun she bought to protect herself from death threats turned up in a Marin County courtroom. During an attempted prison break that turned bloody, after police opened fire on those involved, her gun was found on a young suspect. Afraid that, as a radical Black intellectual, she would not get a fair trial, Davis fled to Chicago. As police closed in on her, she proceeded to Miami and New York. She was still in disguise when apprehended, and the trial of the decade began.

Her defense became a cause célèbre, winning support from Aretha Franklin, Jean Genet, even inspiring a mediocre pop song by artists John Lennon and Yoko Ono. In her landmark *Autobiography*, re-released in January 2022 by Haymarket Books, she stylishly recounts the ordeal which eventually culminated in her acquittal in 1973. Edited by Toni Morrison, who interviewed the imprisoned Davis during her trial, the *Autobiography* recounts how the philosopher became one of the FBI's Ten Most Wanted Criminals.

Dynamite Hill to UCLA

Davis grew up in a part of Birmingham that was bombed so often by the Ku Klux Klan that it was renamed "Dynamite Hill." Her mother told her, as Davis recounted to Shola Lynch in the documentary, *Free Angela and All Political Prisoners,* that "this was not the way things were supposed to be."[3] She held to that as a matter of faith. From her father she learned the importance of self-defense; he kept guns that Davis saw him brandish in response to each new threat. Coming of age in this atmosphere, Davis and her sister Fania tested the boundaries of Jim Crow, easing into French accents to break the color code in retail stores. After being well tended to despite local codes, they laughed in the face of hypocritical white store owners and left without buying anything—an improvised Situationist boycott.

Members of the NAACP, her parents had been partially radicalized by friends and Birmingham neighbors, the Burnhams, a Black family who, as members of the Communist Party, came south to spur anti-racist change. Angela would remain lifelong friends with several Burnhams, including Margaret, who would become an internationally renowned civil rights lawyer. Approaching high school, Davis found herself surrounded by students who were frequently taught by teachers who cared little for Black history (in her textbook, the Civil War was renamed "the war for Southern Independence"). Having spent summers in New York with the Burnhams, Davis found a program that brought students from the segregated south to study in the north. Her timing was ironic, and she lamented missing Birmingham's protests, regretting how she missed the radical change that came to her hometown.[4]

In New York, Davis attended Elizabeth Irwin High School in Greenwich Village, where she was taught by teachers whom McCarthyites had blacklisted for their leftwing views. In a Jim Crow version of foreign exchange study, she lived with a white, liberal Christian Brooklyn family whom she respected as longtime allies of the Black Liberation Movement.

Davis earned a scholarship to Brandeis University, where she studied abroad in France and fell in love with critical theory and French literature. One of very few Black students at Brandeis, she came under the spell of Herbert Marcuse who had written *One Dimensional Man*, a critique of post-war capitalism and the closest thing the 60s generation had to a philosophical manifesto. She would go on to work with Marcuse in Germany and then California.

She returned to the US smoking Gauloises and by her own account she stood out. The rampant penetration of leftwing groups by government agents served as a pretext for the emergence of an understandable distrust of the cosmopolitan and bilingual Davis. Her comrades, Davis admitted with regret, "thought I was an agent. You know, 'Who is this Black woman who is coming from Europe and wanting to know what's going on in the community?'"[5]

She understood that to accomplish anything she needed a collective. But finding herself drawn to groups like the Black Panthers and Student Nonviolent Coordinating Committee, she discovered yet more layers of the mistrust that accompanied her arrival in San Diego. The former's nationalism and uninterrogated chauvinism sat especially uneasily with Davis.

Eventually, she fell in with Franklin and Kendra Alexander. These three were among the seed members of the Che-Lumumba Club of the Communist Party, embedded within the Black Panther movement. She was invited to apply for a position at UCLA, which sought a scholar trained in continental European philosophy who could teach Marxism. When offered the job, she accepted but her political affiliations meant that trouble followed Davis into the lecture hall.

"Are You A Member of the Communist Party?"

On July 1, 1969, in an article in the UCLA *Daily Bruin*, an undercover FBI agent leaked that the philosophy department had recently hired an assistant professor who "is well qualified for the post, and is also a member of the Communist Party." Davis remained unnamed. But a week later, the *San Francisco Examiner* named Davis as the professor cited in the *Bruin*, labeling her a "known Maoist, according to US intelligence reports, and active in the SDS and the Black Panthers...."[6] Two thirds of this was bunk.

"That's when all hell broke out," Davis recalled.[7] The California Regents directed UCLA's Chancellor "to determine whether Professor Davis was a member of the Communist Party, and not to sign any contracts with her pending receipt of this information." The chancellor sent Davis a registered letter, requesting a response that same month, noting, "I am constrained by Regental policy to request that you inform me whether or not you are a member of the Communist Party." The letter went to an old address and Davis never saw it.

As a result of the publicity, her first lecture (on the philosophy of Frederick Douglas), drew 2,000 students. A white student whom journalists interviewed after the lecture suggested that Davis was "trying to overthrow our system of government, and admits it."[8] Whether this sentiment was shared by her colleagues and the rest of the student body mattered little. Lieutenant Governor Ed Reinecke cited her membership in the Party as reason to dismiss her, though an earlier case at Berkeley affirmed that political affiliations were protected under academic freedom.[9]

The Hunt for Angela

While she fought for her job, Davis grew enmeshed in the struggle for prisoners' rights. America was cultivating the world's largest incarceration rate, and these were, in Davis's opinion, political prisoners. A particular case in Soledad State Prison drew her attention.

Convicted for stealing $70 in an armed robbery, George Jackson had spent seven of his eleven-year sentence in San Quentin's brutal solitary confinement. Soon he became radicalized by reading Karl Marx, Friedrich Engels, Leon Trotsky, and Mao Zedong. In 1969, he was transferred to Soledad State, two hours' drive south of San Francisco, where, on January 13, 1970, the guards did something shocking.

Though prisoners were typically segregated by racial identity, that day the guards placed prisoners of color together in the prison yard with members of the murderous Aryan Brotherhood. In the *Autobiography*, Davis accuses the guards of instigating the violence that broke out, during which Jackson's friend and comrade was shot to death by a guard. When another guard was beaten and thrown from an upper prison tier, plunging to his death, it was seen as retaliation.

Jackson and two other prison reform activists—both Black and both convicted for minor property crimes (one for stealing a television)—were "singled out" and charged with the killing. It was a capital offense: in the days of California's death penalty, a successful conviction could end in the state's gas chambers.

Davis met Jackson at a hearing and was drawn to both his in-person tenderness and his cogent prison writings. In a volley of letters, they grew close and ultimately fell in love. Left out of the *Autobiography*, for understandable reasons (it was published quickly, in 1974), their love story is a minor through-line in the documentary *Free Angela and All Political Prisoners*. Lynch develops it judiciously, using the encounter to humanize both figures against the backdrop of bleak events and violence unraveling around them.

Through her advocacy for Jackson, Davis also met his younger brother, Jonathan. Growing up with a beloved brother behind bars, Jonathan's desperation worried his family. His activism was met with a shrug at school, frustrating him. In one letter, George described him as a loyal "man-child" and asked Davis to bring him into the movement.

In August 1970, Jonathan smuggled a gun into a Marin County courtroom to free his brother and other prisoners. The incident ended in a bloodbath in the Marin County Civic Center parking lot—with Jonathan, two prisoners, and Judge Haley shot in a white van (all but the judge shot by police snipers).

Showing solidarity with the Jackson family, thousands turned out for Jonathan's funeral, where whispers confirmed that Davis had been implicated: the guns used were those that she had purchased to protect herself. But as Davis tells Lynch, "That was not the time to make myself available to the police for arrest."[10] The hunt for Angela Davis was under way.

FBI's Most Wanted

During her flight, Walter Cronkite reported that the FBI put Davis on its Ten Most Wanted List. Wanted posters, straight out of cowboy films, accused her of murder, kidnapping and interstate flight. Across the country, tall, young Black women, who might or might not have a space between their upper front teeth, were rounded up and pulled into custody, while Davis planned her escape with little but the clothes she wore when she learned she was wanted.

She considered asylum in Cuba but did not want to live in exile, as this would likely have lasted the rest of her life. She wanted to live in her broken homeland and see its arc bend toward justice. In a wig, Davis flew from Las Vegas to Chicago, where she met trusted friend David Poindexter. They would guide each other into a life underground. But while the two were planning Davis's flight to safety, Poindexter got into an argument with a friend in his apartment building, which worried them.

The FBI called together its countless Communist Party informants, who, according to rumors, outnumbered ordinary members two to one. Against this backdrop, Poindexter feared that his harboring Davis might become known, if agents questioned the disgruntled friend. So they fled to Miami. Holed up among palm trees, Davis worried about friends, family, and comrades. Every noise made her jump, she later recalled.

Unknown to either of them, the police had identified the white Toyota in which the pair traveled. Poindexter's mother was questioned in Florida, and the fugitives fled north to New York. In one of their abandoned crash pads, law enforcement found undeveloped film in the couch cushions. These photos gave away Davis's disguise. Her iconic afro was covered by a wig: agents had pursued the wrong profile.

One afternoon, as she and Poindexter returned to the hotel, Davis's ongoing fear that she was being surveilled was confirmed. A lurking agent leapt at her in the hallway, asking to lift her upper lip. "I'm looking for that gap," he said. The glasses and wig she wore "they snatched . . . off the top of my head, repeating . . . 'Are you Angela Davis?' I did not say yes, I did not say no; I did not say anything at all. I only requested my telephone calls."[11]

When President Richard Nixon signed the Organized Crime Bill a few days later, he boasted of Davis's arrest, proudly declaring that his administration had brought a known terrorist to justice. Told the other inmates would despise her for her communism, she was placed in solitary confinement—for her own protection. Once her lawyers ended this denial of her rights, she found fellow prisoners curious about or favorable toward socialism.

The Fresno Farmer

One night in Greenwich Village—where supporters could be heard yelling slogans from the street below—police barged into her cell. Her lawyer wanted to discuss extradition, they said. It was 3:00 a.m., and she was skeptical. When she went along with them, she was forced violently to the floor, cuffed and taken in a caravan to a New Jersey Air

Force base. "If I so much as stumble," she thought, "they will probably open fire on me and that will be the end."[12]

She was arraigned in the Civic Center where the shootings had erupted the summer before. The Attorney General sought three death penalty charges. "That made me realize how serious they were. But it also made me realize that it wasn't about me. Because, first of all, I couldn't be killed three times. It was about the construction of this imaginary enemy. And I was the embodiment of that enemy," Davis recounted.[13]

Davis fought to write in prison, partly by joining her own legal counsel, striving to maintain "a sphere of freedom." Her emotional relationship to Jackson, who was acquitted of the capital offense, grew "far more intense" while she, too, was behind bars. "Part of that passion consisted in our being able to imagine ourselves as comrades, ushering in a new world."[14] They conspired on legal strategy, occasionally using the privacy of a prison meeting room to express their love. And this salaciously entered into her FBI file, suggesting her defense strategy meetings were illegally surveilled.

Davis's lawyer, Howard Moore, described the difficult task of defending her: "I don't know of any other cases in the last century that presented that degree of difficulty, where the courthouse itself was a crime scene, and the judge, the prosecutor, the jurors and the witnesses were all victims."[15] In response, Davis's collective built what she terms a movement to free her and all political prisoners. One judge describes being moved by the number of letters and phone calls he received. But if it became a long trial, Davis feared the campaign, led largely by Fania Davis, might dissipate.

Before the judge moved her trial to San Jose, Jackson was murdered in prison, latest in the *Autobiography's* long list of comrades and beloved friends killed by police, some (like Gregory Clark) for the crime of driving while Black. Davis was forced to grieve Jackson while defending herself.

As hers was a capital case, she was, de facto, denied bail. But as her trial loomed, California overturned the death penalty (though the ban would not last). Davis was freed, provided she could raise $100,000. Aretha Franklin had offered to front this, but she was on tour abroad when bail was due. A white Fresno farmer, Roger MacAfee—whom Davis did not even know—put up his farm as collateral. The immediate death threats he received led him to milk his cows and bale his hay with an AR-15 close to hand.

Crime of Passion?

Even from his opening statement, the prosecutor played to a McCarthyite fear of subversion, alleging that Davis participated in the kidnapping as a political act and that it was a crime of passion, triggered by her lust for George Jackson. The prosecution moved to enter love letters between Jackson and Davis as evidence, likely a product of illegal surveillance of prisoners. When challenged, three key pages were allowed, in which Davis expressed helplessness, love, and her wish to free him. The prosecution called 104 witnesses, hoping to (in the words of friend and co-counsel Bettina Aptheker) "overwhelm the jury with what had happened" on August 7 in that very same courthouse.[16]

In order to indict the sexism at the heart of the prosecution's case, Davis's lawyer pushed a risky gambit, asking Davis to make her own opening statement. Davis agreed, calling the prosecutor's claim that her love for Jackson had led her to crime "utterly absurd, clear evidence of male chauvinism."[17]

One of Davis's lawyers[18] was a proponent of a theory—which has since been proved by data—that eyewitness testimony is wildly unreliable. He pursued this with a witness who asserted that Davis was present during the August 7 kidnappings. But when asked to identify her in the courtroom, the witness pointed to Kendra Alexander—her friend and legal advisor—who also had natural hair and sat beside Davis.

In the defense's closing statement, her lawyer reminded a jury that had met and gotten to know her, that Davis wasn't stupid enough to buy a gun in her own name and then use it in a conspiracy to kidnap a judge. He knew he "had to prove that Angela's flight was not evidence of guilt,"[19] and asked the jury to imagine themselves as Black, in *this* country. Only then would they understand why she fled. If they knew how white America failed to uphold rights for Black Americans, their only question would have been why she let herself get caught at all, as one Lynch interviewee quips.

When cleared of all charges, Davis was relieved and elated, calling it the happiest day of her life. Citing the Nixon Administration's economic program alongside the dishonesty and brutality of its war on Vietnam, she called upon the press to underline that this is a repudiation of an assumption in the country that "whatever the government does is not, a priori, the truth."[20]

Indeed, White House Counsel John Ehrlichman admitted in an interview in *Harper's Magazine* that even the Nixon administration knew their Southern Strategy (which became Ronald Reagan's blueprint) was morally bankrupt:

> *The Nixon Campaign in 1968, and the Nixon White House after that, had two enemies: the antiwar left and Black people. You understand what I'm saying?*

> *We knew we couldn't make it illegal to be either against the war or Black, but by getting the public to associate hippies with marijuana and Blacks with heroin, and then criminalizing both heavily, we could disrupt those communities. We could arrest their leaders, raid their homes, break up their meetings and vilify them night after night on the evening news. Did we know we were lying about the drugs? Of course we did.*[21]

Angela Davis's story helped instill in liberals and radicals alike a healthy skepticism to the belief that the state and its institutions are neutral. This is a lesson which, during a time of racialized mass incarceration and rampant exploitation of the working class, is more valuable than ever. Davis's *Autobiography* gives a window onto the century-long war on the left, and how the pathological lies of the last phase are renamed, reframed, and amplified to inoculate the state against demands for progress and justice.

1973

Militant: Leonard Peltier and Anna Mae Aquash in Pine Ridge

or how, despite AIM's gains, the wrongly convicted and wrongly accused paid the price for activism

1.

In 1973 rookie reporter Kevin McKiernan smuggled himself onto the Pine Ridge Sioux Reservation in the trunk of a car, hoping to cover the takeover of Wounded Knee, South Dakota. Embedded with activists of the American Indian Movement (AIM)—who clamored for control of their communities and an end to slum conditions—McKiernan filmed their conflicts with Tribal Chair Richard ("Dickie") Wilson, his private militia which called itself Guardians of Oglala Nation (GOONs), and the government agents backing it. Despite a media blackout, McKiernan sat in on AIM negotiations with the Nixon administration, earning on-camera glares from negotiator Kent Frizzell. As a settlement was hammered out between the groups, McKiernan buried his film in a hole and smuggled himself out of the encampment. Arrests followed, his included. Six weeks later, he returned to Wounded Knee to recover his footage.

In his 2019 documentary, which combines the footage of the seventy-one-day occupation with interviews conducted decades later, McKiernan crisply narrates these events, during which government agents shot and killed two Indigenous activists and wounded many more. McKiernan tracks down FBI agents who admit, on camera, a number of shocking but long-suspected claims: that penetrating groups like AIM, getting members to fight each other, and using secret informants to prod them to commit crimes and bury their leaders in litigation—not to mention framing or goading them to kill one another—were all aims of the Bureau's Counterintelligence Program, COINTELPRO.

The enthralling film, *From Wounded Knee to Standing Rock: A Reporter's Journey*,[1] recalls how effective AIM was in galvanizing US institutions to roll back destructive Cold War policies that exacerbated Indigenous poverty, violence and incarceration. From AIM's glorious five-year heyday emerged two decades' worth of reforms. And while these reforms helped restore tribal sovereignty, the history of AIM's achievements, as the Wounded Knee occupation turns fifty, has dimmed—so much so that the United States is backsliding, through law enforcement repression and paramilitary violence against Indigenous activists and allied environmentalists, who are treated as terrorists for petitioning for sustainable policies.

2.

In the early 1970s, McKiernan was an aspiring (white) journalist in his twenties, struggling to mourn "a string of political assassinations and war tearing up my generation."[2] After an Oglala Sioux tribal member was killed in Custer, South Dakota, in early 1973, McKiernan profiled American Indian Movement founder Dennis Banks. Tribes were reeling from two decades of policies of forced assimilation enacted to erode Native sovereignty, rights and culture. Under the Truman and Eisenhower administrations came Termination (ending the federal recognition of tribes and placing them under states' jurisdiction) and Relocation (forcing tribal members off reservations into large Western cities). Postwar conservatives depicted these policies within an anti-communist framework. "We are spending billions of dollars fighting communism . . . [and] perpetuating the system of reservations and tribal governments, which are natural Socialist environments," Montana Senator George Malone complained.[3]

One hundred and nine tribes were terminated during the period, several of which, like the Mishewal Wappo Tribe of Northern California, were never reconstituted—their land taken, their federal funding discontinued.[4] After this sustained assault on tribal sovereignty, poverty and violence became pervasive on remaining tribal lands. Indigenous people relocated to Western US cities often fared worse than those allowed to remain on reservations. In Minneapolis's Southside, tribal members lived in "tenement housing, [in] slum conditions," Banks recalls. "Rats were all over the place." Just as Black Power emerged in African American communities in the face of poverty and a lack of social supports, poverty became "a primary purpose for the birth of the AIM. That, along with high unemployment and the police brutality" their members endured.

Organized by Native inmates in a Minnesota penitentiary, AIM went on to spur protests in Minneapolis to expose and publicize bigotry against Tribal members. It urged that church collections for Native charities go directly to Natives (rather than to church coffers), attacked racist depictions in school textbooks, and delivered legal aid to incarcerated tribal members, which swiftly reduced the disproportionately high arrest rate of Natives in Minneapolis.[5] The Movement spread to Chicago, Los Angeles, and San Francisco. "Years of abuse," including sexual violence against Native women, "that's what started the AIM," Banks tells McKiernan.

From November 1969 to June 1971, members of AIM and other Red Power groups secured national coverage when they occupied the federally governed Alcatraz Island, invoking the 1868 Treaty of Fort Laramie. Signed between the US and the Lakota Nation, activists said, the treaty decreed that retired, abandoned, and out-of-use federal land—like

Alcatraz—be returned to the tribe who once occupied it. Amidst rampant Native deaths in Nebraska and South Dakota, the Movement organized a cross-country march, "the Trail of Broken Treaties," in October 1972. Arriving in Washington in November, activists seized the Bureau of Indian Affairs wing of the Department of the Interior, holding it for a week (a week that spanned Nixon's re-election for a second term). Criticized by some tribal members for its militant tactics and the theft of public records—mostly concerning land deals that were unfair to Natives[6]—this was confrontation politics at its most spectacular.

After the BIA occupation, AIM fatefully announced that it would hold a celebration at Pine Ridge, South Dakota, where US policies were dividing the tribe. There, the Oglala Sioux Civil Rights Commission, OSCRC, was struggling to impeach Tribal Chairman Dickie Wilson, fraudulently elected and covertly tied to the federal government and COINTELPRO. In peaceful protests, OSCRC accused Wilson of misusing tribal funds and firing and strong-arming political opponents using his paramilitary GOONs.

After protesting Wilson's policies, OSCRC formally voted to impeach him. Presiding over the matter himself, Wilson moved immediately to trial—guessing, shrewdly, that the plaintiffs' case was not yet ready. His ploy worked; then it backfired. When they lost, OSCRC appealed to AIM, who were already heading toward Pine Ridge from their Washington march.

On February 27, 1973, an estimated fifty carloads of AIM activists alighted on Wounded Knee. Wilson declared a state of emergency. The following morning, Wounded Knee was encircled by a small army of FBI agents, Bureau of Indian Affairs Police, and US Marshals. On the afternoon of February 28, agents started shooting and AIM members returned gunfire. Each shot was fired on hallowed ground.

In the original Wounded Knee massacre, in late 1890, government forces killed as many as 300 Lakota men, women, and children. Survivors, such as medicine man Black Elk, recalled how it started after tribal members' weapons were confiscated as punishment for performances of the Ghost Dance, a grieving rite in which ancestors lent the living strength to overcome the white onslaughts the Lakota had faced for decades. When Wilson started blocking food to activists, Banks saw a through line, remarking that the government had "been trying to starve us out since 1849." This time, the Lakota and their allies would keep their weapons.

As "Indians from scores of tribes from across the country and Canada" poured into Pine Ridge, McKiernan recounts his good luck in scoring a press pass from Minnesota Public Radio. But he soon heard that reporters who tried to enter the besieged town would be arrested on federal charges. One asked officials, "Is it your contention that the Justice Department may regulate the press whenever it chooses?"

AIM cofounder Russell Means saw the press ban as foreboding, a waiting game until the press gave up and went home, "so that they can come in here and massacre us." One federal agent seemed to confirm Means's fears, asking, "How can you invoke a hundred-year-old treaty . . . shoot guns at FBI agents, and expect to come out . . . alive?"

McKiernan, too, understood the urgency of press coverage and the possibility that it might offer some protection. He enlisted Lakota guide Arthur Chips to smuggle him into Wounded Knee, hiding in the trunk of Chips's car as it navigated secret back roads at night and led him successfully into the compound—despite the two tripping thermal sensors installed by the FBI in the process.

Between Wilson's actions, the government ban on the press, and the surveilling and shooting at AIM activists, tensions were high inside Wounded Knee. Willard Carlson, a Yurok tribal member, recalled the distrust at general assembly meetings each night. "If you didn't know the person sitting next to you, he or she could possibly be an informant, a Fed. So you had to be careful." Though McKiernan didn't know anyone, Banks says, "We'd come to trust Kevin."

Meanwhile, President Nixon appointed Assistant Attorney General for the Environment and Natural Resources Dale "Kent" Frizzell as the administration's lead negotiator. Frizzell heard long-held grievances repeated in negotiations. At one meeting, McKiernan is spotted taking notes and recording–and he captures cold stares from Frizzell on camera. At a press conference before the banned journalists, Frizzell justified the media ban, implying that it fostered candor in negotiations. And it appeared that the negotiations were working.

AIM wanted a meeting with the White House to discuss broken treaties, and the negotiators wanted the activists to turn in their weapons. The administration initially said yes. It was agreed that once Means and three other AIM leaders began their meeting at the White House, Means would telephone colleagues at Wounded Knee to prompt AIM to draw down its arms. Both sides approved of the deal, which was followed by a one-hour photo op of the signing of the agreement. Yet as AIM leaders celebrated the deal on a flight in a government helicopter, Nixon reneged.

On day forty of the occupation, the administration—also bogged down in Vietnam at the time—clarified its position. It would not negotiate with guns still pointed at federal agents. A swift buildup began. Federal bunkers and armored personnel carriers inched closer to the village. Electricity and water were cut. Activists worried about another massacre at Wounded Knee. It emerged later that the U.S. Army was secretly—illegally—running the military operation. Firefights increased; more people were wounded. Then both sides dug in and waited.

Boredom set in. AIM leaders worried that the lull might tempt activists to leave. AIM member Anna Mae Pictou, a Mikmaq Indian from Canada, planned to marry Nogeeshik Aquash after the standoff. Banks nudged them to get married in the village. On April 12, 1973, Wallace Black Elk, grandson of the legendary medicine man, conducted the ceremony, overseeing the couple's exchange of vows.

Black Elk's grandfather had "walked through the same spot after the historic massacre," he says, "and was afraid this was the end of the Indian race, that the tree of life was dying. But he soon had another vision—that of a tree sprouting another root. Thanks to this stand, the tree of life was alive."

3.

On Easter morning, the FBI allowed Chief Frank Fools Crow and a translator through the blockade. One held up a *Denver Post* headline about White House Counsel John Dean's agreeing to testify in the widening Watergate scandal. "See," he said, laughing, "the government is weakening." A group of antiwar protestors delivered food to the AIM activists; federal agents fired on those who scrambled to recover the supplies.

The shooting made forty-seven-year-old Frank Clearwater, who had recently arrived, sit up in bed. He took a bullet in his head, marking him as the first to be killed by government agents. Ken Tiger, a Seminole veteran of the war in Vietnam, recalled, "We had a limited amount of ammunition to begin with, unlike the government. So we were not shooting as much. . . But if you stuck your head up, a bullet might whizz by."

Lawrence Buddy La Monte, an Oglala Sioux Vietnam veteran, was killed on day sixty. His mother Agnes had a great aunt and uncle killed at Wounded Knee in 1890. (Her mother had also been there, though she was just twelve years old.) On day sixty-nine, federal agents opened the roadblock to let LaMonte's body and his relatives proceed to the famous graveyard. The loss demoralized activists.

On May 7, 1973 (day seventy), the night before their surrender, AIM leaders, expecting to face charges, packed up, held ceremonies with their medicine men, and hiked out of Wounded Knee, "hoping to pick their way through FBI lines," McKiernan recalls. Knowing the government would confiscate it, McKiernan wrapped, then buried, his film. He learned that assistant US Attorney General Richard Hellstern had "personally ordered [his] arrest."

The FBI handcuffed him, confiscating his cameras and tape recorder, and charged him with interfering with federal agents in the lawful performance of their duties. Given the irregularities of US behavior, his and many similar cases were dropped. Mass arrests of AIM leaders that followed were among the government's arsenal of tactics. The expensive, time-consuming trials proved particularly effective at keeping the Movement too busy to organize.

Two months after Wounded Knee, McKiernan ran into Anna Mae Aquash, the activist who got married during the occupation, in Minneapolis. When he called out her name, she corrected him. "My name is Joanna now." Had she gone underground? he wondered.

This stayed with him, as his footage remained unused.

4.

McKiernan's film is a thrilling, intimate window into already dramatic events, a work of history in which scoops abound. He interviews one former federal agent who, in retirement, admits that the FBI worked with the GOONs, Wilson's private militia. GOON member Duane Brewer boasts on camera of the relationship, admitting the FBI gave him both information and armor-piercing ammunitions. Why? "To deal with AIM, who we were at war with."

Paid illegally through government poverty alleviation funds,[7] GOONs vowed to "restore order" on the reservation. With impunity guaranteed through federal protection, GOONs and Feds are believed to have killed so many activists that, from 1973 to 1976, the homicide rate at Pine Ridge was among the highest in the nation. In 2000, more than twenty years later, the FBI disputed this.[8]

Another McKiernan scoop comes during the aftermath, when he was in Pine Ridge two years later to interview Banks at an AIM encampment on the Jumping Bulls' family ranch. His visit was well timed. On June 25, 1975, McKiernan left to cover another event in the Black Hills, when he heard on the radio that a shootout had begun at the Jumping Bulls' ranch. Racing back, he witnessed two FBI agents and an AIM member bleeding to death after a shootout from the agents' car. The room where he'd slept the night before was pierced with bullet holes.

Some twenty AIM members escaped into the hills, prompting "the largest manhunt in FBI history." (The hunt for the Unabomber beat the record two decades later.) Special Agent George O'Clock describes how, after the FBI lost the two agents (whom he calls "family members"), "You want to get the individual who did such a thing, and get 'em fast."

Former South Dakota Senator James Abourezk has a different take. "When an Indian is killed, it's hardly investigated. When an FBI agent is killed, they put two hundred more agents out to find out who did it. If that's not a double standard, I don't know what is."

Eventually three members of AIM were charged for the shooting deaths of the agents: Leonard Peltier, Robert Robineau, and Darrelle Dino Butler. The latter two were acquitted for firing in self-defense, after plainclothes agents fired at them. Peltier fled to Canada, but was arrested in 1977 and extradited to the US

After moving Peltier's case to a less sympathetic jurisdiction, the government wrangled a woman named Myrtle Poor Bear, who claimed to be Peltier's girlfriend at the time of the shootout, to sign affidavits attesting to his guilt. In fact, she had never met Peltier and later admitted she was coerced into signing the affidavits. Asking to recant at trial, she was ultimately blocked. FBI agent David Price had threatened her at gunpoint with explicit death threats, she later said. The judge ruled her incompetent on the question of why she signed, otherwise allowing the affidavits as evidence.

Though Amnesty International USA[9] and more than fifty members of Congress[10] criticized the affidavits and called for a new trial, Peltier was sentenced to life in federal prison. Even as a US appeals court upheld the verdict, it criticized federal prosecutors. Appeals Court Judge Donald Ross suggested the FBI had falsified the affidavits. "And if they are willing to do that," he added, "they must be willing to fabricate other evidence."[11] Judge Gerald Heaney of the Eighth Circuit went further. Though he previously denied Peltier's legal appeal, he argued in 1991 for presidential clemency to free Peltier from prison. He suggested authorities should have put their weapons down and "listened to the legitimate grievances"[12] of AIM activists.

When Agent Price appears at a public forum about Wounded Knee years later, McKiernan is in attendance, and—in the documentary's most thrilling segment—raises his hand and reminds Price that Judge Ross deemed the extradition of Leonard Peltier from Canada on the basis of false testimony an example of government misconduct. Listening, Price's face, in closeup, hearkens toward faraway thought. One can almost imagine him contemplating flight, literal or metaphorical.

Agent Price: I don't know how to begin this, so I'll try to begin...

McKiernan: Didn't Myrtle Poor Bear say...

Agent Price: Hold it, hold it. I know where... what you're... you want to go off in a little hole, which can be answered, and has been answered in court many times and I quit paying attention to it.

McKiernan: Well, she claimed that Peltier confessed the murder to her, is that correct?

David Price: Not quite.

McKiernan: Was the court wrong in blaming the FBI as well as AIM for those years?

David Price: Yes.

McKiernan: The FBI's hands were clean?

David Price: Yes.

Though the exchange is satisfying, it nevertheless falls short of an anticipated confession. For this, an exchange with another agent will do.

Douglas Durham, an FBI informant, managed to become head of security for AIM—even becoming the personal bodyguard of Dennis Banks. Durham is a reminder of how rampant informants were in the days of COINTELPRO, Black Panthers, and AIM. (Malcolm X's head of security, Gene Roberts—the man who gave him mouth-to-mouth resuscitation in the Audubon Ballroom—was an informant in NYPD's Bureau of Special Services and Investigations, BOSSI unit.)

But Durham is not the star of McKiernan's final scenes. When he gets an interview with former FBI Special Agent Tom Parker, McKiernan asks if the goal was to sow paranoia in the New Left movements it penetrated. Parker agrees. "That certainly would be one of the objectives," he replies. "I'm being a little coy with you here."

> McKiernan: I know you are. But it was not accidental? The FBI was trying to make people paranoid?
>
> Parker: That was certainly a way to cause disruption and dissension and disorganization, and certainly [it] was talked about as one of the goals of what we were trying to do.

McKiernan puts a pin in this, circling back to the woman he couldn't stop thinking of, whose wedding he filmed. In late March 1976, McKiernan learned by telephone that Anna Mae Aquash had died. The government ruled exposure as the cause; she had frozen to death. But a doctor saw blood on the back of her head. A rancher who found her described it to McKiernan.

"After cutting off her hands and sending them to Washington for analysis," McKiernan reports, "the FBI buried her as a Jane Doe in a pauper's grave." Her family suspected foul play and hired a private pathologist, who found a bullet in the back of Anna Mae's head. With this, the backstory is relit.

Sometime after Durham's cover was blown, Anna Mae entered a relationship with Banks. Through that time, the FBI tried to make her look like an informant, showering her with attention in public and waving to her ostentatiously in front of AIM members. "A snitch jacket," it's called in Bureau circles. In her last letter, she wrote her family: "they're out to get me. They'll kill me."

As Agent Parker returns to his nonchalant confession, he admits that the FBI believed targets like Anna Mae could be goaded into killing each other. "That certainly is one of the possible outcomes, that the dissension would grow to the point that there was violence between the people there," he says in neutral-sounding jargon.

McKiernan: So you would kill an informant?
Parker: That certainly was in the realm of possibility. Ok? And I can say, at that point we weren't real concerned about that type of thing if that happened: the same as with any criminal situation. Say if you had two hostages and they ended up shooting each other, which happens. That's the way it goes.

Since then tribal members have fought for redress of the government's war on Indigenous activists. McKiernan interviews Tom Poor Bear, recent Vice President of the Oglala Tribal Council, who in 2019 continued his push to reopen cold cases from the 1970s, which saw "almost seventy uninvestigated deaths during the reign of terror" of Nixon's Bureau of Indian Affairs, DOJ, and FBI. Before he died of COVID-19 in 2020, Poor Bear called for a review of misconduct by the FBI. And as Oneida-Stockbridge Munsee historian Heather Bruegl recalls, Aquash's story as it is told also needs review. She was a formidable AIM activist, who noted in a letter, "These white people think this country belongs to them. The whole country changed with only a handful of raggedy-ass pilgrims that came over here in the 1500s. And it can take a handful of raggedy-ass Indians to do the same, and I intend to be one of those raggedy-ass Indians."

Bruegl adds, "We don't talk about the women at Wounded Knee the way we talk about the water protectors at Standing Rock. Anna Mae was more than just the tragedy so often told about her. She left her two children in the care of her sisters to come and fight for native rights."

5.

The Wounded Knee occupation ended in the late spring of 1973, fifty years ago. That same year, the Senate Subcommittee on Indian Affairs Hearings convened. A year later, the International Treaty Council followed. In 1975, the Indian Self-Determination Act was signed, and the Council of Economic Resource Tribes and the American Indian Policy Review Commission formed. In 1978, the Indian Freedom of Religion Act and the Indian Child Welfare Act both passed.

The 1979 Supreme Court Ruling on the Boldt Treaty Decision in Northwest Fishing Cases followed. The 1980 U.S. Supreme Court Decision on the Black Hills was followed by the 1982 Indian Mineral Development Act, 1988's Indian Gaming Regulatory Act, and 1990's Native American Languages Act, as well as the Native American Grave Protection and Repatriation Act (in the news recently thanks to museums' lack of enforcement of it). In autumn of 1996, President Clinton declared November to be Native American Heritage Month, as presidents before him had.

The throughline from the 1960s and '70s occupations and the reforms that followed was offset by what Sioux author Nick Estes calls the United States' ongoing "dirty war" against Indigenous activists. Late in the film, McKiernan interviews tribal members present at Wounded Knee who also worked to stop the Dakota Access Pipeline slated for Standing Rock, North Dakota. In 2016, stakeholders in the Dakota Access Pipeline called in a private army, who hired Joel McCullough to pose as a "water protector" among those protesting the pipeline.

A former special forces officer, McCullough's cover was blown when slides were leaked to The Intercept in 2020 showing McCullough to be part of private contractor TigerSwan's scheme to treat environmental protestors as "jihadis," bait them into crimes, and have them charged as terrorists.

Throughout *From Wounded Knee to Standing Rock*, media commentators can be heard describing Wounded Knee occupiers as "militant Indians"—which does similar work as "jihadi" to cast the activists as acceptable targets of paramilitary violence. The protesters at Standing Rock were unarmed. The Pipeline began operation in April 2017.

Meanwhile, police violence against Native Americans remains rampant. Since George Floyd's 2020 murder by police, the CDC tracks police killings. Its data show that police kill tribal members at a rate six times higher than whites. South Dakota remains an especially "anti-Indian" state, Estes writes, with incarceration rates ten times higher than the national average.

Atop this backdrop is where the triumph of McKiernan's film becomes clear. The value of the documentary, and the fact that the footage it includes survived in the first place, is that it creates a record of tactics deployed by the state to destroy AIM members at Wounded Knee—and the resilience of the movement's activists in spite of this.

We can only speculate as to whether his presence at Wounded Knee offered them protection from the FBI's violence at the time, as McKiernan hoped. Nevertheless, the film that emerged from it, and the history of the fifty years since the events in South Dakota, together tell an important story: the American Indian Movement's "militant" tactics worked. In the years after the standoff, much-needed reforms bolstered tribal sovereignty.

Today, as state and corporate forces use tactics honed during COINTELPRO to defang Indigenous protest movements, AIM's actions read like case studies in Indigenous radicalism: testaments to the concrete political power that could be won by committing to an absolute assertion of sovereignty. What was birthed during the Wounded Knee occupation, recalls McKiernan, was "the spirit, the flickering hope of a few that sparked a small prairie fire: the budding flame of unity."

III

"Most wars or military coups or invasions are done in the name of democracy against democracy."
—Eduardo Galeano

1968

Blood Memory:
N. Scott Momaday on Rainy Mountain

or how to remember events beyond our corporeal existence

1.

Just before the turn of the last century, when many Native American tribes were hopeless about the future, a dance was born in the new state of "Nevada." The Paiute spiritual leader Wovoka created it from a vision, and it spread across the plains. Wovoka choreographed the dance to invoke those killed by the United States in the nation's wars of extermination, pacification, and removal.

The ancestors came to him in a dream, promising to return to help fight against the unceasing violent westward expansion of the whites. No Indian should do any of the killing. (A dust would come and bury the white interlopers.) Instead, they should dance, he insisted. While dancing, some fainted, reliving the death of an ancestor.

Three months later, at Wounded Knee, South Dakota, 300 unarmed Lakota men and women were massacred by American soldiers. Why? For the crime of joining the Ghost Dance. Despite this repression, the Dance continued to spread. As it did so, it lent urgency to other dances such as the Kiowa Tribe's Sun Dance. Viewing these dances as proof of the failure of Indians to assimilate, US soldiers at Fort Sill suppressed it. The loss "killed Kiowa culture" and the tribe became "a people whose spirit was broken," recalls Kiowa author N. Scott Momaday.

"My grandmother was there. Without bitterness and for as long as she lived, she bore a vision of deicide." Momaday calls the moment "a kind of trail of tears, when the Kiowas are brought to Fort Sill and their horses are killed in their hearing. They were stifled. This was utter defeat." A brave warrior, Sitting Bear (who once killed an enemy with an eagle's feather) "sang the death song, and took his own life."

"I feel very close to that man," Momaday said. "Things couldn't have been worse, but they changed. They brought about their own survival. That's a big story. It's not only the Kiowa story, of course—it's the Indian story."[1]

2.

Nearly a century after the Ghost Dance, Momaday—who died in January 2024, a month before his ninetieth birthday—composed his debut novel *House Made of Dawn*, which won the 1969 Pulitzer Prize in Fiction. Native Americans were at another low point. Seven decades after the Ghost Dance spread and was extinguished, little had changed. United States' policy was still assimilation. In place of reservations, Indian "termination" and "relocation" meant scattering the tribes.

House Made of Dawn follows a World War II veteran, Abel, who returns to Jemez Pueblo in New Mexico. Struggling with shell shock, Abel is alienated from his family and his tribe. Set against the long trauma of US genocide, Abel's alienation leads him to violence, prison, and relocation to Los Angeles. But removal to the city exacerbates Abel's malady of isolation. When he bottoms out—after being beaten nearly to death by a cruel police officer—a Navajo friend sends him back to Jemez. Only this return reduces his anguish, helping him acknowledge the stories of his ancestral community and the healing ties of his tribe to the land.

The novel hit its mark. The 1969 Pulitzer Prize was the first of many awards in Momaday's long career, along with the 2021 Frost Medal of the Poetry Society of America and the *Paris Review*'s Hadada Award also that year. But as with the broader confrontation politics of the American Indian and Red Power Movements, non-Indigenous commentators observed the poetry and lyricized portrayal of customs selectively, often mistaking a disguised social novel as merely modernist.

Traditions like the Jemez Runners—celebrated in part to restore social power to the tribes—were taken by reviewers as mystique, as magic, as quaint features in a modern novel. Having missed that it was a social novel in the first place, these influential readers rewrote rituals meant to tie the community to the land and therefore protect it, as mere superstition.

But while some readers condescended to Indian magic, others have gone further, banning Momaday's work as part of a broader so-called "school of resentment" aimed to overturn the white majority "canon" in Southwestern American schools.

3.

Born in Oklahoma during the depression, Momaday recalls the devastation of the dust bowl, which added to the economic misery. The dust bowl swept people and livestock away as the crops failed. It was "devastating, the land just blown away," Momaday recalls. "People dying in the dust." White residents undertook a "mass exodus." But "the Indian people remained on their allotments," including his grandfather. Natives had "always been moored to the land." Land given by the government "was what they were allowed to have," so they stayed.[2]

When he was small, Momaday would watch his father, Al, paint. Al Momaday's work was reminiscent of "the Kiowa Six,"* a group of painters who studied at the University of

---

*   It is more commonly known as the Kiowa Five, but I follow those who see this as the result of the erasure of its youngest and only female member, Lois Smoky Kaulaity; Dr. Mary Jo Watson has led the way in restoring Smoky Kaulaity to her rightful place among the group.

Oklahoma in the 1920s and 1930s and who worked in a two-dimensional traditional Indian style.** As well as painters, half were also dancers, dance being important in their work. His mother Natachee ("Little Moon," in Choctaw) went to the Haskell School, where she met a cousin of Al Momaday's, Lila Ware, who introduced Al and Natachee at Mountain View, where Natachee spent the summer.

Scott's first home was his grandparents' homestead on Rainy Mountain Creek. With no electricity or plumbing, it was "considered bottom of the scale in terms of poverty. I think of my grandparents as being very poor, but rich in their lives."[3] For his daughter Jill Scott Momaday, a filmmaker and actor, the homestead has remained populated by the voices of these elders.

"I get close and my heart starts beating and I feel excitement and a kind of sadness. Because the old people are gone and the house is falling into ruin. But it's such a magical and sacred place to stand on that ground and look out across the plain . . . and have that sort of warm wind and the sounds, the crickets, and then I walk into the arbor. . . . I love that place. And my daughters love that place. And my dad loves that place."[4]

Filling the house with books, Natachee was a writer who passed the vocation to Scott. "Writing came to me more or less naturally, because of my mother. She was a writer and there were always books in the house. So I was introduced to literature at a fairly early age." One day, quite young, he announced that he was going to be a writer. His father

---

** One was reprimanded in the so-called Indian Schools for drawing in class, which was not allowed. The group's only female member was reprimanded for using a figurative, narrative style, at a time when women were only allowed to make the abstract decorations, for example, found on parfleches.

supported the calling by regaling him with Kiowa stories. "He knew a great deal of the oral tradition of the Kiowas, and I made him tell them to me again and again, until they were embedded in my consciousness."

One was the story of eight siblings playing in the forest. One of the boys suddenly turns into a bear.*** After a trip to Devil's Tower, Wyoming, where the legend occurred, Momaday returned to the house near Mountain View, Oklahoma, and "an old man . . . took me up in his hands and began to talk. And all the voices in the arbor fell away and his was the only voice, and . . . he looked down at me and said, *You are Tsoai-talee, Rock-Tree Boy.*" It was an allusion to Devil's Tower. No one knows "what happened to the bear," Momaday says. But he considers himself "the reincarnation of that boy, because of my name. So I have bear power. I turn into a bear on occasion."[5]

At the center of the Kiowa world is the sacred land of Rainy Mountain. It is marked today by old tears. Thanks to Euro-American genocide, "morale was abysmal when the Kiowa arrived here. But they have lived on this continent for thousands of years and have developed a moral strength." As Jill recalls, "It doesn't look big. But when you

---

*** First, they were playing and laughing. But the boy "trembled and began to run upon his hands and feet," scaring his seven sisters. "His fingers became claws and his body was covered with fur. . . . His sisters were terrified and the bear ran after them. They came to the stump of a great tree and the tree spoke to them. It bade" the seven sisters "climb upon it, and as they did, so it began to rise into the air. The bear came to kill them, but they were just beyond its reach. He reared against the tree and scored the bark all around with its claws. The seven sisters were borne into the sky and they became the stars of the Big Dipper."

climb it, you are on the top of the world, and can see the most panoramic view."[6]

In addition to being a writer and a painter, Momaday's parents were teachers on reservations in New Mexico throughout his childhood. Because he looked Asian, his friend Billy Don was enlisted as his bodyguard when Japanese Americans were being interned during the war. After the war, he moved to Jemez Pueblo when his parents became teachers at the two-teacher Day School overseen by the Indian Services, a section of the Bureau of Indian Affairs.

"Those were the most impressionable years of my life. The Pueblo life that I saw as a child was very rich, and deeply invested in a spiritual view of the world." In Jemez, Momaday got his first horse, a boon to a young man hoping to explore the world beyond his home. The horse, Pecos, fed his creative imagination. "On the back of Pecos I was in another world," he recalls:

> *I could imagine that I was a Kiowa of the nineteenth or eighteenth century, riding out on the plains, buffalo hunting. But I understood something about my ancestors. The imagination is the power of seeing beyond reality. So I had the extension of my senses into an imaginary world, a very colorful one and a very dramatic one. The imagination was the thing that enabled me to see into the farther world*[7].

Momaday writes of a time, centuries before, when "the Kiowa and the horse came simultaneously upon the Great Plains. Then for 100 years and more the Kiowa and the horse were one. The horse . . . brought about a revolution." With the change, the Kiowa were "given the means to prevail against distance."[8]

At Jemez Pueblo, Momaday aged out of the schools. The Day School, where his parents taught, only went through sixth grade, and the Catholic Mission school only went through eighth. For three years, Momaday attended four different high schools, sometimes riding a bus thirty miles each way. For his senior year, he went to Augustus Military Academy in Fort Defiance, Virginia, where he received college preparation that wasn't available in reservation schools.

After high school, Momaday studied political science at the University of New Mexico, then for a year he studied law at the University of Virginia, where he joined the prestigious Jefferson Literary and Debating Society. Through the Society he met a Southern American writer who served as the university's writer-in-residence: William Faulkner. Meeting Faulkner urged him toward literature and the storytelling he loved as a boy. Back at the University of New Mexico, he finished his undergraduate degree in 1958, then he followed his parents' path, spending a year teaching in the Jicarillo Apache reservation school in Northern New Mexico.

The following spring, after receiving one of its highly sought fellowships, Momaday did graduate work in creative writing at Stanford, where he studied poetry—"the crown of literature," as he calls it. "Indians had song and prayer," he adds, "not poetry, per se. So I spent my whole time there writing poetry. And when I went to teach at [University of California at] Santa Barbara, which was my first post, I had grown tired of writing poetry. I had something in me that I wanted to express."[9]

Of *House Made of Dawn*, which started as a series of poems, he recalls the indirect journey, and how he fought through many genres for the book. "I once heard that William Gass was asked . . . *Who do you write for?* And he said, 'Well,

I don't write for myself; that would be self-serving. I don't write for an audience; that would be pandering. I write for the thing that is trying to be born.'"[10]

4.

When we meet Abel, he is so inebriated that he doesn't recognize his own grandfather. As he sobers up, he reflects on the moment his mother died and his grandfather protected him. He recalls the pain, too, of his brother's death, and the other haunting rites of passage that influenced him before the war. But then we witness Abel's first eagle hunt. It begins with a dazzling display of "golden eagles, a male and female, in their mating flight . . . cavorting, spinning and spiraling on the cold, clear columns of air . . ."

The female eagle carries a rattlesnake in her talons, darting up through the sky like a missile. She flew "upward at an angle from the rim until she was small in the sky, and she let go of the snake . . . The male swerved and sailed . . . sliding down in a blur . . . [and] . . . hit the snake in the head . . . rolled and swung upward [and] . . . let go of the snake in turn . . ."[11]

This memory of delight and survival segues into Abel's fear of the sky, as he flashes back to his terror on a European battlefield. "He awoke on the side of the wooded hill . . . He didn't know where he was, and he was alone."[12] Alone and yet surrounded by

> *the bodies of men; he could barely see them strewn among the pits . . . But there was sound: something low and incessant . . . The mortar fire had stopped; there someone, some human force far away and out of sight, was making way for the machine that was coming . . . For hours, days perhaps, the whir and*

explosion of fire had been the only mooring of his mind to sleep, but now there was nothing but silence and the strange insinuation of the machine upon it.[13]

As Abel struggles with trauma that spurs his self-annihilation, he finds work through the reservation's Mexican priest. Hired to cut firewood for a glamorous white woman named Angela, he begins an affair with her. Their affair triggers his trauma, spurring Abel into a violent act. As his hatred of himself and others reaches a pinnacle, he kills an albino man and goes to jail.

Of the book's inception, he tells Kiowa director Jeffrey Palmer, for his 2019 documentary *N. Scott Momaday: Words From a Bear*, "The seeds of the book began in my life at Jemez. And it was soon after the Second World War. Some of the veterans were coming back to Jemez. They had been in combat and they had been torn from their traditional world. And they were trying to get back into it, and some of them were having a terrible time. They were wounded people. Abel is an example of that."[14]

The book is polyvocal, each section told by a different witness. Faulkner's early use of a shifting stream of consciousness between characters inspired Momaday. We learn of Abel's trial through the mockery of Tosamah, Kiowa Priest of the Sun. Described in the section told by Ben Bennaly, the brotherly Navajo roommate, Tosamah is at once a classic preacher and a caretaker of Kiowa stories. But he also acts as the assimilated tribal scold who bashes Abel during his freefall over the question of Native American representation in the broader culture.

"You take that poor cat . . . They gave him every advantage . . . a pair of shoes and told him to go to school. They deloused him and gave him a lot of free haircuts . . . But . . .

He was too damn dumb to be civilized. So what happened? They let him alone at last. They thought he was harmless. They thought he was going to plant some beans, man, and live off the fat of the land . . ." Momaday's tongue-in-cheek stand-in, Tosamah adds, "Can you imagine what went on at that trial?"[15]

> *There was this longhair, see, cold sober, of sound mind, and the goddam judge looking on, and the prosecutor trying to talk sense to that poor degenerate Indian . . . "Well, your honors, it was this way, see? I cut me up a little snake meat out there in the sand." Christ, man, that must have been our finest hour, better than Little Bighorn. That little no-count cat must have had the whole Jesus scheme right in the palm of his hand. Think of it! What's-His-Name v. United States. I mean, where's the legal precedent, man? When you stop to think about it, due process is a hell of a remedy for snakebite.*[16]

Upon his release, Abel is sent on Relocation to Los Angeles, finding himself in a community of tribal members who are also displaced. Unlike Tosamah, Bennaly proves more critical of the government than of their confrere Abel. "He didn't have anyplace to stay," Bennaly recalls, acting as Abel's witness. "The Relocation people were looking around, I guess, but they hadn't found a place, and he was going to spend the night at the Indian Center. There's a storeroom down there in the alley, where they keep the food and clothing that people have donated, you know. You can stay there sometimes if you don't have anyplace else to go."[17]

Rather than logistics like finding Abel a place to stay, the government focuses its resources on surveilling him. Its officers remind him at every turn of the threat of incarceration. "Everything went along all right for about two months, I guess," Bennaly recalls. "And it would have gone all right after that, too, if they had just let him alone." Instead:

> *the parole officer, and welfare, and the Relocation people kept coming around, and they were always after him . . . They wanted to know how he was doing, had he been staying out of trouble . . . They were always warning him, you know? Telling him how he had to stay out of trouble, or else he was going to wind up in prison again. I guess he had to think about that all the time, because they wouldn't let him forget it . . .*[18]

When the Bureau of Indian Affairs agents and parole officers start hounding Bennaly, he admits he "could see why" Abel wasn't getting along well, "but I didn't know how to tell them about it. They wouldn't have understood anyway." He elaborates on what it's like to be relocated to a city you never lived in, along with a new lifestyle expressed in a language and landscape which are not your own.

> *You have to get used to everything, you know; it's like starting out someplace where you've never been before, and you don't know where you're going or why or when you have to get there, and everybody's looking at you, waiting for you . . . They have a lot of words, and you know they mean something, but you don't know what, and your own*

> *words are no good because they're not the same; they're different.*[19]

Language and geographical dislocation combine with condescension, a lack of resources, surveillance, and capitalist alienation. In writing about the move from New Mexico to Los Angeles, Momaday embeds an array of critiques by a Navajo witness to a Pueblo relocation victim's severe, deepening alienation. It is, in effect, Momaday's portrayal of the staggering failures of mid-century US policies, many of which linger.

In the worst of the era's Native American ghettos in Minneapolis, the activist Russell Means recalled that in the mid to late 1960s—thanks to Relocation—Natives grew to ten percent of the city's population but made up a whopping eighty to ninety percent of its prisoners. The American Indian Movement (or AIM), which Means joined early enough to be considered a co-founder, reversed that trend quickly with little more than walkie-talkies.[20] But the problem isn't gone.[21]

Through an anguished protagonist, Momaday made the social and political problems facing US tribes familiar. While Abel's fate in the city worsens, culminating in police brutality by a sadistic cop, Bennaly proves his brother's keeper, singing a blessing and putting him on a train home. The novel takes its title from the Navajo Chantway healing song that Bennaly sings to him. Abel arrives as his beloved grandfather is dying and he must summon enough strength to reverse the caretaker roles with his dying elder.

Arranging traditional Pueblo rites through the Mexican priest, he participates in the Run of the Dead, an annual Jemez ceremony that combines the Day of the Dead ritual with a marathon. Of many traditions of which Abel partook in his youth, it is especially those that tie him to the contours and seasons of the everlasting land that help him endure new depredations of change, age, and time.

5.

House Made of Dawn appeared in 1968 to wide acclaim. But some missed the point of the return that Momaday dramatized in the narrative, hinting that it was not about sovereignty, but was instead about sorcery, or otherwise somehow nefariously vague. In "Anglos and Indians"—three days after Robert F. Kennedy's assassination (and only months after Martin Luther King, Jr.'s)—Marshall Sprague[22] reviewed the novel in *The New York Times*, calling it "as subtly wrought as a piece of Navajo silverware," and "superb in its own right."

At the review's end, however, he breaks his pledge at the beginning not to patronize, lamenting the novel's plentiful "haze," concluding through a marginalizing "we" that "the mysteries of cultures different from *our own* cannot be explained in a short novel, even by an artist as talented as Mr. Momaday." Presuming that the novel was for him and non-Indigenous readers, he misses the polyvocal mastery that made it a novel for Kiowas, Navajos, and readers of other tribes. Beneath the casual dismissal, Sprague mentions none of the mid-century policies of Relocation, Termination, and erasure that made the situation dire for tribes for two decades (and for centuries before that).

Not everyone missed the point. The novel was awarded the 1969 Pulitzer Prize.[23] Writing for the judges, Boston College's P. Albert Duhamel noted, "Our first choice is N. Scott Momaday's *House Made of Dawn*, because of its [. . .] 'eloquence and intensity of feeling, its freshness of vision and subject, its immediacy of theme' and because an award to its author might be considered a recognition of 'the arrival on the American literary scene of a matured, sophisticated literary artist from the original Americans."[24]

Whatever condescension the author found tucked into his accolades, it was met by an awareness of absence, of the gatekeeping that had kept Indigenous writers largely out of the canon. The social function named was that of inclusion, while the inclusion was meaningful largely for the Indigenous history smuggled in through Abel's story.

"To be a Native person and win that was astounding," noted Joy Harjo. "It still is. So, yes, it opens doors, because we were [now] recognized as being *literary* versus having our work put under a folk category . . . . that's what I've been trying to say everywhere. It's just like orality . . . . It's literature. It has a standing."[25]

Although Momaday is savvy enough to deny the mantle of social writing, he cops to two kinds of social mission in *N. Scott Momaday: Words from a Bear*. In his long interview with Kiowa director Jeffrey Palmer, he admits to being part of the American Indian and anti-Vietnam war movements, and to being an environmentalist. "I do feel good about being a part of that movement [AIM]. I think there are two books that were very influential in bringing to light the possibility of an American Indian Literature. One was *House Made of Dawn* and the other was [Dee Brown's] *Bury My Heart at Wounded Knee*, which was a wonderful history of a thirty-year period in American history. They were both successful and I think made a difference. They convinced the publishing world that here is something we overlooked, and we can give this some emphasis."[26]

When he reviewed *Bury My Heart at Wounded Knee* for *The New York Times*, however, Momaday went further, diagnosing the malady that led white Americans to extirpate and mass-murder Indigenous people, and connecting this to the ongoing atrocities in American wars abroad, including war crimes in Vietnam exposed by Seymour Hersh:

> *It will come as a surprise to many readers of this book (and I sincerely hope that there are many indeed) that so much of great drama and moment actually took place in the three decades of this remarkable story . . . Having read Mr. Brown, one has a better understanding of what it is that nags at the American conscience at times (to our everlasting credit) and of that morality which informs and fuses events so far apart in time and space as the massacres at Wounded Knee and My Lai.*[27]

As important as this mainstream recognition was, the story he told of the hopelessness of the Kiowa a century before and of their survival was more visceral to fellow Indigenous than to non-Indigenous readers. A good strategy for the latter is to listen to what Indigenous readers found so exciting in the book, which is recorded in Palmer's *Words from a Bear*.

"What happened during the Eisenhower administration?" asks Comanche activist LaDonna Harris. "The government removed . . . Indian people from the reservation, from their home. This was a federal policy, because at that time there weren't any jobs on the reservation":

> *They told them, "This will really be good, we'll pay for your way." But there was no program for them. After they got them there, they just let them go. We're a communal society. All of our tribes are, and so to take you away from that organization of community and put you in major cities and kind of isolate you . . .*

> *they were having problems. And* House Made of Dawn *talks about these issues, how we were always perceived to be a problem. And we always said, "If you see us as a problem, we'll be a problem."*[28]

"Huge numbers of our uncles and fathers and grandfathers went to serve in the US military, who were like Abel," recalls Pueblo writer Simon Ortiz. "In that way, there was real connection, real identification with and real example of—ourselves . . . Scott Momaday for the first time was able to really lay down the impact of World War II upon warriors, illustrating the terrible toll the war took on young men from various tribal cultures, the terrible toll that that took. Not only the story of returning veterans from World War II, but the impact of the larger society, the larger world on young men who have seldom ventured far from their home villages."[29]

Both scholars and allies agree. Professor Susan Scarberry-Garcia tells Palmer that in Abel, Momaday created a Native protagonist who was "shell shocked," who "must imagine his way back into wholeness and there's a lot of pain and suffering that goes with that." Letitia Chambers of the Heard Museum told Palmer, "He treats the search for identity and the conflicts between traditional cultures and Anglo society with great insight," adding that the Native voice has largely been excluded from Native histories.[30]

In this way, *House Made of Dawn* proved to be the literary companion to the American Indian Movement, articulating the movement's grievances through cinematic and novelistic lyricism that would ensure the book was translated into many languages. It broadened the stream of consciousness technique beyond Faulkner, Joyce, and Woolf, stretching it into a stream of *historical* consciousness.

The novel refuses to reduce grievances to militancy, occupations, or "violence"—the buzzwords by which the mainstream media defined AIM. As told through Abel's witnesses, what appears on the surface in Abel's troubles were responses to prior violence. The violence is located in the land. The novel's place of redress is not centered on magic or "haze" but the all-important tribal ties to land. As Scarberry-Garcia writes, healing in the novel "occurs when the characters internalize images of the land by means of the symbolic acts of singing and story-telling. The [Navajo] songs are models of the process of composition and reassemblage of inner energies, and the stories from oral tradition are models of redefining or remaking one's place in the natural world."[31]

If land is central to the non-Indigenous as a commodity, how much more central is it to its longtime stewards, whose connection stretches a dozen or more millennia and is defined by this kinship? "They must know the long journey of the sun on the black mesa," Abel's grandfather prays for his offspring, "how it rode in the seasons and the years, and they must live according to the sun appearing, for only then could they reckon where they were, where all things were, in time . . . "

> *There, at the rounder knoll, it was time to plant corn; and there, where the highest plane fell away, that was the day of the rooster race, six days ahead of the black bull running and the little horse dancing, seven ahead of the Pecos immigration; and there . . . the secret dances, every four days of fasting in the kiva, the moon good for hoeing and the time for harvest, the rabbit and witch hunts, all the proper days of the clans and societies; and just there at the saddle,*

> where the sky was lower and brighter than elsewhere on the high black land, the clearing of the ditches in advance of the spring rains, and the long race of the black men at dawn.
>
> These things he told to his grandson slowly and at length, because they were old and true, and they could be lost forever as easily as one generation is lost to the next, as easily as one old man might lose his voice . . .[32]

6.

Fifty-five years after its publication, the book's canonical status endures. But even a Pulitzer Prize winner will have his run-ins with that long American habit of erasure. During the Obama administration, bans sponsored by John Huppenthal, Arizona's Superintendent of Public Instruction (who campaigned on the promise to "stop la raza") targeted the spread of Mexican American and Chicano studies. Caught in the crossfire was an anthology that included work by Momaday.

With the threat of millions in state funding being withheld, these books already in use in Arizona's public schools were forcefully confiscated. "Students said the banned books were seized from their classrooms and out of their hands, after Tucson schools banned Mexican American Studies, including a book of photos of Mexico. Crying, students said it was like Nazi Germany, and they were unable to sleep since it happened."[33]

Along with work of Pueblo author Leslie Marmon Silko, Momaday's poem, "The Delight Song of Tsoai-talee," appeared in this anthology, which the censors proclaimed was in violation of Huppenthal's ban, as it was aimed at "classes that are primarily designed for a particular ethnic group or that 'promote *resentment* toward a race or class of people,'" *The Los Angeles Times* reported.[34]

It was twenty years prior, in an interview with *The Paris Review*, that the critic Harold Bloom called the multiculturalists fighting for their place in the canon "The School of Resentment," adding that "we can't really ask literature or the representatives of a literary culture, in or out of the university, to save society. Literature is not an instrument of social change or an instrument of social reform."[35] Before "wokeness," the ban on social consciousness in art and education has been articulated both by cultural gatekeepers in the academy and right-wingers in the halls of power, nearly in unison, using the same rationale but different vocabularies.

But you can't hurt a man who's a bear inside. In *Words From A Bear*, Momaday recalls a "spectacular" red mesa, west of Jemez, on top of which "are the ruins of an old Pueblo." At seventeen, preparing to leave Jemez for school in the East, in Virginia, where he would meet Faulkner, he recalls, "I wanted to climb that mesa one last time."

On the climb down, he grew disoriented as he came to an impassable funnel, one "with a ledge at the bottom." If he could get to the ledge, he might make it "the rest of the way without too much trouble." But when he got there, "the ledge that had appeared at the top vanished; it was an optical illusion of some kind. I was looking down and there were boulders . . . way below." It dawned on him, "Oh, I'm in trouble."[36]

"Some awareness of my mortality came at that point. I thought . . . 'I'm going to die here.'" Then he "looked out across the valley and saw the corn fields and the squash fields, and I saw the late golden sun on the Pueblo walls, and the mountains beyond. I thought, 'This is a beautiful world. I see it as I never really saw it before.' And then I found myself sitting on the ground, looking up at the funnel. I have no idea how I got down." He recalls it as "a kind of religious experience and a mystery," deciding finally that "moments like that define who you are . . . One lives moment to moment and gathers those that define him and casts the others away and finally he ends up being who he is . . . I write out of those moments."[37]

Momaday believes in blood memory, describing this as "the capacity for remembering things beyond our own corporeal existence." In this way he conceives of his identity broadly, "gathering myself in terms of my ancestors. The Kiowa part is crucial . . . The Kiowas had a colorful history. Their mythology is very highly developed. It's a whole oral tradition in itself . . . Indians are storytellers. Those stories were passed on by word of mouth only, and so they were always just one generation from being just gone."[38]

Momaday's voice endures and his creativity continues. As he proclaims in the poem in the anthology banned in Arizona:

> I stand in good relation to the earth
> I stand in good relation to the gods
> I stand in good relation to all that is beautiful
> I stand in good relation to the daughter of Tsen-tainte
> You see, I am alive, I am alive.

1954

Anachronistic: Miguel Ángel Asturias on his grandparents' finca

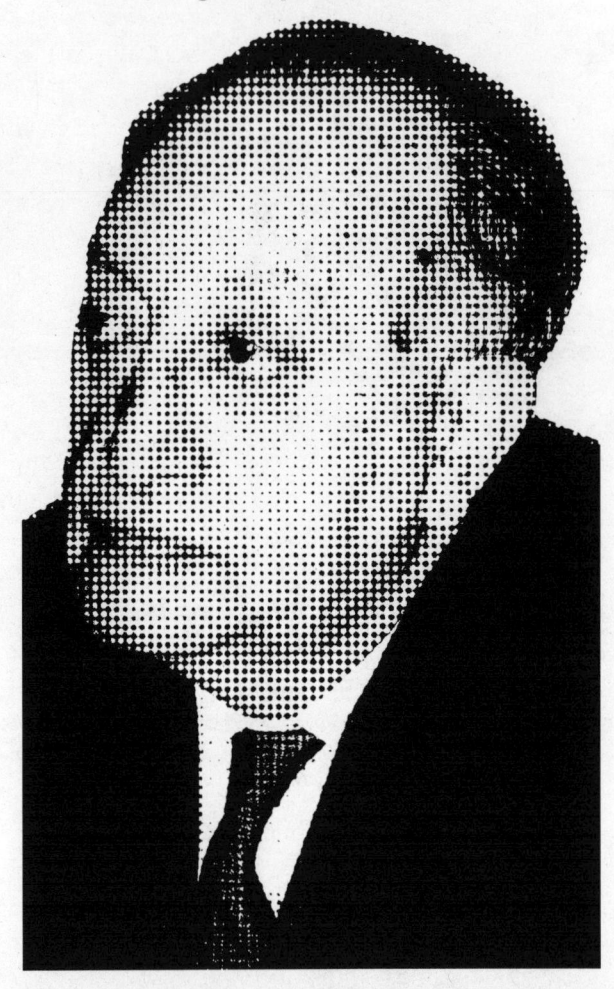

or how an innovator of magical realism learned his craft from the Maya

"Our Latin American literature has always been a committed, a responsible literature," argued Guatemalan novelist Miguel Ángel Asturias in 1973. "[T]he great works of our countries have been written in response to a vital need, a need of the people, and therefore almost all our literature is committed . . . Only as an exception do some of our writers isolate themselves and become uninterested in what is happening around them; such writers are concerned with psychological or egocentric subjects and the problems of a personality out of contact with surrounding reality . . ."[1]

It was the bourgeois writers, he wants to say, who ignore the looting of their resources by the rich behemoth to the North which then turns around and redeploys those riches on death squads and dictators. It is no surprise, then, that Asturias's landmark novel, *Mr. President* confronts its readers with similar frankness. *Mr. President* examined the rampant corruption of a fictional Guatemalan dictator. But the country's *real* dictators disrupted the novel's genesis and sent its author into exile a decade later. In this act of suppression, Asturias's censors and exilers were aided by the United States—and, specifically, the CIA. Such suppression has long impaired Asturias's career, reputation, and recognition.

In the introduction to *Mr. President*—from David Unger's lucid new translation—the literary scholar Gerald Martin calls the novel "the first page of the Boom."[2] "The Boom" was the nickname for the clutch of new Latin American novels emerging in the 1960s, including those by future Nobel laureates Gabriel García Márquez and Mario Vargas Llosa. The ascent of these young, brash talents in fiction was twinned with the mid-century magazine *Mundo Nuevo*, which spotlighted their work.

"Without Asturias," Martin assures us, "[the Boom] might not have developed."[3] But while *Mundo Nuevo* championed the younger writers Asturias inspired, its editor disparaged Asturias himself. Why? *Mr. President* shared the Boom authors' modern aesthetics, blending surrealism with a reportorial tone, even inserting magical elements. As Martin sees it, the conspicuous conceit at the heart of the most acclaimed of the Boom novels, *One Hundred Years of Solitude*, was even preempted in *Mr. President*. Asturias called it "magical *sur*realism."

But the problem with Asturias, for *Mundo Nuevo*'s backers, was not strictly aesthetic. It was Cold War politics that was at issue. The United States not only supported or helped install these despots; it also quietly backed the Congress for Cultural Freedom, an anti-communist front created to push pro-American narratives through magazines like *Mundo Nuevo* and dozens more around the world.

As the Congress disparaged Asturias, Martin, then a young scholar, spoke out both to defend the author and challenge *Mundo Nuevo*'s biases (though at the time he couldn't know about its American patronage, which was classified). Martin assailed its editor in chief for refusing to recognize the Boom's undeniable forerunner. Amidst Martin's incensed critiques, Asturias remained a thorny problem for *Mundo Nuevo*. His work challenged the Boom's creation myth, part of which held that American freedom had inspired and would promote the new oeuvre. But like many great books, *Mr. President* refused to go away—culminating, in 1967, with Asturias being awarded the Nobel Prize for literature.

But that very year that Asturias won the ultimate accolade for writers, the Congress was discredited as a CIA front. Now, Guatemalan-American novelist David Unger's masterful, clear translation presents an opening for the Nobel laureate (who died in 1974). A new generation of

North American readers will gain access to his witty, influential, and defamed masterpiece.

In his introduction, Martin repeatedly forces readers to look at *Mr. President* as a work that, had it not been suppressed, was contemporary to *Ulysses*, early Faulkner, Woolf, and Elliott. To understand this is to understand the Guatemalan as a modernist innovator, just as the Nicaraguan poet Rubén Darío was for poetry.

Rival Dictator Stories

Asturias was born on October 19, 1899, the year after dictator Manuel Estrada Cabrera assumed power. Asturias's father Ernesto was a judge and his mother Maria was a school teacher. "My parents were quite persecuted," Asturias recalled, "though they were not imprisoned or anything of the sort."[4] When he was a toddler, students protested the dictatorship of Cabrera. When Asturias's father showed sympathy and released them, Miguel's parents lost their jobs. The family relocated from the capital to Salamá, in Baja Verapaz. Miguel learned the rhythms of the countryside, traversing his grandparents' farm on horseback with his beloved grandfather. But it was his Maya nanny, Lola Reyes, who instilled a love of folk legends that remained with him, infusing his literary work for decades to come. "Although he returned with his family to Guatemala City [in 1908]," writes translator Gregory Rabassa, "those early rural memories became constant in his vision of life and legend in Guatemala."[5]

After returning to the capital, Miguel spent time at the family's supply store, which they opened in response to their blacklisting. In pursuit of his degree at the National Central Institute for Boys, Miguel watched as the unthinkable unfolded. On Christmas Day, 1918, a powerful earthquake buried much of the city. Aftershocks stretched into the New Year. As rescue efforts faltered, the once-powerful Estrada Cabrera's support plummeted. Joining the so-called Generation of 1920, Asturias saw an opening to become politically active in the wake of the crisis and helped organize strikes. The dictator's failure to deal with these mass protests led the National Assembly to declare him unfit to rule. Refusing exile, Estrada Cabrera was sent to prison.

Meanwhile, Asturias had switched his studies from medicine to law. As a law student, he took a position as secretary to the court that tried the dictator. "Cabrera had come completely under the spell of his own myth," Rabassa notes, surrounding himself with astrologers, mystics, and soothsayers. "It was in his association with Cabrera that Asturias's most famous character was formed," first as a short story.[6] Asturias wrote that he "saw him almost every day in the prison. And I found that there's no doubt that men like that have a special power over people. To the extent that while he was a prisoner people would say: 'No, that can't be Estrada Cabrera. The real Estrada Cabrera escaped. This is some poor old man they've locked up . . .'"[7] This intermingling of weakness and omnipotence flowed into his literary style.

In 1923, Asturias graduated at the top of his class, and earned a prestigious award for his thesis on social problems affecting Guatemala's Indigenous community. The booming family supply store exposed him to Indigenous Maya traders. "His contact with these Indians brought Asturias back to his earlier sojourn in the country," Rabassa recalled.[8] But soon he was on the run. Remarking critically on the power of the military in *Tiempos Nuevos*, a weekly launched by Asturias and his colleagues, one colleague was assaulted by government thugs. Asturias was briefly arrested. His parents took the hint and sent him abroad to safety.

But even in Europe, events bolstered his fascination with Guatemala's Maya. He visited the (looted) Maya collection at the British Museum in the early 1920s. In France, he met Professor Georges Raynaud of the Sorbonne, a scholar of Maya religion and culture. Asturias was inspired to translate the *Popol Vuh*, based on Raynaud's French translation. He also published poetry that combined surrealism and Maya legends—as well as a novel, *Legends of Guatemala*, which brought these legends together with childhood recollections. Throughout the 1920s, Asturias reworked "Political Beggars," the dictator story he had begun in 1922, imbuing it with surrealism and modernist techniques.

"Arriving in Europe," Asturias told the writer Jimena Saenz, "we reunited with friends in the cafes of Montparnasse, and in the cafe chatter there began to grow what we might call a rivalry between the Venezuelans, Guatemalans, Mexicans, as we shared various anecdotes of our respective dictators . . ."[9] What rushed back to Asturias in those coffee-fueled duels was an almost intimate, clandestine atmosphere around the dictatorship.

Rumors about dictators infiltrated the private lives of Central Americans and imbued the resulting novel with noir undertones: how families would close up their house fronts, receding into the kitchen to whisper not directly of "Estrada Cabrera but of 'the man' . . ." speaking "in a low voice of what was happening in the country . . . of political personalities or situations involving political prisoners, of peoples in the penitentiary . . . or those killed by the bomb that exploded near the church by the Callejón del Judío."[10]

Asturias took the opportunity to befriend and read not only Joyce, but also André Breton and Paul Valéry.

Valéry praised *Legends of Guatemala* in its preface. But Asturias also continued to study Maya culture as he dredged up the minutiae of the grotesque dictatorship haunting his youth—details that stretched into more material than would fit in a mere short story.

The Model

Published in the half-decade before Orwell's *1984*, *Mr. President* captures the mass propaganda use of new technologies like televisions: "Every night a movie screen was raised like a gallows in the Plaza Central. A hypnotized crowd watched blurred fragments, as if witnessing the burning of heretics. . . . Society's crème de la crème strolled in circles . . . while the common folk gazed in awe at the screen in religious silence."[11] This fear proves atmospheric, as the president's favorite advisor, Miguel Angel Face, undertakes a secret mission to prompt the president's main rival, a general, to go on the run. Why? He needs a scapegoat, and running is a confession of guilt, he says.[12]

Unaware the President has orchestrated the general's escape, a judge advocate shouts, "I want to know how he escaped! . . . That's why telephones exist; to capture government's enemies."[13] This judge also warns a suspected witness: "Lying is a big mistake. The authorities know everything. And they know you spoke to the general."[14]

During celebrations at the presidential residence, a sudden melee on the stairs erupts into gunshots. Finally, the shots end. "It was nothing," Asturias writes. "Little by little, the guests formed groups; some peed in their pants out of fear, others lost gloves, others recovered their color but were scared mute . . . At the foot of a small staircase, the military band's first drummer lay on the ground. He had rolled down from the second floor, drum and all, setting off the general panic."[15]

"What could I say?" a paid informant complains over a beer to an aspiring informant. "It's tougher now to get into the Secret Police than when I joined. Everyone knows where the future lies."[16]

Mr. President is at its most magical-realist when the disembodied hands, eyes, ears, and surveillance networks blossom into dream-scenes. This happens in later chapters, such as "Tohil's Dance," a reference to the K'iche Maya god of fire and warfare, who drinks blood as a ritual sacrifice.

Rival Dictators

After much of *El señor presidente* was written, Asturias traveled through the Middle East and Europe, where he encountered explicit fascism. In 1933, he returned to yet another Guatemalan dictatorship, that of Jorge Ubico, who had taken power two years before. Prone to calling himself Napoleon, Ubico relied on a Nazi-supporting police chief named Anzueto, who embezzled properties for his boss. When a minister refused to condone this corruption, he was accused of plotting to overthrow the government, was imprisoned, and was forced under torture to confess. When a journalist exposed the cover-up, he too was imprisoned.

Asturias watched as a new generation of protestors—largely teachers—challenged Ubico, who had initially hoped to install the Nazi police chief as his puppet successor. But throngs of well-educated dissidents challenged the dictator and brought about Guatemala's "Democratic Spring." Under a new Guatemalan democracy, Asturias became a diplomat. And it was in this window that he finally published *El señor presidente*. Funded by his family, the novel was published in 1946 in Mexico, where he served in the embassy. Two years later, the book was published properly, to greater fanfare, by Losada in Buenos Aires—his next ambassadorial post.[17]

But this democratic moment where Asturias's work flourished was short lived. It was the nation's last peaceful transfer of power for decades. In June 1954, with the support of the CIA, the United Fruit Company, and President Dwight D. Eisenhower—who also had United Fruit stakeholders on his cabinet—right-wing factions of Guatemala's military led by Carlos Castillo Armas overthrew the elected President Jacobo Arbenz. As Asturias was sent into exile again, the CIA's new outfit—the Congress for Cultural Freedom—was nearing its five-year anniversary.

Weaponized Culture

The Congress for Cultural Freedom was born at a conference in Berlin in 1950. In the occupied city, American officers had seen their own and other allied troops flooding into the Soviet quarter for concerts and culture. Simultaneously, dozens of magazines were established with the aim of reaching Europe's cultural set. Like a tycoon's array of new luxe mansions, London's *Encounter*, Berlin's *Der Monat*, Paris's *Preuves*, and Rome's *Tempo Presente* were launched to signal American sophistication through literary achievement. Heeding a call to engage the so-called Third World, a second batch followed—*Notebooks of the Congress for Cultural Freedom* among them.

Launched in 1953, a year before the long-planned US coup in Guatemala, *Cuadernos* would be part of the greater constellation of coup-and-cleanup maneuvers that swept out democratic socialist, nationalist, populist, and reformist regimes like Arbenz's and installed US friendly dictators with impunity. But if the United States wanted to sound urbane and liberal in these magazines, it therefore risked blowing its propagandistic cover. Could US-backed, right-wing dictatorships don the veneer of cultural sophistication?

By the 1960s the Congress's top official, Mike Josselson (a covert CIA officer) defended *Cuadernos'* politics from Keith Botsford, the roving editor who bristled at the magazine's lack of uptake on the left. Botsford was an American born in Europe who remembered being brought up in a household filled with "help" and privilege. But he also understood the failures of the CCF to reach the right people in Latin America, calling the current magazine and its editors "the paralytic wing of the liberal reaction."[18]

Especially after the failed 1961 US invasion of Cuba at the Bay of Pigs, Botsford argued for a new magazine that might offer an "opening to the left" in Latin America. After years butting heads, Botsford persuaded Josselson that *Cuadernos* was too conservative. Latin America's left ignored it. Conservatives read it, but it was preaching to the choir. A new magazine was needed.

"Sleazed" by the CIA

In 1965, Botsford invited Emir Rodríguez Monegal—a Uruguayan literary critic, mentioned in previous chapters—to travel to Yugoslavia for a meeting of PEN, the literary organization for freedom of expression. Botsford and Monegal had never met, and, when the letter arrived, Rodríguez Monegal had never heard of either PEN or the CCF. Botsford and his colleagues at the Congress for Cultural Freedom had been "eying Monegal" for an editing job. But they broke the ice by insisting he "cast a vote for the president of the International PEN Club."[19] The candidates were Asturias and the American playwright and Pulitzer Prize winner, Arthur Miller.

Botsford disparaged Asturias, a diplomat in France at the time, as an "exquisite sleaze," stipulating "that Monegal should vote for Miller if he wanted the [Congress] to foot the bill" for his trip.[20] The invitation was alluring and heralded Rodríguez Monegal's enthusiastic conscription into the war on Asturias. From then on, he would be an avid critic of the author and a determined campaigner against his literary recognition. He would also become the editor in chief of the CCF's newest magazine, *Mundo Nuevo*.

The Americans prevailed and Miller became PEN's new president. Miller came to suspect that he'd been used for a new style of prosecuting the Cold War: "One of the early people who approached me about PEN—I can't remember his name now—but people would later say about him, 'Why, that guy was an agent all the time.'"[21] Though the Americans got their way with the PEN presidency, they were apoplectic after Asturias was awarded the Nobel Prize in 1967. Emir Rodríguez Monegal, more than anyone, threw a literary conniption.

After the prize, the young British scholar, Gerald Martin, watched the suppression of Asturias grow overt. A few years earlier, he had no sooner learned of Asturias's work than decided to do his PhD thesis on him. He was smitten, a literary crush, writing and researching it quickly. But thanks to a new translation out the year he was finishing it, he learned that Asturias would come through the UK for a publicity tour. While he eagerly hoped to meet Asturias that May, he wound up getting to spend a full hour with him before others came to interrupt.[22]

Martin would go on to win many awards and write the official biography of Gabriel García Márquez—and his official Mario Vargas Llosa biography is due next. But before he was seasoned by literary feuds, he had no idea, since it was done in secret, that Asturias was shadow-banned out of an important job at PEN. In the years to come, he came to recognize the dishonesty at the heart of the movement to suppress his idol, and fought back.

Initially, when Asturias won the Nobel—the first Latin American novelist; first and only Central American writer—so soon after Martin began work on him, he decided he had been lucky. But in the late 1960s, he read vague dismissals of Asturias's work. The author of many such dismissals was Rodríguez Monegal. Over the next five years, Monegal derided Asturias's "slow, rhetorical tone" that "belongs to that generation which believes literature to be something sacred." Reviewing Asturias's *The Green Pope* (from the *Banana Trilogy*, which is a lacerating critique of US policy in Latin America) Monegal wrote in *The New York Times* in 1971, "Asturias's failure is not on the documentary level. It is in the fictionalizing of reality."[23]

The novel unfolds through the lens of "Tropical Banana, Inc.," a doppelganger for the United Fruit Company. Monegal complained that Asturias's "protagonist and his rivals are unreal not because they do unbelievable things; they are unreal because the presentation of their more than believable actions carries no conviction whatsoever." He went even further, saying: "To believe that Asturias's trilogy represents the best of the Latin American novel today is to be as wrong and outdated as the Swedish Academy was when it gave him the 1967 Nobel Prize."[24]

Others in the CCF fold were no less gratuitously dismissive of Asturias's achievement. Writing in *Encounter*, for instance, Hans Habe described the Nobel Prize as having less than a remarkable record picking winners. Somewhat hilariously, Habe also suggests that recently "the Peace Prize became a piece of political partisanship . . ."[25]

Asturias's most vehement defense probably came from Martin, who was contemptuous of the idea that Asturias's work was invalidated by its political themes. Martin warned that, in forcing a dichotomy between literary versus protest writing, Rodríguez Monegal risked reducing the phrase "protest writer" to an excuse not actually to read literature. It implicitly demeaned criticism and reading by only valuing the kind of spontaneous chatter found in a *Mundo Nuevo* interview. He was, in other words, calling Rodríguez Monegal a tin-eared hack with a political off-switch.[26]

In *Mr. President* itself, the atmosphere of double-dealing thwarts the protagonist Angel Face's relationships not unlike the way Asturias was thwarted by the CIA's cultural gatekeepers. Unlike the many characters tortured and sent to prison in the novel, Angel Face in the end is tortured and sent, like Asturias himself, into exile. How does it feel to be the author's roguish but exiled stand-in? "He felt buried alive," writes Asturias, "open eyed."[27]

Asturias died in June 1974, about a week before the twentieth anniversary of the US-sponsored coup in Guatemala. *Mr. President* is decidedly hard to translate, relying on poetic alliterations, onomatopoeia, devices learned from surrealism's inventors and other avant-garde movements. But it also relies on Asturias's very keen ear to the street, his love of myth and Indigenous culture.

Much of the translation is truly of another time, rendering not just Central American Spanish, but Guatemalan neighborhood-, class- and period-specific slang. Unger proves to be a masterful transformer and renderer of this ear. The praise for Unger's translation is highly deserved. But as for Penguin Classics and Unger retranslating this unfairly suppressed book, it is long overdue, like being unburied—with your eyes open.

1979

Clarification: Rigoberta Menchú in Oslo

or how 626 Mayan villages across Guatemala's
northern highlands were eradicated

"It is said that our Indigenous ancestors, Mayas and Aztecs, made human sacrifices to their gods," Rigoberta Menchú once quipped. "It occurs to me to ask: How many humans have been sacrificed to the gods of Capital in the last five hundred years?"[1] The activist's 1983 memoir, *I, Rigoberta Menchú*, recounts the shocking story of an American-sponsored counterinsurgency against the majority Maya population.

Acting largely in self-defense in a system of exploitation and forced labor going back centuries, Menchú's fellow Maya were attacked in the name of anticommunism. Tens of thousands of villagers were massacred, whole villages were eradicated, women were raped, and children were killed.

But even before her family was dragged into the insurgency for their humble fight to keep their small parcel of land, Menchú suffered unimaginable losses. Before her decade-long exile to Mexico and Europe—where she told her story in a spoken testimonial that became the acclaimed memoir—she was orphaned by the military regimes that she and her family lived under, losing almost her entire family.

For her candid—if contested—memoir, and for her work on behalf of human and equal rights for Guatemala's Maya, she won the 1992 Nobel Peace Prize, in a year that marked the 500th anniversary of Columbus's arrival to Indigenous America, an anniversary that Maya look upon as a catastrophe.

As the memoir turns 40, it's worth remembering that her story didn't end with the Nobel Prize. Menchú founded Winaq, the country's first Indigenous political party, and ran as Guatemala's first Indigenous candidate for president, twice. Though she lost, Menchú paved the way for others by helping spur the movement to prosecute Guatemala's corrupt and genocidal Cold War regimes and by creating a Maya-peasant infrastructure that spurred another Maya woman's run for the presidency in 2023.[2]

"Discovery" or Catastrophe?

Rigoberta Menchú Tum was born in Laj Chimel, a village in the remote central highlands of the department of El Quiché. Without electricity or roads, the village felt far away from the Guatemalan Army. "My land is very magic and ... has mysteries," Menchú told Dawn Gifford Engle, the director of the 2016 documentary, *Daughter of the Maya*.[3] Menchú's grandfather, who lived well past 100, regaled the family with stories that had been passed down over millennia from the civilization of the Maya.

The accomplishments of the culture of the Maya can hardly be overstated. As *National Geographic* put it, "They built a culture that flowered while Europe languished in the Dark Ages and that survived six times as long as the Roman Empire. They lived by a calendar the equal of [any], developed the concept of zero in mathematics, predicted eclipses of sun and moon, and traced the path of Venus with an error of only 14 seconds a year." When Diego Rivera first saw their Classical murals in the Yucatán and the jungles of Chiapas, he is said to have wept. They rivaled the Renaissance murals of Europe and invented a pigment of blue known today as Mayan blue that is close to immortal in how little it fades over centuries on the walls of their temples; and it took modern science a century to decode.

Despite the repression of Indigenous groups that came with European "discovery," the Maya community survived as a majority in Guatemala. It viewed the destruction of its culture when Europeans arrived as a catastrophe. Stewards of Maya book culture and learning were targeted in particular by the Spanish, who declared themselves the New World's new lords and carved up the continent. In constant danger, Maya elders practiced their traditions in secret.

By the 1700s, Spain was the world's largest empire. It renamed the Maya world "the kingdom of Guatemala." Spanish laws put in place trustees over the Indigenous groups, and Spaniards enslaved Mayas on *encomiendas*. Indigenous Americans had no gold, so the Spaniards made their fortunes on slave labor. "There are still elder Indigenous people who suffer the consequences of being treated as slaves," Menchú reminds us. "It's just that today, different methods are used."[4]

After Spain's decline in 1821, all of Central and most of Latin America declared their independence. Maya leaders organized to participate in the creation of independent Guatemala. But they were arrested, imprisoned, or executed. The new authoritarian state benefited a privileged few, but it excluded most Guatemalans from citizenship or owning land.

In 1904, Estrada Cabrera gave vast tracts of Guatemala to the United Fruit Company. Founded in 1899, the United Fruit Company became the biggest landowner in Central America and controlled the railroad, the port facilities, and major shipping routes. It also ran its own postal, radio, and telegraph services. By the 1930s, it controlled eighty percent of the US banana trade. Having given it so much land, government forces were often called in to suppress workers who organized against it.

Rigoberta's father, Vicente Menchú, was a farmer who never went to school and who spoke little Spanish. Her mother, Juana Tum, was a traditionalist who taught her children the spiritual roots of Maya culture. A healer and midwife, Juana assisted the mothers in eighteen surrounding villages during childbirth. As someone was going into labor, Juana was led to the distant village to provide medical care. Without factory medicine, she used the community's traditional medicinal plants.

In Menchú's youth, Maya families were forced to work on plantations owned by the country's large landholders. Her village worked these plantations, where Menchú bore the hardships of subsistence child labor from a young age: long hours, wage theft, and brutal conditions. Living as migrants in their own country, the hellish lifestyle took them to the sweltering coast for months each year.

Civil War

In 1950, Vicente Menchú fought for a piece of land of his own. He tried to get the rights to his plot documented. Organizing to unite with other farmers and campesinos instilled a political consciousness in the family. But early in the 1950s came the "Guatemalan Spring": the democratically elected reformist President Jacobo Arbenz took over from his democratically elected reformist predecessor, Juan José Arévalo. Arbenz's landslide victory promised land reform, the freedom to organize, and freedom of speech.

At the time, two percent of the richest families owned two thirds of the arable land. When Arbenz sought to buy back unused excess lands from United Fruit, the company accused him of "communism" and worked with the CIA to topple him. US Vice President Richard Nixon traveled to Guatemala in the wake of the coup to thank General Carlos Castillo Armas, who got a ticker-tape parade and honorary degrees at two universities in New York, Fordham and Columbia.⁵

With democracy overthrown, Maya farmers burned crops in protest as the lands granted to them were retaken for the oligarchs. As punishment for joining these protests, Menchú's father was persecuted as a communist and sent to prison many times. "The community had to make a huge sacrifice to get him out of jail," she recalled.⁶ At the farmer's organization, the Comite de Unidad Campesina (CUC), Menchú learned the art of organizing from her father. The CUC was their outlet to forge solutions to the ongoing problem of land rights.

Menchú recalls how people from surrounding villages "asked him for advice, and that increased the persecution." But her father sought to open doors especially for his favorite daughter, who "was accepted by the sister nuns of the Holy Family, and I worked there for three years. After that, they gave me the opportunity to study, and I completed the first four years of primary school in just one year."⁷ But more trouble awaited her.

When Carlos Castillo Armas was assassinated, General Miguel Ydigoras Fuentes ballot-stuffed his way into the presidency. This would spur a civil war that would alter Menchú's fate. The CIA Station Chief described Ydigoras Fuentes as "a moody, almost schizophrenic individual" who "disregards the advice of his Cabinet."⁸

Ydigoras Fuentes's widespread corruption spurred mass protests out of which emerged the MR-13 guerrilla group. These left-wing generals tried to oust the erratic Ydigoras Fuentes but their coup failed, resulting in the 1960 civil war. Meanwhile, to prevent the center-left former president Juan José Arévalo from retaking power in the chaos of Ydigoras Fuentes's rule, a right-wing coup toppled the general in 1963. Opposition was met with brutal force that spread to the Maya highlands.

Irregular Locals

In *I, Rigoberta Menchú*, the author recalls her transformation as military violence came to El Quiché. As the counterinsurgency violence spread, she learned of an epidemic of women being raped in Maya villages, including the brutal murder of a friend. Villagers were subject to such rampant violence that they had no choice but to defend themselves, mobilizing to create improvised weaponry and to capture guns in ambushes. This placed Menchú in a category the military defined as "Irregular Local Forces." Initially, maneuvers were nonviolent but the regime targeted them as fighters anyway.

The first soldier Menchú's defense unit captured was Maya. They let him go with a plea to desert his command. But having gotten little information, they immediately regretted this. The second time they captured a soldier "we got a lot of information . . . about how they treat the soldiers in the army." According to the sympathetic captive, "From the first day I arrived in the barracks, they told me that my parents were stupid . . ." because they couldn't speak Spanish and promised that the army would teach them Spanish. "Then they told me I had to kill the communists from Cuba and Russia. I had to kill them all."[9]

When challenged, he replied, "I'm not to blame for all this, they grabbed me in the town." Hearing him cry, they "felt sorry for him, because we are all human."[10] Behind the recruitment of Maya was a centuries-old practice of forced labor. But what greater forces were enabling it?

Acknowledging how the Church has often meant "to divide us and keep the poor dormant," Menchú describes how she maintained Christian faith while observing what Maya ancestors and history have taught. "[W]e have understood that being a Christian means refusing to accept all the injustices which are committed against our people . . . the discrimination committed against a humble people who barely know what eating meat is . . ."[11]

Beyond the bible, "reality teaches us . . . that we don't need a Church . . . which knows nothing of hunger . . . This awakening of the Indians didn't come . . . from one day to the next, because Catholic Action and other religions . . . have all tried to keep us where we were. But I think that unless a religion springs from within the people themselves, it is a weapon of the system."[12]

While joining this Maya awakening, Menchú serves as witness to and documenter of massacres that spurred left-wing movements across Guatemala to unite. In Panzós, an area of Cobán "they discovered oil and began throwing peasants off their land . . . They were Kekchi Indians and the army massacred them as if they were killing birds . . . Blood ran in the main square . . . "[13]

She finds that anticommunism is the most common excuse used to enable counterinsurgency violence. Ironically, she recalls whole "villages in El Quiché . . . unable to perform their [Maya] ceremonies because they were . . . called subversives and communists."[14] But under the next US-backed dictator in the late 1970s, it grew even worse. "Lucas García came to power with such a lust for killing, that the repression really began in El Quiché." The region "was like a . . . rag in his hands":

> *He set up military bases in many . . . villages and there were rapes, tortures, kidnappings. And massacres. The villages of Chajul, Cotzal and Nebaj suffered*

> massacres as the repression fell . . . above all on the
> Indian population.[15]

On September 9, 1979, her brother Patrocinio Menchú Tum was kidnapped by the army. "He disappeared for 15 days," Menchú told an interviewer. The family knew people "had been detained in the area, so my mother started to look for him." The family learns that Patrocinio had been tortured, set on fire, and burned alive in Chajul.

"Together with another 20 or so young men around the same age, he was cruelly tortured." But they "had no idea where his body was left." Learning of this cruelty "was precisely the moment . . . when I finally felt firmly convinced that if it's a sin to kill a human being, how can what the regime does to us *not* be a sin?"[16] As many campesinos did, Menchú and her family redoubled their commitment to their cause, as she longed to tell her people's history to the world.

Embassy Fire

On January 31, 1980, Vicente took part in a march in Guatemala City to protest the army's ongoing kidnapping and murder of poor Maya. It was organized by the CUC. Denied their moment before Congress, protestors were chased into the Spanish embassy. The ensuing police raid—over objections of the Spanish ambassador—culminated in the fire-bombing of the embassy where 36 protestors were burned alive.

"My father," she recalls, "was one of those burned to death at the Spanish embassy. There was a general in power who ordered the massacre . . . " The sole survivor (and sole witness to what happened inside the embassy),

Gregorio Yuja Xona was dragged from his hospital bed, tortured, and killed.[17] Spain broke off diplomatic relations with Guatemala over the incident.

After the fire, Menchú returned to Chimel. "I knew that the risk was very high," she recalls, "but I went back, and found my mom very brave, very strong." Juana told her daughter, "I know that your brother has died, and I know that your father has died, but we will keep on fighting.'" Menchú begged her mother to flee into exile with her. Her mother refused.

She soon disappeared. "I was told that my mother was kidnapped," she tells Engle. "Her clothes were taken away. They cut her hair and she was tortured." Menchú later learns that her mother's body was left "on the road that goes from Uspantán to Sicachal." The army ordered a guard to prevent her burial, so that she "was eaten by wild animals."[18]

It felt like her village was being targeted and being wiped out. Though denials were widespread in the Guatemalan media, this is precisely what happened to many Maya villages. "A lot of people from the community were massacred. A helicopter came and bombarded and burned the houses. But because of all this, there are very few people still alive from Chimel, where I was born."[19]

With Menchú orphaned, how could it get any worse?

Evangelical Genocide

After a coup d'etat by General Efraín Rios Montt in 1982, what had been an unspoken genocide became more open. Rios Montt lost his campaign for the presidency in 1974 but was paid off to accept the results and to take a diplomatic post in Madrid before the fire-bombing would sever ties between the two countries. Leaving government, he returned in the late 1970s and converted from Catholicism to a stringent Evangelical Christian sect, the Church of the Word. He befriended right-wing clerics like Jerry Falwell and Pat Robertson. The dictator also sought training (and funding) from Israel and honed his genocidal campaign with the slogan, "If you cannot kill the fish, you must drain the sea."[20]

Meanwhile, left-wing groups forged a united coalition, the Guatemalan National Revolutionary Unity, or URNG. It had only grown stronger as a result of the extremist violence of prior administrations. Viewing the movement as communist, Rios Montt's regime envisioned insurgents closing in on Guatemala's populous areas from the rural regions. So his generals continued the army's genocidal atrocities. Beginning in the city and suburbs, the army fanned outward in concentric circles.

But they did so under the cover of "protecting civilians." In areas that were "secure," they offered social programs. After US aid was curtailed under Carter as a result of Guatemala's rampant human rights violations, the Reagan administration sent aid through Evangelical Christian networks in an operation code-named "International Love Lift." But the thinly veiled love was a cover for more overt genocidal eradication of the left-wing movements and the nation's Indigenous majority.

By Rios Montt's second year the concentric rippling circles of murderous counterinsurgency came to the western border. Just as elsewhere in the country, massacres in the highlands targeted the Maya poor. In July, 1982, twenty-five kilometers from Asturias's grandparents' house, 268 Maya were massacred in the village of Rabinal. Soldiers moved from house to house, grabbing children and beating them to death. Women were raped and killed. The rest were shot. The next day, survivors were forced to dig mass graves before joining the Guatemalan Army.

In Dos Erres, in Petén, 160 Maya residents were massacred by government soldiers. In Rio Negro, 440 were killed, while 5000 were killed in the area between 1980 and 1982. During the long civil war which lasted until 1996, 626 Indigenous villages were destroyed, vanishing from the map. Of the more than 200,000 casualties that would haunt the nation for years, most were Maya.[21] A third of these casualties, an estimated 70,000 to 75,000 occurred under Rios Montt's sixteen months in power.[22]

In Exile

Her village decimated, and without siblings, Menchú turned to the Sisters of the Holy Family, whose nuns helped her escape to the safety of exile in Mexico. "I live near your country. I see your country every day," Bishop Samuel Luís García, of Chiapas, told her.[23] With few options, she crossed the border to the Diocese of San Cristóbal de las Casas. "The compañeros got me out on a plane to Mexico, and I felt a shattered, broken woman, because I'd never imagined that one day those criminals would force me to abandon my country. All the same, I also hoped to come back very soon and carry on working."[24]

The Monsignor gave her sleep medicine for PTSD and she slept for two weeks. When she emerged better rested, he told her, "You must come with me to the communities."[25] For six months, Menchú and the cleric traveled through the jungle, visiting Indigenous communities in the most remote parts of Chiapas, where a revolutionary movement was already under way. Though the more famous Zapatista uprising went public in response to NAFTA on January 1, 1994, the Zapatista National Liberation Army emerged from the National Liberation Front in the period when Menchú was touring the jungles and villages of Chiapas.

What they finally would build was an autonomous zone for Indigenous people who radically reimagined how sovereign nation states should be run. The registered inhabitants received free healthcare and schools for all, while maintaining land sovereignty and control over agriculture and other resources. "Those people gave me a forward-looking perspective," she said of her experience.[26]

By 1982 and for nearly a decade, thousands of other Maya fled over the border into Mexico. Many were en route to the United States to escape General Rios Montt and successor dictatorships supported and trained by the United States. In Mexico, the Guatemalan refugee community grew to more than 50,000. Menchú became active in the community, campaigning to tell the world what was happening to her people.

She traveled to New York to meet with United Nations delegates and to Geneva to warn European leaders of the atrocities. During a week spent with Venezuelan sociologist Elizabeth Burgos-Debray in Paris, Menchú told her story in what became her widely translated testimonio, *I, Rigoberta Menchú*. She offered voiceover narration for the film *When the Mountains Tremble*; and for ten years she traveled and spoke before global audiences, sharing tales of her awakening as a result of her people's suffering in Guatemala. The book became a best seller.

"The World is Watching!"

When she returned briefly from exile in October 1992, she was greeted by Adolfo Pérez Esquivel of Argentina, a Nobel Peace Prize winner. She joined her community in marking

500 years since Columbus had landed in the Americas. Millions of Indigenous people across the continent held protests that day. "I believe this is a very important day. Many brothers and sisters around the world, especially on this continent, are demonstrating in the same way," she said.[27]

On October 16, 1992, she was awarded the Nobel Prize for Peace as a result of Pérez Esquivel's nomination. The committee granted the prize "for her struggle for social justice and ethno-cultural reconciliation based on respect for the rights of Indigenous peoples." On a post-award tour in a pickup truck, she told crowds of fellow Maya who lined the streets, "Today, the world is watching." Her words were met with shouts:

"Long live Rigoberta Menchú, long live the Maya Quiché! Long live peace!"[28]

In tears, she replied, "This is the first official press conference I am giving after the great happiness of learning that I won the Nobel Peace Prize. I would like to offer a tribute to all my Indigenous brothers and sisters of America. I know that you are listening to me in every single corner. You have fought for this. This is not because of the personal merits of Rigoberta Menchú. It is for the memory of America."[29]

Indigenous activists now had the world's attention. But the brutal atrocities by the Guatemalan military continued. The Maya resistance was chased through mountains in the country's unyielding campaigns of eradication and scorched earth. Villagers in many cases were asked to identify the Catholic leaders who helped protect and feed them. When they did so, they were mowed down, followed by the leaders they had named.

In January, 1993, as a tentative ceasefire was being negotiated, a wave of Civil War refugees returned home.

"Our children need a guarantee for their future," Menchú declared. "We cannot leave them a world of uncertainty. We want to leave a more secure world so that the land becomes their land, today and forever. Then they can live here and cultivate their greatest potential and creativity."[30]

"Historical Truth"

Menchú married fellow refugee Angel Canil Grave, and they adopted a son, Maj. During peace talks in Mexico City beginning in 1994, Menchú said that her group listened at the door. "And when they came out, we pressured them. We told them, 'This needs to happen. You have to write this down.' And we proposed content for the peace agreement. We were very active with the refugees. There were more than 50,000 in Mexico. The refugees were a very strong force, with the muscle to say no to war. 'No more war. Yes to peace.' And this put pressure on both sides . . . . The mothers said, 'I don't want my son drafted into the war, not by the guerrillas, nor by the Army . . . It was the mothers who were pushing hardest to end the war."[31]

When the peace deal was signed in Oslo in 1996, Menchú was invited to speak. "When in this solemn place we received the Nobel Peace Prize, we had the hope that one day we could talk of peace."[32] But negotiations stalled on questions over whether mass murderers and torturers could be forgiven or forgotten. Yet once the accords were finally signed, Menchú immediately campaigned for justice.

"The people fought for their land, they fought for a piece of land, to farm it, to have a future for their children, a secure life," she said. "And the security they were seeking led them to death. I think that if it was a personal offense, it would be easier to forgive, forget, and start a new life. But this is not a personal horror, or a personal offense. It's a collective offense. It is the collective memory of Guatemala."[33]

In 1998, Larry Rohter, writing in *The New York Times* and citing the work of anthropologist and Middlebury College Professor David Stoll, accused Menchú of fabricating or conflating key parts of her autobiography.[34] But when a truth commission—the Commission for Historical Clarification—was launched under the auspices of the United Nations, Menchú and her allies remained focused on demanding justice for loved ones who were abducted, tortured, and killed during the civil war. It was a country littered with clandestine graves.

As the truth commission proceeded, it made sure not to accuse any of the Army's officers before verifying the facts. "We the victims are the ones who should be in charge of everything having to do with claims for justice," Menchú said. "This justice we seek would be meaningless if we only learn what happened, because the victims already know what happened."[35]

The findings, indeed, were clear. In 1999, *The New York Times* reported that "The truth commission . . . concluded that the United States gave money and training to a Guatemalan military that committed 'acts of genocide' against the Mayans during the most brutal armed conflict in Central America, Guatemala's 36-year civil war . . . The report, by the independent Historical Clarification Commission, contradicts years of official denials of the torture, kidnapping and execution of thousands of civilians in a war that the commission estimated killed more than 200,000 people. The commission listed the American training of the officer corps in counterinsurgency techniques as a key factor that 'had a significant bearing on human rights violations during the armed confrontation.'"[36]

But when her father's killer, Pedro Garcia Arredondo, former head of "Command 6," a special investigations unit of the now-defunct National Police, was convicted of homicide and crimes against humanity in 2015 for his leadership of the 1980 siege of the Spanish embassy, Menchú was "vindicated," as Pulitzer Prize-winning historian Greg Grandin described the matter in *The Nation*.[37]

Indeed, Menchú helped set the tone and forge the climate that convicted him and condemned many others guilty of genocide. Her lawsuit also led to the conviction for genocide of the dictator Rios Montt. Finally "there'll be a time," she vowed, "when things will be different, when we'll all be happy, perhaps not with nice houses, but at least we won't see our lands running with blood and sweat."[38]

1992

Unearthed:
Jennifer, Efraín and the CIA in Guatemala

or how during its dirty war the agency lied to, killed, and spied on its own citizens

As poor Maya refugees crossed into the United States in the early 1980s, immigrant rights lawyer Jennifer Harbury discovered that they were being denied asylum hearings, though they were claiming danger from conflict back home. Curious about the cause and hoping to verify their stories, Harbury went to Mexico and Guatemala to trace their flight route north.

Heading south from the Texas-Mexico border, she climbed a Guatemalan volcano, and interviewed a guerrilla fighter with the armed resistance, Efraín Bámaca Velázquez. Coming to admire his mind and plight, Harbury fell in love with him and they were married.

Soon the unthinkable happened.

The two spent the 1991 Christmas holiday on the border, as Bámaca Velázquez attended clandestine peace negotiations in Mexico. When he returned to the Sierra, and his base near the cloud-covered summit of the 13,000-plus foot Tajumulco Volcano, he was caught in a firefight. On March 12, 1992, he was wounded. A comrade injured next to him woke and saw that the comandante—nom de guerre: Everardo—had vanished. Guatemalan officials reported a captured fighter; Bámaca Velázquez was the only missing fighter that day. This much was clear.

But the rest is shot through with military propaganda, allegations of US-enabled torture, cover-up, and disinformation. When the military wrote it up, they included a description that matched Bámaca Velázquez's—down to his height, facial traits, hair color and the location and time of his capture. There could be no mistake. Yet this was the end of the trail: he vanished into the labyrinth of the death squads.

When officials told her that he shot himself rather than be taken, Harbury asked for the body. When they dug up his grave, she used forensics to prove they had swapped another body for his. Why? To hide that they had tortured the high-ranking comandante for information on the Maya-led uprising against the genocidal dictatorship. Harbury's incredible tale culminates in her testimony before Congress, triggering CIA reforms at the close of the Cold War.

Her searing 1997 memoir *Searching for Everardo: A Story of Love, War, and the CIA in Guatemala* recounts her difficult hunger strikes in 1993 in Guatemala City, which threatened to pierce the husk of Guatemalan impunity. As the Bámaca-Harbury Affair turns thirty, a new Democratic administration is using bipartisan buzzwords and unfair deals with Mexico to block asylum hearings. Reflecting the cruel, illegal policy, Vice President Kamala Harris traveled in June 2021 to Guatemala, and told would-be refugees from a region that the US has helped destabilize, "Do Not Come." Harbury's story highlights why this is wrong. As Suketu Mehta says, speaking for immigrants and refugees arriving in Western countries, "We are here, because you were there."

Recruited by a Fictional Character

Efraín Bámaca Velázquez was born to a campesino family in El Tablero in San Marcos. The hamlet located in Guatemala's southwest was a "very poor and isolated place," where his parents worked on a plantation earning "wages of hunger." "Like many compañeros," he told Harbury, "I grew up on a coffee plantation. My family is Mayan. So of course we were not the owners—only the serfs. My father labored long, hard hours in the fields, just to keep us alive."[1]

From a young age, Bámaca Velázquez worked picking coffee. His mother died because the family "had no money for doctors or medicine."[2] Simple antibiotics would have saved her. With no one there to care for Bámaca Velázquez and his sisters (one caretaker had beaten them), they spent their days hungry until their father returned from the fields. When Bámaca Velázquez was old enough to work in the cornfields, he worked long days, wishing he could study in the nearby school. He learned to read by going to church with his grandparents.

In Harbury's *Bridge of Courage*, he says he began to run away to the mountains at sixteen. Like many young people, he wanted time to think, to analyze his alienation and the harsh injustices in his homeland, "time to be a person, instead of a donkey."[3] Sometimes he took friends into the hills. On one trip, they met "compañeros," guerrilla fighters who talked to him and his friends like they were intelligent. Among them was Rodrigo Asturias, son of the author Miguel Ángel Asturias.

"Rodrigo was not one to sit at home and write," Harbury recalls. "He had once worked openly for reforms and had seen .... his civilian friends .... hunted down and killed and he himself came under frightening reprisals .... he learned that the only chance for genuine change was through an armed revolution."[4] To protect his identity, Asturias adopted the *nom de guerre* "Gasper Ilom." The name came from his father's novel, *Men of Corn*.

Up in the hills, Asturias discussed history with the youngsters and gave them books. As high as Asturias climbed in the armed resistance, his bird's-eye view of his homeland was not unlike Bámaca Velázquez's, "even though he came from the other end of the social ladder." "You can imagine what they meant to me, and how I loved them," Bámaca Velázquez recalled of meeting them.

As he shared ideas with Bámaca Velázquez, "Asturias saw a society not unlike South Africa's." It was "a nation where the great majority were Mayan peasants, the original inhabitants, yet where the Mayans had no political rights, no lands, and no power."[5] "Eighty percent were illiterate," Harbury recalls,

> and eighty percent suffered from malnutrition so severe that the average village woman was under five feet tall, with bones too frail to heal after breaking. The infant mortality rate was one of the highest in the hemisphere. Minimum wage did not cover basic dietary needs, let alone housing or health care. Any civil rights efforts were crushed with a frightening cruelty. All this went on as the tiny blond and blue-eyed upper class enjoyed the greatest of wealth and luxury, and looked down upon the villagers.[6]

Bámaca Velázquez returned from the mountain to see his family, and reflected on their suffering. But now it seemed cruel—more unfair and unnecessary than before. Asturias believed that the Maya majority should be reflected proportionately in the movement's leadership, and Bámaca Velázquez became the tenth member of the Organization of People in Arms, or ORPA.[7] Telling his sister three times that he would leave, she no longer believed him. But one day, as she called for his help chasing pests from the cornfields, she couldn't find him.

"And so it was that before dawn on my eighteenth birthday," he recalled, "I ran away from home once and for all, up the dark trails to join the compañeros."[8]

"A Tunnel So Dark"

Raised in Connecticut by a father who taught at Yale, Harbury went to college at Cornell. But at a time when the

National Guard was killing student protestors in the US during the Vietnam war, she left before graduating. On a journey of self-discovery, she backpacked from Switzerland to Afghanistan.

She decided she needed a law degree to do the civil rights work to which she felt committed, and in 1978 she graduated from Harvard Law School. Knowing she wanted to work in immigration rights, she moved to the border near the Rio Grande Valley. "I loved my work, and I spent my days with the farmworkers, learning some Spanish, hurrying to strike lines, and fighting for health rights, bilingual education, and [higher] minimum wages."[9]

When the White House flipped from Carter Democrats to Reagan Republicans, something changed. Harbury witnessed "thousands of Mayans swimming the Rio Grande and running in terror from the death squads and massacres in Guatemala. Their stories stopped me dead in my tracks. I didn't want to believe what I was hearing, for the cruelty and suffering they were describing left me in despair."[10]

As a result of the 1980 Refugee Act, asylum seekers are promised protections, even before the hearings to which they are entitled to prove their concerns. "A refugee is inherently a refugee even if a government hasn't yet made that determination," says International Rescue Committee immigration director Olga Byrne. "If you meet that definition and you're fleeing danger, you should not be penalized for your manner of entry, and you should not be turned away at the border to a country where you'd face persecution."[11]

But this legal assurance wasn't being afforded to these refugees. "A man covered with acid-burn scars, fresh from a torture chamber where his brother had died, was declared to have no reasonable fear of persecution should he be deported. That lit my fuse," she recalls.[12]

In 1985, Harbury moved to Guatemala to collect testimony on why so many were fleeing. Refugees arrived lacking documentation and Harbury thought her research might help when they arrived. She stayed for two years, as she told director Patricia Goudvis for the 1998 documentary *Dirty Secrets: Jennifer, Everardo, and the CIA in Guatemala.*

During that time, she lived in the homes of the Grupo de Apoyo Mutuo (GAM) or Mutual Aid Group, whom she describes as advocating for the Disappeared. Staying in their houses, she marched beside them, hoping that a foreigner's presence might prevent them from being killed.

On the National Plaza, she heard them cry: "They were alive when you took them. Give them back alive!"[13] But how did it get so dire?

"The truth is," recalls human rights activist Amilcar Mendez, "that ever since 1954, with the intervention of the CIA" in its coup against Jacobo Arbenz,

> *it's as if they put Guatemalan society in a tunnel so dark that none of us knew . . . . when morning would come. The persecution began with communists and anyone with progressive ideas. Many people were detained or disappeared. With the 1960s came military coups, military governments, fraudulent elections and then in the 70s and 80s, this whole process of violence that was fed by the CIA reached inconceivable levels.*[14]

Hundreds of thousands of poor Guatemalans like Bámaca Velázquez faced this tunnel of violence. Those fleeing, whom Harbury met at the border, were men and women running from terror, protected by law, but whom the administration sent back to the death squads.

Exchanging Spoons

"There is a crackled response" on their walkie-talkies, "and a sudden clattering of boots; then four other compañeros appear in the shadows," Harbury writes. "They look quickly at me, evaluating my readiness, then give me welcoming hugs . . ."[15] Hiking to the guerrilla base, Harbury climbs the Tajumulco Volcano, something of a midpoint on the American *cordillera*.*

Harbury has entered into guerrilla territory to meet, if not join, the armed resistance—who have taken up arms to defend themselves. On short rests, she is charmed by the forest and its defenders. "It is beautiful here, the sharp black outlines of the volcano etched against the night sky with its scattering of brilliant stars. A rich silence envelops us . . . We are out of the military's grim reach, and it is time to rest. We are safe."[16]

She crosses rivers, and even falls into one. But the compañeros help her out. One by one, she learns the fighters' names. In this cordillera of freedom, their sense of humor underscores their happiness, and she is brought into camp where she will interview the comandante.

Meeting Bámaca Velázquez, she expects a giant, given the respect in which his combatants hold him. But to her astonishment, he is soft spoken and curious, far from the alpha male stereotype in which media portray men like him.

---

*   The American Cordillera stretches from Hinton, Alberta in the foothills of the Canadian Rockies—where Peltier hid from the FBI—through the Sangre de Cristo Mountains in Momaday's childhood New Mexico, morphing into the Sierra Madre Oriental as it sidesteps Paz's Mexico City, continuing south to García Márquez's Andes.

"His mind is like an enormous vortex, spinning everything inward toward this hungry center," she recalls.

He asks "about public schools and private schools and field trips and museums and child nutrition programs and special education and my opinion on bilingual classes . . ." as well as the 1960s, "race rights and the Vietnam War, of details about Freedom Summer and descriptions of Jimi Hendrix and Janis Joplin and my evaluation of the impact of Watergate."[17]

At a celebration, they dance. She finds him gentle, humble, shy. When it becomes clear their feelings are mutual, he pulls her gently aside—into a kiss. She soon finds him conflicted. As they both realize, it is a doomed relationship. "I love you," he tells her, "but in this life it is all so impossible." They maintain an epistolary romance: each letter a risk to his safety.

When the separation weighs on them, they decide to spend spring in Mexico. It is 1991. The Cold War is ending—but not here. Not yet. He is summoned to Mexico for secret peace negotiations, and the secrecy infuses the first part of her memoir with the breathless urgency of a forbidden romance—the insider account of a spy thriller. They come to know each other better in Mexico, and she records this intimately. (Years later, some question they were ever married).

For Harbury—prone to statements like: "People think there is repression because of the armed revolution; there is an armed revolution because of the repression"—none of it is uncomplicated. Literarily, it is unusual. How many guerrilla fighters do you know any of the following about: flavor of their dreams, bits of diary entries, most recent playlist?

During a Mexican carnival, she watches Bámaca Velázquez use a pretend gun to win her a prize, making her "think about the fact that he has killed other human beings." To gauge his heart, she asks what it is like to kill. "Killing, he answers . . . is the most terrible task of the war . . . Lives must be taken in combat but not elsewhere. Prisoners should never be killed, for they are but brothers."[18] Fellow Maya are routinely kidnapped into the army, pitted against their own.

She dreams of having kids with him but finds that this is not possible. "He has learned that, inexorably, attachments bring pain."[19] Despite this, he is quietly considering marriage. Yet they cannot be sure they can even trust each other. "He cares for me, but how can he know I am not an infiltrator? . . . His heart trusts me but . . . the heart is the fastest route to betrayal."[20]

They share a time of peace, which he cherishes on a level she cannot fathom: "we curl up together on the sofa under an old blanket, he making notes for the next day's meetings while I try to read."[21] The subtext is like living with a condemned man. She memorizes his scars, tracing "the round white scar over his heart. A bit of shrapnel struck him in the breastbone . . . an old gash on his upper lip" and "a thick scar on his left arm."[22]

In Texas, they are married "in that small farmhouse in the woods." They pen their own vows, forging them together late into the night, "tailoring them to fit our notions of what a true marriage should be. We want no rings . . . Instead we decide on the compañero tradition from the mountains: We will exchange spoons."[23] No sooner are they married than he is called away, as the war has entered a critical new phase, "and the compañeros will either make great advances or suffer grim setbacks."[24]

Labyrinth of the Unthinkable

Late one evening, when Harbury is in New Hampshire, she gets a call. She is visiting a friend who is dying of cancer, and is expecting something related to this. But instead she hears static and the voice of a comrade in Spanish. "He offers no introduction, and for a moment I am disoriented." Gathering her thoughts, she listens to the voice's "repressed note of sadness and in that moment I know the unthinkable has happened."[25] Bámaca Velázquez has disappeared in a firefight at a river bend, and she rushes back to the Mexico-Guatemala border.

From the bits the compañeros are able to share with her, Harbury helps them reassemble the story of her husband's last battle. "The compas were out of the volcano . . . and in the dangerous terrain of the coffee plantations. Everardo knows the region like the back of his hand . . . On March twelfth they had divided up, the combatants going in different directions on different missions. The command post was hidden away at a bend in the river. Everardo stayed behind with half a dozen . . . of the most trusted compas to . . . coordinate the patrols."[26]

A young villager had come "to warn . . . that an army unit was nearby." Bámaca Velázquez and his troops frantically gathered their supplies, including maps, code books, and communications equipment, when suddenly "a hail of smoke and bullets broke out."

> They threw themselves to the ground and took cover in the deep foliage . . . Everardo was with Amílcar, but Amílcar was seriously wounded and lost consciousness. When he came to a few minutes later, the army was gone and the others were bending over him, frantically asking for Comandante Everardo. They combed

the area and found nothing—no boots, no backpack, no rifle, and no body. He had simply vanished.[27]

Harbury's fear was that the military had taken him alive in order to torture him for his knowledge of the organization that it is trying to eradicate. According to the reports, his alleged body was brought to an Army base called Retalhuleu. Wondering how to proceed, she proposes that they force the army to dig up the corpse.

"No one likes the subject," she recalls, "for they all loved Everardo."[28] One comrade "argues that I am quite mad. The body has been buried in a tropical trench for a month now. It will be horrifying and I am far too close to be clinical about this."[29] But she has no illusions.

To prepare, she studies videos of exhumations. First she convinces the comrades and then the army. Maneuvering through Guatemalan institutions, she is granted an exhumation. But the first of these is canceled at the last moment by Attorney General Asisclo.

"Asisclo," she writes, "is . . . saying that the exhumation must be canceled . . . because foreigners are present . . . My heart sinks. This is what they warned me about, the presence of foreigners raising the stakes too high." She tells "Asisclo that if our presence is a problem, we will gladly" leave "and wait. He turns a darker shade of red. This will not be good enough at all."[30]

Asisclo introduces a Catch-22. He declares that for the exhumation to continue,

> *Someone from the [Guatemalan National Revolutionary Unity guerrilla group] must come in person to identify the body. Are any of us from the URNG? The police crowd a bit closer and [her lawyer's] jaw drops open. The judge is white-faced and silent.*

A young man steps forward with a video and pans us carefully. Are any of us from the URNG? * ³¹

Harbury has withheld the fact that Bámaca Velázquez is her husband. With the exhumation canceled, she decides that this was a mistake. A wife could insist that the exhumation go forward. Following the law, she secures a second exhumation. This time, though, she declares herself to be his wife.

To find the body indicated in the report, the team she has assembled opens three graves—as several are piled on top of one another. Finally, the third corpse is said to be the alleged body taken at the river that day. But the cadaver is 15 years younger than Bámaca Velázquez. Shorter, with his skull smashed in, the young man's ankles and wrists are tied.

It is not Bámaca Velázquez, but the fact that the corpse doesn't match the military's description confirms that they lied. For Harbury, the lie suggests they are keeping him alive to torture him for information, as he is the highest-ranking fighter they have captured. If the military, accustomed to controlling the narrative, had expected to be vindicated by their bait and switch, Harbury has flipped the script.

Her hunch proves to be backed up by an eyewitness, a fighter named Santiago who escaped from a secret army prison. Harbury met him researching her first book. Santiago saw her husband alive on the day he disappeared and for several months afterward. He reported seeing him badly bloated from torture, with an officer named Alpírez standing over him, holding what appeared to be torture devices.³²

---

*   URNG is the united groups of leftwing guerrilla fighters.

A Hunger Artist

Interlaced with the exhumations is a series of meetings with Guatemalan and American officials, including the US Ambassador to Guatemala, Marilyn McAfee. Some of the meetings are triggered by Harbury's two hunger strikes, the second of which lasts a risky thirty-two days. McAfee appears gussied up for television, visiting Harbury at her encampment on the National Plaza during the month-long fast. Throughout their interactions, Harbury wrestles with the question of whether McAfee is on her side.

Initially, McAfee snipes at Harbury, directly or through proxies. One of McAfee's staffers remains skeptical. As Harbury petitions the embassy for help, the staffer plays bad cop and hectors or mansplains in response to her concerns. Given his odd countenance and consistent needling, she begins to refer to him as "Needle Nose." Downplaying the brutality of Guatemala's military, "Needle Nose" assures her

> that the guerrillas also kill all their prisoners of war. I tell him that this is ridiculous, that most of the compañeros have brothers who were forcibly recruited into the army and that they routinely release all their prisoners unharmed . . .[33]

She urges him to talk with a Guatemalan bishop

> who once retrieved a young prisoner from [a guerrilla front]. The army had refused to take the soldier back, claiming that he was a deserter and should be shot . . . After twelve months, the compañeros returned him to his home village and handed him over to the bishop for protection. The public meeting is on film.[34]

His point (that the guerrilla movement was equally responsible for reprisal killings and disappearances) has been refuted in multiple reports, including a UN study by the Commission for Historical Clarification. Despite her correct analysis, *Searching for Everardo* is filled with lacerating self-doubt. During a key moment with McAfee, Harbury is given a falsified report that makes her question Santiago's sighting of Everardo. The report places Everardo's body at the river, describing him perfectly. But she continues reading until the file includes two key words:

"Scars: none."

This, we know from Christmas 1991, is not her husband. "I remember Everardo's battered body, the faded gash in the upper lip."[35] She devises a new theory before American officials, who are left speechless, if muttering. "What happened, I tell McAfee, is that the army took Everardo alive, just exactly as Santiago told us. To conceal this from the outside world, they took another young man to the battleground . . . and beat him to death."

This, she says, was followed by press briefings in which they "announced that they had 'found' the cadaver of a guerrilla member out there and had sent the body to Retalhuleu [military base] for burial."[36] "When the [guerrillas] asked for a description," she adds, "the army sent a perfect description of Everardo, not of the young man. This international hoax was carried out . . . as they were sitting at the peace table with the URNG and discussing . . . human rights. Not good, I say. Not good."[37]

Her precise hypotheses frustrate the careerist officials, and she records each "deafening silence in the room . . . Needle Nose is appalled and says nothing at all." Another staffer's eyes fill with tears. "Marilyn McAfee is pale and motionless . . . . She is going to help me."[38]

Graverobbers?

Harbury's debriefings with General Mario René Enríquez Morales, the Guatemalan defense minister, are as frustrating as her discussions with Needle Nose. She pulls no punches in dialogue that stands out as satire powerful enough to make Asturias jealous. To the man in charge of the army, she repeats her allegations of army fraud.

"So you see . . . the army took Everardo alive and carried out an international hoax, faking his death so that he could be tortured in secret." Elucidating the coverup, Harbury insists that the general act, releasing her husband or charging him and arranging a trial. "Otherwise," she warns, "I am going to make one hell of a racket."[39]

Harbury is at her finest butting heads with two-bit despots, theirs and ours. "Enríquez keeps a studiously blank and courteous expression on his face, wincing only when I suggest he talk with Colonel Alpírez and Major Sosa Orellana." She depicts his wide smile as he responds. "Well, he says, this is all very tragic indeed, and he would be delighted to help me. But I must understand that the army never had my husband . . . this is just a terrible misunderstanding."[40]

Unaccustomed to fact checking, Enríquez is one of many who underestimate her. "They found a body. I myself say the body is not my husband's so they never had him. Who knows where he is? If I would just tell him where I *think* Everardo might be hiding out, Enríquez himself will be glad to escort me in person to the place in his own helicopter."

"Well, the problem," she says,

is last year the army gave a description of the body that matched Everardo feature by feature and to the

> centimeter. If they never had Everardo in the first place, where did they get the description and why did they send it? The body in the grave is completely different.[41]

"Well, he says, clearing his throat, the subversivos must have switched the body in the grave to make us look bad. They do things like that, you know."[42] She expresses her concern that her husband is being held in one of the well-known, "secret" military prisons.

"For many years now, the military has been accused of having secret prisons and secret prisoners," he acknowledges. "But even [President] de León Carpio," a former human rights official, "says there is no such thing. Haven't I heard? He gives a smug smile."[43]

"Well if there's no such thing," she replies, "how do you explain the case of Sister Dianna Ortiz? . . . a young and beautiful Ursuline nun who was kidnapped from a convent garden in Guatemala, placed in a police car, and taken to the [military's] Politécnica [base]. There she was gang-raped, left with more than one hundred cigarette burns on her back, and lowered into a pit filled with rats and humans, most of them dead, some of them dying."[44]

"She was a U.S. citizen," Harbury adds,

> and at the end of the day a mysterious North American came into the room and took her away. De Leon Carpio himself had denounced her case back when he was [still a human rights official].[45]

"Enriquez stiffens," she recalls, as her brazen reply "hits him between the eyes."[46]

"When I Stand, My Heart Beats Far Too Fast"

Faced with their record, officials reply in person and in writing that the Geneva Conventions do not apply; there is "no war in Guatemala, only illegal sedition, and that therefore no prisoners of war exist." "Reading the churlish answer," she recalls, "I gloat a bit, happy that the army is showing its true colors."[47] But she is going in circles. Ever curious and increasingly desperate, Harbury comes to believe that Enríquez may be speaking in code.

When he suggests that her husband may turn up at the Mexico-Texas border, she hopes he might be acknowledging a possible solution to their impasse. She pursues it, and he lights up; his "diplomatic" demeanor returns. "He tells me that he is quite pleased that I have come forward to clarify this matter and that I am quite right to offer to correct my mistakes. I interrupt and tell him that until I find Everardo alive, of course, I will be forced to continue my battle against the army . . . What else . . . can a wife do?"[48]

She stumps him, and he reveals his true colors. "She loves him even though he's a subversive, a villager, homely . . . " she overhears him muttering. "He does not mean this comment unkindly," she stipulates, "but the racism outrages me nonetheless. I protest sharply that Everardo is a beautiful man. Enríquez looks at me and shakes his head. That's love, he murmurs, clearly baffled."

Returning to the question of compromise, he adds "that perhaps, someday, he will attend our child's baptism up there in Texas."[49] But again she finds him stonewalling. McAfee too. Finally Harbury's multi-pronged activism settles on a House of Representatives Resolution warning of atrocities in Guatemala that might place the country in violation of the Leahy Law.

Building on the 1961 Foreign Assistance Act, the 1997 Leahy Law prohibits the United States from giving aid to countries in violation of human rights. Under any such resolution, her husband's case, brazen as it was, would offer key evidence. But Harbury stumbles upon "a copy of a letter sent by" McAfee "to [Maryland] Representative Connie Morella," who is drafting the resolution.

"It . . . requests certain modifications be made . . . I skim through the recommendations and stop dead at the line that asks for my case to be removed altogether. There is no request to remove the other human rights cases. Only ours . . ."[50]

This upsets her, and as she carries out a second hunger strike in the fall of 1994, her misery nearly causes her to commit suicide during her thirty-two-day hunger strike.[51] At her lowest point, healthcare workers check her vital organs and warn her. "My blood pressure is very low," she recalls. "When I stand, my heart beats far too fast. My left eyelid is drooping closed and will not obey my commands to remain open . . . how much longer will I last?"[52]

A Test Case

Enter *60 Minutes* reporter Mike Wallace, who presents Harbury with memos showing the US knew Bámaca Velázquez was taken alive, but lied to her. "So they have known all along," she recalls. "They have been watching me go through this hell, knowing all along and saying nothing." For five years, State Department and Central Intelligence Agency officials lied as she tried to save her husband from torture, while nearly killing herself with hunger strikes.

Livid and bereft, she recalls the army's "blistering campaign against me in the press, claiming that I am trying to destroy the Guatemalan economy, that it is all a hoax, that I actually gained weight during my hunger strike, that I am just after money for my book, that I could never have loved or married that uncultured indio Bámaca."[53]

In a meeting with Congressman Robert Torricelli of New Jersey, Harbury repeats her damning litany. Continuing her tale of mass graves and gaslighting, Torricelli grows "openly angry . . . He cuts me off in mid-sentence and says that . . . Everardo was indeed captured by the army and he was killed in 1992, upon orders of Colonel Julio Roberto Alpírez. Alpírez was a CIA asset . . . and he was also implicated in the death of Michael De Vine, an innkeeper and US citizen who was murdered by the army in 1990."[54] She learns, too, that the same day he was seen interrogating Bámaca Velázquez with torture devices, he was paid $44,000 by the US

Harbury once hoped to represent immigrants at the border in asylum cases. Then she married a "subversive" who was fighting for one battered side in another country's civil war. What was her point? "I want people to know what it feels like to have someone disappear in your family," she tells director Goudvis. "And I want people to understand what that . . . system of terror against a civilian population is about."[55]

The answer is impunity.

"If they kill my husband in the face of UN orders, OAS orders, Congressional and Senate resolutions and cries of protest from Amnesty, Americas' Watch, the Kennedy Center and [President Bill] Clinton . . . if they kill him in the face of that and get away with it, with total impunity, and no one does anything about it, who are they not gonna kill later? This is a test case. If they get away with this, they can get away with anything, and they know it."⁵⁶

Along with another widow of a husband murdered in Guatemala, Carol Ann DeVine, Harbury testified to the Senate on April 5, 1995, ending with a powerful plea: "The army is still the president," she began, adding,

> They control the courts. A judge rules wrong, he's dead. We have brave lawyers . . . like mine, who has a bomb go off in her office right after the exhumation . . . I'm therefore asking that if they continue to shoot, to murder, to torture, to rape . . . There are many things we can do. We can stop the training exercises. We can cancel their visas here . . . Why don't we extradite them? Why are we selling them helicopter parts? Why are we sending them bullets? . . . There are many things we can do to get a clear message through to the army, if [they] don't respect the law and if [they] don't respect the agreements in the peace process that [they] have just signed . . . I'm asking you to do that. It's too late for my husband. It's too late for Mrs. DeVine's husband. It's too late for both of us as women who loved their husbands. Please don't let it be too late for anyone else.

*

Long after Harbury's book was published, *The New York Times* reported that Ambassador McAfee was surveilled and targeted for blackmail. Guatemalan G-2 intelligence officers recorded McAfee at night engaged in baby-talk with her presumed lover, "Murphy." They listened as McAfee, a married woman, told Murphy—her secretary, they believed—how pretty she was, what a good girl she was, how much she loved her. A client of the CIA, G-2 had her over a barrel.[57]

Poised to blackmail McAfee not to go off script, not to speak out on human rights abuses like the Harbury-Bámaca affair, they threatened to leak the story of her illicit lesbian affair with her secretary (whose last name *was* Murphy). This, as Harbury warned, was the epitome of impunity. It was backed with inconceivable violence and cruelty—but also by startling ineptitude. These experts who listen in (tap tap, is this thing on?) missed a vital clue.

McAfee's dog was named Murphy.[58]

2009

Hard Choices:
Manuel Zelaya and Berta Cáceres on the Run

or how newly elected Democrats' refusal to say
"coup" affected two Hondurans

One of the first casualties of the Honduras coup was the nineteen-year-old son of a pastor who was shot in the back of the head by US-outfitted snipers. On July 5, 2009, Pastor Jose David Murillo, a well-known environmentalist, attended a rally in Tegucigalpa to welcome home the rightful Honduran president, Manuel "Mel" Zelaya, who planned to repatriate himself. Murillo, along with his wife and children, had come to Toncontín International Airport to meet Zelaya's plane a week after he was deposed. When the charter plane was denied landing rights—with trucks and a grounded 737 blocking the runway—the celebration turned into a protest.

Unbeknownst to Pastor Murillo, who had taught his children the value of peaceful resistance in his work against deforestation, Honduran military snipers had taken position on the airport's roof. Watching the president's plane veer back into the sky, the crowd that had come to welcome him—many of whom wore crimson and carried banners that read "Bloque Popular"—began shouting and pushing toward the runway. That's when the snipers shot live rounds and tear gas at the unarmed protesters.

"I stood up in front of the soldiers and cried, 'What are you doing? Do not attack us.' We had done nothing to provoke them," Murillo recalled. In the chaos, he was separated from his sons, including his nineteen-year-old, Isis Obed Murillo, the youngest of five. An hour later, he got a call from his oldest, who said that Isis had been shot in the back of the head by snipers. Ten minutes later, he was dead. When they identified their son that evening, Murillo's wife, Sylvia, said they "did not have any words sufficient to our grief."[1]

It was an eventful and tragic week for Hondurans. Zelaya had been arrested in the early morning hours the Sunday before and whisked out of the country. Like Guatemalan President Jacobo Arbenz fifty-five years prior, Zelaya was sent into exile in his pajamas.

The day of the coup, a referendum on reforming the Honduran constitution was scheduled. If approved by voters, a constitutional convention, or *constituyente*, would have designed a more inclusive constitution. "Zelaya was trying to re-create recent constitutional conventions in Ecuador, Bolivia, and Venezuela that had approved new constitutions expanding democratic rights and the power of Indigenous people, women, small farmers, and others at the bottom," writes Dana Frank, a history professor at the University of California, Santa Cruz.

Though the right-wing media in Honduras and the US painted this as an attempt to win Zelaya a constitutionally banned second term, the convention wouldn't have taken place until long after his term was up, Frank writes. In her 2018 book, *The Long Honduran Night: Resistance, Terror and the United States in the Aftermath of the Coup*, Frank tells of being blindsided by the overthrow, especially after it was certified by the Obama administration. Frank was an activist with the labor rights nonprofit USLEAP at the time of the coup. She said that the protests organized by a coalition of groups, what she calls the "resistance," were what most sustained her and her Honduran friends in the coup's aftermath, and deaths like those of Isis Obed Murillo were what haunted and motivated her.

The Honduran coup turns ten this summer, and the list of the dead grows, both inside Honduras and at the US border. The world's great democracy spent years debating whether children forcibly separated from their parents and placed in cages with no access to showers—and with limited due process—are considered to be in concentration camps. Against this backdrop, Frank's book is useful for understanding the United States' role in the tragedy at the border and its origin in Honduras. While one accusatory finger in Frank's pages points to distortions of the American right, many others point back at the previous Democratic administration for enabling the violence that helped send so many Hondurans into flight in the first place.

'From the Outset Let Us Bring You News of Your Protagonist'

Ramon Amaya-Amador was born in 1916 of a relationship between a priest and his secret lover. He wrote his first book while he was a schoolteacher in Olancho Province. According to one scholar, he "lacked the self-discipline to conform to small-town ways," and abandoned the classroom to begin working in Honduras's banana fields in the north. When industry stalled during the Depression, worsened by "yellow sigatoka" blight, Amaya-Amador joined the Communist Party and launched a magazine, *Alerta*. Serialized in *Alerta*, *Prision Verde* (Green Prison) became Amaya-Amador's—and Honduras's—"most famous novel."

Scholar Janet Gold recalls the 1950 novel's prophetic thrust: "By dramatizing the contrasting situations of local landowners who are convinced . . . to sell their land and one . . . who refuses," Gold writes, Amaya-Amador "creates sympathy for the independent-minded character only to . . . reveal that government troops in league with the foreign company force him off his land":

> The unhygienic living conditions in the camps, the dangers of working with pesticide-laden fruit, the absence of educational facilities for workers' children,

> *the government's corruption and complicity in the exploitation of Honduran citizens are just a few of the injustices ... in the novel. A leader emerges ... to lead a strike ... and the leader is killed, but his memory lives on to inspire a glimmer of hope.*[2]

Beyond the novel's litany of exploitation, *Prision Verde* "was uncannily prophetic, for on May 2, 1954, some 25,000 United Fruit Co. and 15,000 Standard Fruit Co. workers began a strike that lasted sixty-nine days. Workers from other sectors joined ... which finally resulted in official recognition of the right of workers to unionize, the creation of an eight-hour workday, overtime compensation, and paid vacations."[3]

As a result of fears of another Hugo Chavez in Honduras, all these and other gains would be attacked after the 2009 coup.

The Waffling Obama Administration

Elected in 2006, Zelaya was moving politically to the left when he was ousted. He brought Honduras into regional coalitions like Petrocaribe and the Bolivarian Alliance for the Peoples of Our America (ALBA), founded by Cuba and Venezuela in 2004. He was on the verge of signing over land to 300,000 small farmers to grow the country's working-class base. These moves were beyond the pale for the Northern Behemoth, and he was removed because of them.

The interim government of Roberto Micheletti that followed immediately began a program of repression to consolidate and legitimize the coup. But the countercoup, in the form of massive protests, sit-ins, and occupations of various offices, was immediate and widespread. A collision was coming: "The terror escalated," Frank writes; "one by one, activists disappeared or were assassinated." The message was clear; dissent would not be tolerated. During those first days of the coup, CNN, Radio Progresso, and Cholusat SUR were shut down. The government "shut off electricity to neighborhoods where protests were particularly strong. In Olancho, where [ousted President] Zelaya came from"—as did Amaya-Amador—"the military reportedly began breaking into houses and capturing young people, forcing others to flee into the hills."[4]

On July 11, two weeks after the coup and six days after Isis Obed Murillo was shot, Roger Bados—a local union president and anti-coup activist in San Pedro Sula—was shot to death by armed men. That night, three men boarded a bus in Santa Bárbara, ordered the opposition activist Ramón García off the bus, and murdered him.[5] A month later, police grabbed twenty-five-year-old Irma Melissa Villanueva from a protest in Choloma outside San Pedro Sula, and—according to Frank—"took her away to a remote location, where four policemen gang-raped her for hours. 'Now, bitch, you're gonna see what happens to you for being where you shouldn't be,' they told her." She told her story three days later. For her courage, she faced a second rape, this time with her family forced to watch. We'll "see if you report us this time," her attackers said.[6]

That fall, Micheletti suspended four articles of the constitution, "restricting freedom of transit, banning public meetings not authorized by security forces, and barring the media from criticizing the government—[while] thirty-five hundred to four thousand people had been illegally detained for peacefully demonstrating." On September 26, the thirty-sixth anniversary of the use of the national stadium in Chile to house political prisoners after the US-sponsored coup, the BBC published a photograph of a Honduran stadium being used to detain more than 600 political prisoners.[7] Wondering what she can do to assist, Frank also wonders if the Obama administration, sworn in just five months before the coup, could help?

"We knew that a coup attempt had been stopped in Bolivia the year before and that in 2002 a coup in Venezuela had been reversed after two days," she writes. "We could feel how surprisingly strong the Honduran resistance was. We knew that the Organization of American States and dozens of countries throughout Latin America and all over the world had condemned the coup ferociously and called for Zelaya's immediate restoration."[8] Was President Obama, the "Yes, we can!" candidate, a cause for hope?

In fact, the administration waffled. On the day of the coup, Obama spoke in general terms about respecting "the rule of law." The day after, Frank writes, the administration was "willing to call it a coup, but by mid-week the State Department had backed off from demanding Zelaya's immediate return."[9] "Despite the obviously criminal and illegitimate nature of the regime . . . the Obama administration began treating de facto President Micheletti as Zelaya's legitimate diplomatic equal."[10] Ten days after the coup, "Secretary of State Hillary Clinton announced that the United States had persuaded both sides to negotiations in San José, Costa Rica," thereby "successfully transferring power over the situation onto US-controlled terrain [sic] and away from" the Organization of American States (OAS), a majority of whose members "were adamant that Zelaya had to be returned to full powers."[11]

Furthermore, "Obama and Clinton pointedly refused to ever use the phrase 'military coup,' which would have legally obligated the United States to stop almost all foreign aid to Honduras immediately," Frank writes.[12] She addresses a question that hung in the air: Did the US pre-approve this coup, as it had so many times past? "We don't yet have concrete evidence that the United States promoted the coup or approved it in advance," Frank acknowledges. "We do know that the plane in which the Honduran military flew Zelaya out of the country stopped to refuel at Soto Cano Air Force Base, a joint US-Honduran base, and we can presume that it would not have done so without US permission." Is that all? "We know that four of the six top generals who oversaw the coup were trained by the United States at the School of the Americas/Western Hemisphere Institute for Security Cooperation in Fort Benning, Georgia, and that it is unlikely that they would have perpetrated a coup without US approval."[13] Citing *The Intercept*, Frank reports further that "top Honduran military officials attended a party thrown by the US Embassy's defense attaché. At nine o'clock that night, Kenneth Rodriguez, the commander of US forces in Honduras, left the party to meet with [Honduran] General Romeo Vazquez Velasquez, then returned to the festivities. The next morning, Vazquez led the coup."[14]

By claiming that it did its best to discourage this coup, the Obama administration tacitly admits to know about it in advance. Writing in *The Guardian*, Mark Weisbrot wonders what that discouragement might have sounded like: "Did administration officials say, 'You know that we will have to say that we are against such a move if you do it, because everyone else will?' Or was it more like, 'Don't do it, because we will do everything in our power to reverse any such coup'? The administration's actions since the coup indicate something more like the former, if not worse."[15]

Media Blockade, North and South

Like their US counterparts, many Honduran newspapers "loved the coup," Frank writes. "They were full of fantastic, alarmist fictions: Zelaya is a drug dealer! The Venezuelan and Nicaraguan armies are amassed at the Honduran border, ready to invade to restore him!"[16] As US media have done with anti-leftist demonstrations in Venezuela, the Honduran media considered small gatherings in support of the coup as significant, while ignoring protests denouncing the coup that were attended continuously by hundreds of thousands of activists. "To its eternal shame," Frank writes, "[the newspaper] *La Prensa* even ran a doctored photo of the men at the airport carrying the body of Isis Obed, the young man killed by government snipers, in which the blood streaming down from his head had been airbrushed out."[17]

While the interests of the elite were amplified in the media, "President" Micheletti continued to preside over a regime of violent censorship. He confiscated the equipment of broadcast stations that questioned the official narrative of the coup plotters, closing down such stations as Radio Progreso or ordering them off the air, as happened with "three radio stations and television Channel 36." The opposition called this blockade the *cerco mediatico*. Frank recalls how in the US she too "ran head-on into our own *cerco mediatico*."[18]

Although she estimates that about half of the coup opponents had been opposed to Zelaya during his incumbency, media outlets like The Associated Press reduced the opposition to "Zelaya supporters," or even (as the AP wrote), "die-hard supporters of ousted President Zelaya," "implying that the opposition was merely fanatical groupies who should have politely given up long before." That Zelaya had sought a second term was the right-wing shibboleth that US media would not let die. *Newsweek* "even uncritically quoted Jorge Castaneda of Mexico claiming Zelaya was illegally trying to get a third term,"[19] though there'd been no second term.

Indeed, the dishonesty of *The Wall Street Journal*'s Mary Anastasia O'Grady stands out. With such headlines as "Honduras Defends Its Democracy: Fidel Castro and Hillary Clinton Object" and with opening paragraphs that read, "It seems that President Mel Zelaya miscalculated when he tried to emulate the success of his good friend Hugo [Chavez] in reshaping the Honduran Constitution to his liking,"[20] one sees the paralytic wing of establishment media trying to push the newly elected Obama to the right. "Those few academics who did have knowledge of Honduras" seldom "stepped in to challenge the administration's narrative," according to Frank.[21] Was this the result of timidity after the high emotions surrounding Obama's election, the slow caution of academics, or both?

Don't Be Shy, Madame Secretary

With President Obama getting hammered in the right-wing media for his gestures toward following the law, and with little support from the already marginalized left, the administration began to stall for elections coming that fall. But given Honduras's media blackout, its abridgement of the constitution, and its war on the opposition, the outcome was a foregone conclusion: "Ongoing repression of basic civil liberties made a free and fair election clearly impossible," writes Frank, "while the very same army that perpetrated the coup controlled the physical ballots. All international bodies—including the United Nations, the Carter Center, and the OAS, with the exception of the US Republican Party and a few delegates from the Democratic Party—refused to observe the process."[22]

Emerging from one of two right-wing parties that dominated Honduras's two-party system, Porfirio Pepe Lobo assumed the presidency. This sent the signal that violence and impunity would continue. With the administration looking for an escape from this trap, given its legal obligations to defund any officially declared coup, Assistant Secretary of State Thomas Shannon wrote Secretary Clinton to suggest the US merely wash its hands of the entire mess.

"As we think about what to say, I would recommend that we not be shy. We should congratulate the Honduran people, we should connect today's vote to the deep democratic vocation of the Honduran people, and we should call on the community of democratic nations (and especially those of the Americas) to recognize, respect, and respond to this accomplishment of the Honduran people."[23] There was nothing shy and everything shameless about this stance.

More Spaces for Our People?

"High on the list" of Lobo's spoils, Frank writes, was a radical revanchist economic agenda—a rollback of good laws. One hard-won advance for Honduras that was reversed, the Land Reform Law, dates back to the decade after the 1954 strike, with the result that the years 1973 to 1977 were sometimes dubbed the "Golden Age" of land reform. In fact, 120,000 hectares of land were distributed to *campesinos* during those years. According to one scholar, "Over three decades a total of 409,000 hectares (the equivalent of 12.3% of the agricultural area of Honduras) were handed over to 60,000 peasant families (or . . . 13% of the rural population)."[24]

But post-coup, campesinos were murdered, their homes within legally redistributed lands were burned, and thugs forced them out of their homes with the threat of armed violence, although the leadership hoped to overwrite this violent expropriation with a legal screen.

To speed up the theft of these lands on behalf of the "market," a scheme was born that Frank calls "so far-fetched it seemed unthinkable."[25] Spread via a viral TED Talks brainstorm, the "charter cities" proposal sought to redraw cities outside a nation's usual rule of law or sovereignty where others could migrate, or "vote with their feet."[26] The initiative would, in practice, appear to liberate markets from human, labor, and civil rights protections won via historic struggles and inscribed into the Honduran constitution or reflected in other laws, such as the Land Reform Law.

The mastermind behind the proposal was Paul Romer, a New York University economist, who argued that cities in the developing world should be allowed to develop free of regulations and under the watchful eye of a first-world economy—a Big Brother economic protectorate (Romer would later head up the World Bank as its chief economist). Grover Norquist, the no-regulation mastermind behind the Tea Party who also helped create Trump's birther narrative against Obama, sat on Romer's advisory committee.

At the "Honduras is Open for Business" conference, Mexican entrepreneur Carlos Slim was slated to talk, as was former President Bill Clinton, who eventually pulled out. "Whether the event generated any actual investments was unclear," Frank writes, "but it certainly generated a host of mocking parodies in the solidarity world up North: 'Honduras, Open for Repression.' 'Honduras, Busted Open for Business.'"[27]

A few weeks later, presidents Juan Manuel Santos of Colombia and Hugo Chavez of Venezuela announced a deal they had finalized with the Lobo regime, which allowed for Zelaya, who had been holed up in the Brazilian embassy, to return legally to his homeland. "The Cartagena Accord, as it was known, contained three key provisions: first, all criminal charges against Zelaya and his top ministers, still in exile as well, would be annulled. Second, the government of Honduras would commit itself to protecting human rights. Third—and here the plot thickens—a legal path would be made clear for the National Front of Popular Resistance to become a political party."[28] Also known as the FNRP, this was the coalition of labor, land reform advocates, government opposition, and former establishment figures surrounding the ousted Zelaya. Unfortunately, rank-and-file members had recently voted *not* to enter electoral politics, but rather to work outside the party apparatus—this third provision therefore threatened a rift in the coalition.

But Zelaya finally came home and Honduras was then back in the OAS. When Obama appeared with Lobo in the Oval Office, the US leader proclaimed, "Today begins a new chapter in the relationship between our two countries. In part because of pressure from the international community, but also because of the strong commitment to democracy and leadership by President Lobo, what we've been seeing is a restoration of democratic practices and commitment to reconciliation that gives us great hope." Lobo responded by noting, "We have affirmed our democratic vocation. We have reaffirmed the road to democracy that we are on and that we will be continuing on. We will be opening even more spaces for our people to be able to express themselves."[29]

The US president's optimism would prove premature. In fact, only one month after the accord, "even more spaces" were *closing off* to Hondurans, certainly to members of the Campesino Movement of Rigores, a town in the northern Aguan Valley where peasants were being brutalized into leaving their homes. During a typical incident on June 24, Frank writes, "the Honduran police and the military destroyed almost the entire campesino community... turning a seven-room schoolhouse, three churches, a community center, and more than a hundred houses into burnt-out rubble in a single afternoon. The nearly 500 residents had an hour's notice to pull out their belongings, then watched as their homes were torched by security forces and crushed by a bulldozer."[30] No judge was present at the site and so the order was illegal.[31]

Nor would these "new spaces" for Honduran self-expression apply at work. In September, the Lobo administration passed the Employment Law, "breaking up full-time jobs and turning them into part-time, temporary employment ineligible for unionization or the government's system of healthcare and pensions," Frank writes. In October, members of Operation Xatruch, a military-police task force deployed to aid in fighting crime and resolving the land conflict, "captured, detained without charges, and tortured Walter Nelin Sabillón Yanos," a campesino land activist. "Sabillón testified... that while... in detention... authorities beat him, repeatedly placed a hood on his head, and... applied electric shock to his hands, abdomen and mouth while interrogating him about the campesino movement," Frank writes.[32] One of the richest landholders, Miguel Facussé, whose private security guards exchanged police and military uniforms for plain clothes when convenient—all while torturing and killing campesinos—even appeared in a US diplomatic cable, collaborating with drug cartels.

After helping break Honduras's institutional safety nets, the Obama administration didn't appear to know how to fix things using the same dynamite with which it had broken them. Yet it wasn't Obama himself, but one of his former Cabinet members (and the people of Honduras) who would pay the price.

Model City Rollout, Interrupted

In May 2012, Adam Davidson (of NPR's "Planet Money" podcast) published a profile with the honest title, "Who Wants to Buy Honduras?"[33] As Frank points out, the article was accompanied by an "outrageous cartoon that depicted a broad, green jungle, punctuated only by a tiny city in the middle, rising amid construction cranes. A yellow plane flew over the city carrying a banner reading 'THE NEW HONDURAS, EST 2010.' In front, a sign poked up out of the jungle reading 'GOOD HONDURAS,' with an arrow pointing toward the city, and 'BAD HONDURAS,' with an arrow pointing off the page. A second sign read: 'WELCOME TO THE NEW HONDURAS (DON'T WORRY, IT'S NOT REALLY HONDURAS).'"[34]

Featuring a short profile of Romer and his big idea, the article admitted that Romer, "who is expected to be chairman [of the area carved out of Honduras], is hoping to build a city that can accommodate 10 million people, which is 2 million more than the current population of Honduras." Davidson adds that Romer's "[model] city will have extremely open immigration policies to attract foreign workers from all over. It will also tactically dissuade *some* from coming. Singapore, Romer said, provides a good (if sometimes overzealous) model. Its strict penalties for things like not flushing a public toilet may make for late-night jokes, but they signal to potential immigrants that it is a great place if you want to work hard and play by the rules."³⁵ Before Donald Trump told Hondurans that they weren't good enough to come across the border into the US, in other words, Obama administration allies told them that they weren't good enough for their own country.

Two days after Honduras was declared "open for business," in the pre-dawn hours of May 15, 2012, "two State Department helicopters carrying Honduran security forces and US 'advisors' from a DEA FAST team shot and killed four Afro-Indigenous Honduran civilians—two of them pregnant—and injured four others," writes Frank.³⁶ Claiming falsely that the Drug Enforcement Administration agents had participated only in an advisory role, the State Department distanced itself from the action. Assistant Secretary of State Victoria Nuland deferred to an investigation underway by Honduran authorities.³⁷ Frank calls that investigation, which was skewed to protect the state murders, "incompetent, corrupt and extremely limited."³⁸

The government of Honduras "used its autopsy report to insist that [one of the women killed] wasn't in fact pregnant."³⁹ State Department staff even showed a selectively edited video to members of Congress attempting to prove that the victims fired on the agents, telling those who hoped to analyze the video further that it was classified. But five years later, a 400-page report by the Office of the Inspector General of the US Department of Justice confirmed the version reported by the victims and their families. "DEA agents had in fact been in the helicopter yelling at the Honduran forces to 'FIRE, FIRE,' on the victims in the boat," Frank writes. Video segments, in fact, "didn't show any fire from the victims' boat at all—but it did show shots from the other boat aimed at the victims. The Inspector General concluded that both the DEA and the State Department had misinformed and misled Congress and the public and then obstructed the subsequent investigation."[40]

For a while, US media actually paid attention and Congress wrote memos threatening to withhold funds, which had been the key to Frank's previously fruitless campaigns. Between early 2012 into mid-2014, the Obama administration was largely on the defensive over its post-coup Honduras policy—rightly so, as Frank and other Honduras-watchers published scathing indictments of its failures. The murder rate in Honduras rose (on its way to the world's highest), women became unsafe (with Honduras becoming the world's most unsafe place for women), police corruption grew rampant, and human rights failed to improve.

To stop the bleeding, Lobo flew to Miami to meet with senior US officials. Vice President Joe Biden flew to Mexico and Honduras. Mexico and Guatemala wanted to decriminalize cocaine, because the renewed US war on drugs was not working. During his visit, Frank wrote that the administration "sought to adeptly reframe the police corruption scandal, the murder rate statistics, and alarm over human rights abuses by US-funded security forces, all within the rubric of the drug war: police killings were subsumed under a generic 'security crisis,' and the 'security crisis' was the result of drug trafficking."[41] Yes, drug trafficking was a reality. But to put it in context, it helps to recall the degree of corruption that the Obama administration tolerated and sponsored. For example, when Honduras's supreme court banned model cities because the plan invalidated the Honduran constitution (arguably a worse outcome than Zelaya's protections for poor people), the legislature—under Juan Orlando Hernandez's direction—illegally replaced four of the justices.

By 2014, when Hernandez assumed the presidency after a highly irregular election, he was in control of the courts (which he had filled with friendly justices), as well as the legislature, in which he'd played a leadership role, as well as the military and police, which Lobo and the post-coup regime had continuously conflated. Laws were passed shielding the government from accountability. Eighty percent of criminal cases weren't prosecuted. Ties between drug traffickers and officials were growing evident. The director of national police, Tiger Bonilla, was leading death squads. For the US to continue working with Bonilla was a violation of the Leahy law. But officials created a *Catch-22*-style workaround that effectively said, "Even though he was the head of police, we will work only with people in the force who aren't him, although every single one of them" *works for him*. The US even turned out to be lying about this. It actually worked directly with Bonilla.

Corruption watchdog Sarah Chayes wrote that under the post-coup regimes in Honduras, "It is no longer possible to think of corruption as just the iniquitous doings of individuals. Corruption is the operating system of sophisticated networks that link together public and private networks and out-and-out criminals—including killers." Chayes linked Honduran emergency migration to corruption enabled by the US, faulting US support explicitly. "Urban violence and out-migration . . . are by-products of the corruption of the very government that enjoys US (and European Union) support to combat those ills."[42]

The Caravans

In June 2014, the website Breitbart ran a story with the headline, "Leaked Images Reveal Children Warehoused in Crowded US Cells, Border Patrol Overwhelmed." The article reprised a UN report investigating why Central American children were fleeing their countries, unsupervised by adults. The site followed that story, seemingly motivated by humanitarian concern, with the headline, "8 Reasons to Close the Border Now." Among those reasons, it alleged "disease," "threat of terrorism," "safety of U.S. citizens," and "American culture is under attack." In other words, right-wing distortions. A third Breitbart story came out the same day: "More than Half of Central American Immigrants on Welfare."[43] CBS News and the *Los Angeles Times* followed suit. And the media also claimed that "fifty-seven thousand undocumented, unaccompanied minors from Central America had swarmed across the border from Mexico," with more on their way.[44] Frank writes, "Overall, this transformation of the public conversation in the United States about Honduras was stunning, and rapid—it took only around three weeks." She continues:

> *In the right-wing version, children were taking advantage of lax border enforcement to invade the country, posing a national security threat. In the liberal version, gangs and drug traffickers were producing terrifying violence in Honduras, making children flee northward, where they were met with scary conditions within the US border enforcement system.*[45]

With midterm elections looming, 2014 was a turning point. Up to that point, activists had been making modest progress in challenging US funding to a country ruled by illegitimate, irregularly elected, or unelected leaders who presided over a system that murdered or jailed journalists, activists, and the opposition, and whose anti-corruption measures appeared toothless and designed to appease

State Department sponsors without actually challenging the leadership. Now, the story shifted to border crossings, gangs, and drugs. The context was erased.

Indeed, even Frank herself turned to writing about gangs and drug traffickers. But unlike most of the newly urgent coverage of Honduras, she added important caveats that contextualized the gangs as having a history while showing the hard work that activists, judges, journalists, teachers, honest politicians, and other civil society upstanders had been trying to achieve in a society otherwise wrecked by support from the giant to the North.

"But let's be clear," she writes, "those gangs and drug traffickers took over a broad swath of daily life in Honduras in part because the elites who ran the government permitted and even profited from it. Who was the gang, in this story? ... The judiciary was [now] largely corrupt; the criminal justice system functioned to protect the crooked and the murderous. The police were deeply interwoven with the gangs and drug traffickers." In short, it was yet another US-funded quagmire.[46]

Ax Murderers for Allies

In a 2015 *New York Times* op-ed titled "A Plan for Central America," Vice President Biden helped the administration manage the destruction it had wrought by promising three things: first, security (though he alludes to his role in crafting the punitive 1994 Crime Bill as a measure of his skills); second, transparency (though under the same leadership that the US had championed in the previous six years); and third, international investment (though the chaos wrought by the rampant impunity would make it difficult to attract such investments).[47]

Since lots of money hadn't worked before, the administration threw lots more at Honduras ($1 billion newly pledged). It did so while maintaining its decision not to hamstring the money with any real accountability. It did get the Honduran leadership under Juan Orlando Hernandez to agree to some on-paper anti-corruption measures, with Transparency International's logo affixed. But by now it was clear that the United States would send money no matter what.

Much of the American cash was spent on billboards promising children that if they left the disorder in Honduras—where certain death lurked—and hired a coyote to pursue life in the North, they would be equally doomed.

While the funding ballooned, the failure of the rule of law in Honduras got so bad that when Frank happened to see then-Secretary of State John Kerry in a Washington, D.C., restaurant in 2016, she introduced herself and said she was working on Honduras policy. "How are we doing down there?" Kerry asked. "We're supporting the ax murderers," she said, and walked off.[48]

The Murder of Berta Cáceres

The altar carved into the rock at La Gruta in La Esperanza honors the shelter that these caves provided to Hondurans hiding from their enemies. In the courtyard beneath is where Berta Cáceres was given a final mass before being buried in this coldest Honduran city. Cáceres grew up during the dirty wars and disappearances in Central America that were largely funded by the United States. In Guatemala, an estimated 200,000 people—mostly Indigenous—were killed. In El Salvador, US-funded counterinsurgency operations contributed to an estimated 70,000 killed between

1980 and 1992. Cáceres's mother, Austra Bertha Flores, a midwife, sheltered and cared for these refugees. Later serving as mayor, Austra Bertha taught her children the importance of solidarity in defense of the disenfranchised.

In 1993, Cáceres founded the National Council of Popular and Indigenous Organizations of Honduras. Its mission was to better the lives of Indigenous Lenca people in the face of illegal logging and regional territorial disputes. Cáceres's work against the Agua Zarca dam began in solidarity with the people of Rio Blanco, who told her that mysterious construction equipment had appeared there. At the time, dams were being planned all over Honduras as a means of amping up the country's electrical power capacity to fuel a patchwork of new mines. A joint project of Desarollos Energeticos, S.A., (DESA) and Chinese state-owned Sinohydro, the Agua Zarca dam targeted the Gualcarque River, a waterway protected for the Indigenous because it is culturally and environmentally crucial to the Lenca.

Using a variety of means to maintain pressure—petitions, court actions, international appeals to the rule of law and Indigenous rights, plus roadblocks that denied access to the site—protesters were tireless, and the Chinese investors withdrew. Death threats followed. In order to protect Cáceres and honor her important work, she was given a battery of high-level meetings (with the Pope, for instance) and such awards as the 2015 Goldman prize, which "honors grassroots environmental heroes." In Cáceres's case, the award was given to her for "a grassroots campaign that successfully pressured the world's largest dam builder to pull out of the Agua Zarca Dam,"[49] and resulted in a celebration at then House Minority Leader

Nancy Pelosi's office. But these were Cáceres's last days and they were numbered.

Before her death, she witnessed colleagues like Rio Blanco community leader Tomás García shot and killed while protesting. Other activists were attacked by machete, discredited, arrested arbitrarily, and tortured. In 2016, while on a trip to the region, the Mexican environmentalist Gustavo Castro visited Cáceres to use her internet. When he learned she was living alone and unprotected, he insisted on staying over. That night, in the pre-dawn hours of March 3—a day before her forty-fifth birthday—assassins entered her house and shot Cáceres and Castro. Having surprised the assassins, whose surveillance had assured them that she lived alone, Castro survived the shooting by playing dead. When they left, Cáceres died in Castro's arms as he awaited medical assistance.

Authorities initially tried to pin the murder on Castro, launching a whisper campaign suggesting a crime of passion. They detained him as suspect rather than victim, illegally suspending his lawyer. His own government was blocked from advocating for his rights. But culpability inevitably pointed back to the military and privatized security teams associated with DESA, whose members had trained at Fort Benning, Georgia, the former School of the Americas.

Cáceres's final mass took place on the steps beneath La Gruta, dedicated to the Virgin of the Immaculate Conception. The environmentalist's casket was surrounded by thousands of grief-stricken supporters, many of whom vowed to continue her work. The first of the now ubiquitous photographs of her joyous face were held up by the crowd.

The DESA-tied suspects were eventually convicted. While gratified that there was some closure, her family—speaking through Cáceres's oldest daughter, Olivia—believed that the verdict represented only partial justice. Honduran leadership, funded by the US, should also be held accountable, as should the US itself.

Cáceres's Voice and the Presidency

By certifying a coup eight years before, Frank argues, the Obama administration was stuck with and responsible for the highly corrupt President Hernandez, who presided over the world's highest per-capita murder rate and the most dangerous country for women. For Democrats, the outcome would turn to a more direct form of fiasco, though one that was far less publicized than the one in Iraq. The Honduras nightmare would nevertheless play into the sobering defeat of Obama's coronated successor.

In a 2014 interview that resurfaced after the assassination, Cáceres responds to Democratic presidential nominee Hillary Clinton's justification for her Honduras policies in her memoir, *Hard Choices*:

> *We're coming out of a coup that we can't put behind us. We can't reverse it. It just kept going. And after, there was the issue of the elections. The same Hillary Clinton, in her book,* Hard Choices, *practically said what was going to happen in Honduras. This demonstrates the meddling [note the word choice] of North Americans in our country. The return of the president, Mel Zelaya, became a secondary issue. There were going to be elections in Honduras. And here, she, Clinton, recognized that they didn't permit Mel Zelaya's return to the presidency. There were going to be elections. And the international community—officials,*

> the government, the grand majority—accepted this, even though we warned this was going to be very dangerous and that it would permit a barbarity, not only in Honduras but in the rest of the continent. And we've been witnesses to this.[50]

Cited widely in US media, Cáceres's words were another form of Latin American history's long arc, bending toward justice, however sloppily, in this case as a kind of imprecise blowback. But other examples were cleaner: in 2022, ousted President Mel Zelaya's wife, Xiomara Castro was elected as Honduras's first woman president.[51] And in 2023, Bernardo Arévalo was elected as an anti-corruption candidate for president of Guatemala. His father, Juan José Arévalo, had become president after a teachers' strike toppled US-backed dictator Jorge Ubico, spawning the republic's "Democratic Spring."

But as mentioned above, this democracy was abridged by the US-sponsored overthrow of Arévalo's successor, Jacobo Arbenz. And yet another coup overthrew dictator Ydigoras Fuentes's regime in 1963, in part because its rampant corruption was lending momentum to the democratic candidacy of Arévalo the Elder, who campaigned against the dictatorship for a second term, and for democracy's return. And so, it was a long arc from father to son.

Although Arévalo the Younger is expected to take office on January 14, 2024—nearly sixty years after his father's second term was blocked—as I write, one of Guatemala's conservative bastions, the electoral registry, has voted arbitrarily to disband Arévalo's party, the SEED Movement Party. Arévalo has vowed to appeal this decision.[52]

ACKNOWLEDGEMENTS

Immense thanks to the people of Gaza, their relatives and their allies for teaching us what true courage in the face of unrelenting horror looks like.

Thanks to Joe Baker, Hadrien Coumans & Curtis Zuniga for your inspirational work at the Lenape Center; for trusting me on various collaborations and for your work unerasing the previously erased. Thanks to Joe and Hadrien for reading this book, too. Thanks to scholar and historian Heather Bruegl (citizen of the Oneida Nation & first-line descendant Stockbridge Munsee) for giving the essays the historical accuracy test and helpful suggestions around Leonard Peltier, Anna Mae Aquash, AIM, and more. Thanks to my first and early readers: Jake Whitney, Stephen Kosloff, Chase Madar, Stephen Reynolds and Regina Lenaburg. Two thirds of the chapters were published as book and film review essays. Thanks to the brilliant writers and filmmakers whose books and films proved their subjects' minds timely (and timeless) again: Imani Perry and Tracy Heather Strain on Lorraine Hansberry, in *Looking for Lorraine* and *Sighted Eyes/Feeling Heart*; Richard Greene, Norman Sherry and Jonathan Naschel for work on Graham Greene and his dispute with Edward Lansdale; Martin Duberman, Gerald Horne and Paul Robeson, Jr., for work on the great Paul Robeson; Gerald Martin, Ilan Stavans, Angel Esteban and Stephanie Panichelli for work on Gabriel Garcia Marquez, and the archivists at Princeton University's Firestone Library for access to Emir Rodriguez Monegal's papers;

Rachel Blau duPlessis and Eric Hoffman for work on George and Mary Oppen.

Thanks to Peniel Joseph, Abdur-Rahman Muhammad, Rachel Dretzin and their colleagues for insights on the life and death of the great Malcolm X; Eliot Weinberger for translations and knowledge of Octavio Paz; Patrick Marber for work on Diego Rivera; Shola Lynch for her film on Angela Davis, *Free Angela & All Political Prisoners*; Nick Estes, Ned Blackhawk & Kevin McKiernan for work on the American Indian Movement.

Thanks to Jeffrey Palmer and Jill Scott Momaday for work on N. Scott Momaday in respective films, *Words From A Bear: N. Scott Momaday* for American Masters & *Return to Rainy Mountain*; David Unger for his translation of *El senor presidente*, as well as Gerald Martin, again, Patrick Iber and Russell Cobb for work on Miguel Angel Asturias; Dawn Gifford Engle, Greg Grandin and Elizabeth Burgos-Debray for work on Rigoberta Menchu, and RM herself for her vision and courage; Patricia Goudvis for work on Jennifer Harbury and Efrain Bámaca Velázquez; Dana Frank for work on Honduras in the aftermath of the June 2009 coup in *Long Honduran Night*.

Thanks to Seymour Hersh for his lifelong work captured so well in *Reporter*, and for sitting down with me onstage in Brooklyn and in Washington, D.C.; thanks to James Risen for sitting down with me and more; and to Frances Stonor Saunders for her illuminating *The Cultural Cold War* and for sitting down with me to discuss the book›s birth and near-death.

Pieces in this book were published previously in magazines, in print and online, with thanks to editors: Micah Utricht, Shawn Gude and John-Baptiste Oduor at *Jacobin*; *The Baffler*'s Chris Lehmann and Dave Denison;

ACKNOWLEDGEMENTS

Jeremy Lybarger at the Poetry Foundation/*Poetry Magazine*; Colin Kinniburgh and team at *Dissent*; Deborah Chasman at *Boston Review*; Ben Platt and team at *Public Books*; and Robert Scheer and Kasia Anderson at *Truthdig*.

Thanks to all at OR Books, including Colin Robinson, John Oakes (who edited *Finks*), Justin Humphries, Emma Ingrisani, Fatema Merchant, Antara Ghosh, Sam Cartwright, and Maria Green; to Everything Studio's Thomas Griffiths and Jessica Green for work on the cover and illustrations of the book's subjects.

Thanks to Victoria LaLonde, my mother, and Peter Whitney, my father, for reading and inspiring this book. To my brothers and sister, Jake, Ben, Delia and Blake for numerous acts of kindness and solidarity. And to friends, family, fellow writers and colleagues for endless conversation and inspiration.

ENDNOTES

Prologue: My Father's House

1 "Washington: The Massacre of Song My: Who is to Blame?" James Reston, *The New York Times*, Nov 26, 1969 https://timesmachine.nytimes.com/timesmachine/1969/11/26/79439043.html?pageNumber=44.
2 While BBC, ("Al Qaeda Origins & Links," BBC, July 20, 2004, http://news.bbc.co.uk/2/hi/middle_east/1670089.stm), describes the U.S. training as direct, most historians of this period deny direct contact between bin Laden and the CIA. Even taking these historians at their word, Saudi Arabia, when it was effectively a CIA cutout for funding the *mujahideen*, worked directly with bin Laden, funneling CIA money to Arab fighters in Afghanistan. Local Afghani fighters who became the Taliban were directly funded by the CIA, and would later harbor bin Laden during his years of anti-US terror.
3 $18 billion is the amount of US aid given to Pakistan between 2002 and 2011.
4 "The New Yorker Passed on Seymour Hersh's bin Laden Story," Dylan Byers, *Politico*, May 11, 2015, https://www.politico.com/blogs/media/2015/05/the-new-yorker-passed-on-seymour-hershs-bin-laden-story-206933.
5 "The Avenger," Scott Sherman, *Columbia Journalism Review*, July – August 2003, https://web.archive.org/web/20051228214929/http://www.cjr.org/issues/2003/4/hersh-sherman.asp.
6 Seymour Hersh, *The Reporter*, Vintage Books, 2018, 325.
7 Ibid., 326–7.
8 Ibid., 327.
9 "Schmidle defends sources in New Yorker's 'Getting Bin Laden' Story, while narrative editors suggest improvements," Mallory Tenore Tarpley, *Poynter Institute*, Aug 11, 2011 https://www.poynter.org/reporting-editing/2011/schmidle-defends-sourcing-in-new-yorkers-getting-

bin-laden-story-while-narrative-editors-suggest-improvements/.
10. See the Bureau of Investigative Journalism, https://www.thebureauinvestigates.com/blog/2020-09-04/ten-years-investigating-us-covert-warfare.
11. Seymour Hersh, *The Reporter*, 135. (He noted this in the context specifically of his My Lai reporting, to Bob Loomis.)
12. Seymour Hersh, "How America Took Out the Nord Stream Pipeline," Substack, Feb 8, 2023, https://seymourhersh.substack.com/p/how-america-took-out-the-nord-stream.
13. CSPAN, "President Biden on Nord Stream 2 if Russia Invades Ukraine: 'We Will Bring an End To It,'" February 7, 2022, https://www.youtube.com/watch?v=OS4O8rGRLf8.
14. Allie Malloy and Maegan Vazquez, "Biden calls Nord Stream leaks 'a deliberate act of sabotage,'" CNN, Sept 30, 2022 https://www.cnn.com/2022/09/30/politics/biden-ukraine-putin-pipeline/index.html
15. Sarah Ellison, "What Was *New York Times* Reporter James Risen's Seven-Year Legal Battle Really For?" *Vanity Fair*, March 17, 2015, https://www.vanityfair.com/news/2015/03/james-risen-anonymous-source-government-battle.
16. James Risen and Eric Lichtblau, "Bush Lets US Spy on Callers Without Courts," *The New York Times*, December 16, 2005, https://www.nytimes.com/2005/12/16/politics/bush-lets-us-spy-on-callers-without-courts.html.
17. For several examples, see Harrison E. Salisbury's *Without Fear or Favor: An Uncompromising Look at* The New York Times, Times Books, 1980.
18. Margaret Sullivan, "Lessons in a Surveillance Drama, Redux," *The New York Times*, Nov 10, 2013 https://www.nytimes.com/2013/11/10/public-editor/sullivan-lessons-in-a-surveillance-drama-redux.html.
19. Natasha Vargas-Cooper, "Enemy of the State," *The Advocate*, Nov 12, 2013, https://www.advocate.com/print-issue/current-issue/2013/11/12/enemy-state.
20. Toni Morrison, *Song of Solomon* (New York: Knopf, 1977) 179.

Amplifier: Lorraine Hansberry in Midtown

1. Imani Perry, *Looking For Lorraine: The Radiant and Radical Life of Lorraine Hansberry* (Boston: Beacon Press, 2018),163.
2. Ibid., 167.
3. Ibid., 173.

4   *Sighted Eyes/Feeling Heart*, Documentary, dir. Tracy Heather Strain, US, 2017, 118 min.
5   *Looking For Lorraine,* 165.
6   Ibid., 9.
7   Ibid.
8   Ibid., 138.
9   Ibid., 10.
10 *Sighted Eyes/Feeling Heart.*
11 *Looking For Lorraine,* 13.
12 Ibid., 16.
13 Ibid., 18.
14 Ibid., 17.
15 Lillian Ross, "How Lorraine Hansberry Wrote 'A Raisin in the Sun,'" *New Yorker,* May 2, 1959, https://www.newyorker.com/magazine/1959/05/09/playwright.
16 *Looking For Lorraine,* 42.
17 Ibid., 47–8.
18 Ibid., 47.
19 Ibid., 49.
20 Ibid., 51.
21 Ibid., 52.
22 Ibid.
23 Ibid., 56.
24 Ibid.
25 Ibid.
26 Ibid. 58.
27 Ibid.
28 Ibid. 62.
29 Ibid. 64.
30 Ibid., 77.
31 *Sighted Eyes/Feeling Heart.*
32 *Looking For Lorraine,* 97.
33 Ibid., 92.
34 *Sighted Eyes/Feeling Heart.*
35 *Looking For Lorraine,* 102.
36 Ibid., 102.
37 Ibid.
38 Ibid., 99.
39 Ibid.
40 Ibid., 100.
41 *Sighted Eyes/Feeling Heart.*
42 Lorraine Hansberry, "The Negro Writer & His Roots: Toward a New Romanticism," speech given at the American Society of African

Culture, First Conference of Negro Writers, March 1, 1959. *The Black Scholar*, Vol. 12, no. 2 (March/April 1981), https://www.jstor.org/stable/41068050.

43 Ibid.
44 *Sighted Eyes/Feeling Heart.*
45 Ibid.
46 Ibid.
47 Ibid.
48 "Right Off the Newsreel," https://archive.org/details/1959businesss1960creenmav20v21rich/page/n601/mode/2up?view=theater&q=Briskin.
49 "Freeman Names Members of Pix Defense Committee," *Film Daily*, October 31, 1940, https://archive.org/details/filmdail78wids/page/n253/mode/2up?view=theater&q=Briskin.
50 I wrote about this in *Finks*.
51 *Sighted Eyes/Feeling Heart.*
52 Obviously that second term would never come; but *before* 1963, as James DiEugenio writes, the Kennedy administration focused its civil rights efforts in the courts, rather than in Congress, making important gains: James DiEugenio, "The Kennedys & Civil Rights: How the MSM Continues to Distort History, Part 3," Kennedys & King website, Oct 20, 2018, https://www.kennedysandking.com/reviews/the-kennedys-and-civil-rights-how-the-msm-continues-to-distort-history-part-3.
53 *Sighted Eyes/Feeling Heart.*
54 Ibid.
55 *Looking For Lorraine,* 164.
56 Ibid. 165.
57 Ibid. 167.
58 Ibid. 171.
59 Ibid. 172.
60 Ibid. 169.
61 Howard Nemiroff, "Born Black and Female," from liner notes for the 1971 cast recording of *To Be Young, Gifted and Black* (Caedmon Records, TRS 342), https://www.lhlt.org/born-black-and-female.

Nonsense of All These Years: Graham Greene in Vietnam

1 David Gritten, "The Film That Scared a Studio," *The Telegraph*, Nov 26, 2002, https://www.telegraph.co.uk/culture/film/3586238/The-film-that-scared-a-studio.html.

2. Jennifer Schuessler, "Bans on Critical Race Theory Threaten Free Speech, Advocacy Group Says," *The New York Times,* Nov 8, 2021, https://www.nytimes.com/2021/11/08/arts/critical-race-theory-bans.html.
3. Such as MIT's Walt Rostow.
4. Graham Greene, *The Quiet American* (New York: Penguin Classics, 2004) 132. Greene admitted later that he wrote the novel in a "fit of pique" after being denied entry into the US as part of McCarthyite America's weaponization of passports and visas to enforce an anticommunist political correctness.
5. Greene, *The Quiet American*, 134.
6. Ibid.,154–5.
7. Ibid.,149.
8. William S, Bushnell, "Paying the Damage: The Quiet American Revisited," undated, published online.
9. Jonathan Nashel, *Edward Lansdale's Cold War* (Amherst: University of Massachusetts Press, 2005) 165.
10. Ibid.,166.
11. Ibid.
12. Ibid., 165.
13. "Greene Criticizes Film Adaptations of his Books," Anonymous AP Article in *The New York Times,* Sept 6, 1984, https://www.nytimes.com/1984/09/06/movies/greene-criticizes-film-adaptations-of-his-books.html.
14. Norman Sherry, *The Life of Graham Greene*, Vol II. (New York: Penguin Books, 1994) 429.
15. "Author Viet Than Nguyen Discusses The Sympathizer and His Escape From Vietnam," NPR, May 17, 2016, https://www.npr.org/2016/05/17/478384200/author-viet-thanh-nguyen-discusses-the-sympathizer-and-his-escape-from-vietnam.
16. Nashel, *Edward Lansdale's Cold War*, 159.
17. Ibid.
18. Matthieu Aikins, "Times Investigation: In U.S. Drone Strike, Evidence Suggests No ISIS Bomb," *The New York Times*, Sept 10, 2021, https://www.nytimes.com/2021/09/10/world/asia/us-air-strike-drone-kabul-afghanistan-isis.html.
19. Greene, *The Quiet American*, 143-4.
20. Graham Greene (David Parkinson, editor), *The Graham Green Film Reader: Reviews, Essays, Interviews & Film Stories* (Hal Leonard Corporation,1994) 443.

Wake Up, America!: Paul Robeson in Peekskill

1. Iver Peterson, "The Importance of Being Princeton, *The New York Times*, Nov 22, 1991 https://www.nytimes.com/1991/11/22/nyregion/importance-being-princeton-map-stars-mostly-eclipsed-modest-best-seller.html.
2. Tom Deignan, "How Eugene O'Neill Took on the Ku Klux Klan," *Irish Central*, May 15, 2023 https://www.irishcentral.com/roots/history/eugene-oneill-ku-klux-klan.
3. Martin Bauml Duberman, *Paul Robeson: A Biography* (Pan Books, 2014).
4. Joseph Dorinson and William A. Pencak, *Paul Robeson: Essays on His Life & Legacy* (McFarland, 2001).
5. *Paul Robeson: Here I Stand*, Documentary, directed by St. Clair Borne, US, 1999, 117 minutes.
6. *Paul Robeson: Here I Stand*, Documentary, directed by St. Clair Borne, US, 1999, 117 minutes.
7. *Paul Robeson: Here I Stand*, Documentary, directed by St. Clair Borne, US, 1999, 117 minutes.
8. Duberman, *Paul Robeson*, 307.
9. Ibid.
10. Mary E. Cygan, "A Man of His Times: Paul Robeson and the Press, 1924-1976," *Pennsylvania History: A Journal of Mid-Atlantic Studies*, Vol. 66, no. 1, Paul Robeson (1898-1976)—A Centennial Symposium (Winter 1999), 27-46, https://www.jstor.org/stable/27774175?seq=6.
11. As described by Robeson, Jr., in *Paul Robeson: Here I Stand*.
12. *Paul Robeson: Here I Stand*.
13. I was alerted to this video interview with Seeger by local friend Bryan Cafaro.
14. Pete Seeger with Majora Carter, Video by The *Nation* Magazine: https://www.youtube.com/watch?v=wuO7XpFelNw.
15. Duberman, *Paul Robeson*, 369.
16. Ibid., 369-70.
17. Ibid., CLII.
18. Charles H. Martin, "Internationalizing the 'American Dilemma': The Civil Rights Congress & the 1951 Genocide Petition to the United Nations," *Journal of American Ethnic History*, Vol. 16, no. 4 (Summer, 1997), 35-61. See also Bill Knight, "Paul Robeson defied racism in Peoria," *The Community Word,* Oct 31, 2018 http://thecommunityword.com/online/blog/2018/10/31/paul-robeson-defied-racism-in-peoria/.

19 Paul Robeson, *Paul Robeson Speaks: Writings, Speeches & Interview, a Centennial Celebration* (New York: Citadel Press, 1978) 406.
20 Gerald Horne, *Paul Robeson: The Artist as Revolutionary* (London: Pluto Press, 2016) 2.

Fifty Years of Disquietude: Gabriel García Márquez in *Mundo Nuevo*

1   Gerald Martin, *Gabriel García Márquez* (New York: Knopf, 2009) 285.
2   Paul Elie, "The Secret History of One Hundred Years of Solitude," *Vanity Fair*, January 2016 https://www.vanityfair.com/culture/2015/12/gabriel-garcia-marquez-one-hundred-years-of-solitude-history.
3   Ilan Stavans, *Gabriel García Márquez: The Early Years* (New York: St. Martin's, 2010) 26.
4   Ángel Estéban and Stephanie Panichelli, *Fidel & Gabo: A Portrait of the Legendary Friendship Between Fidel Castro and Gabriel García Márquez* (New York: Simon & Schuster, 2011), 11.
5   Ibid., 13-4.
6   Mike Evans of the National Security Archive sent me a dossier of documents supporting this as well as this: Douglas Sofer, "Gaitán Y La Cia: La Evidencia," *La Semana*, May 6, 2001, https://www.semana.com/nacion/articulo/gaitan-cia-evidencia/45925-3/.
7   Estéban and Panichelli, *Fidel & Gabo*, 20.
8   Ibid., 23-5.
9   See Estéban and Panichelli, *Fidel & Gabo*, 29-30, and Peter Stone, Gabriel García Maquez: The Art of Fiction, no. 69," *Paris Review*, Issue 82, Winter 1981 https://theparisreview.org/interviews/3196/the-art-of-fiction-no-69-gabriel-garcia-marquez.
10 Stavans, *Gabriel García Márquez: The Early Years*, 14.
11 Salman Rushdie, "Magic in the Service of Truth," *The New York Times*, April 21, 2014, https://www.nytimes.com/2014/04/21/books/review/gabriel-garcia-marquezs-work-was-rooted-in-the-real.html.
12 Gabriel Garcia Marquez, *One Hundred Years of Solitude* (Quality Paperback Book Club, 2001), 201.
13 Ibid., 329-330.
14 Gabriel García Márquez, *Living to Tell the Tale* (New York: Knopf, 2003).
15 Stavans, *Gabriel García Márquez: The Early Years*, 152.

16 García Márquez to Rodríguez Monegal, March 30, 1966, Princeton's Emir Rodríguez Monegal Papers, Firestone Library, Princeton University.
17 Keith Botsford to Dan Bell, May 27, 1967, Princeton's Emir Rodríguez Monegal Papers, Firestone Library, Princeton University.
18 García Márquez to Rodríguez Monegal, May 24, 1967, Princeton's Emir Rodríguez Monegal Papers, Firestone Library, Princeton University.

Indestructible: George and Mary Oppen in Mexico City

1 Mary Oppen, *Meaning: A Life* (Los Angeles: Black Sparrow Press, 1978) 123.
2 Ibid., 125.
3 George Oppen, "The Mind's Own Place," The Poetry Foundation, Undated, https://www.poetryfoundation.org/articles/69407/the-minds-own-place.
4 Oppen, *Meaning: A Life,* 136.
5 Ibid., 138.
6 Ibid., 144.
7 Ibid., 146.
8 Ibid., 151.
9 Ibid.
10 Ibid.
11 Ibid.
12 Ibid., 153.
13 Ibid.
14 Ibid.
15 Ibid., 155.
16 Ibid., 173.
17 Ibid., 176.
18 Eric A. Hoffman, *Oppen: A Narrative* (Brooklyn, NY: Spuyten Duyvil, 2018), 65.
19 Ibid., 66.
20 Oppen, *Meaning: A Life,* 178.
21 Ibid., 193.
22 The Freedom of Information request was filed in 2017, and in 2018 the FBI sent me 200 pages from case file 100-HQ-422023, of which I only have the hard copy.
23 "Veto of the Internal Security Bill," The American Presidency Project at University of California at Santa Barbara https://www.presidency.ucsb.edu/documents/veto-the-internal-security-bill.

24 Jean Rouverol, *Refugees from Hollywood: A Journal of the Blacklist Years* (Albuquerque: University of New Mexico Press, 2000), 57.
25 Ibid.
26 Ibid., 58.
27 Oppen, *Meaning A Life,* 198.
28 Ibid.
29 Ibid., 199.
30 Gerald Horne, *Communist Front? The Civil Rights Congress, 1946-1956* (New York: International Publishers, 1921).
31 Oppen, *Meaning A Life,* 200.
32 Ibid., 201.
33 Ibid.
34 Ibid.
35 Ibid., 202.
36 George Oppen, "The Mind's Own Place," The Poetry Foundation, Undated, https://www.poetryfoundation.org/articles/69407/the-minds-own-place.
37 Such as Hoffman.
38 See my 2016 interview with Viet Thanh Nguyen for the National Book Awards website: https://www.joelwhitney.net/vietthanhnguyen.html This BBC article, "Was My Lai just one of many massacres in Vietnam War?" downgrades 6 million to 5.3 million, but others cite the full six million, estimated. https://www.bbc.com/news/world-asia-23427726
39 George Oppen, *The Selected Letters of George Oppen*, edited by Rachel Blau DuPlessis (Durham: Duke University Press, 1990) 114.
40 Ibid., 135-6.
41 Louis Simpson, "Poets of the Sixties: Long Live Blake ! Down with Donne!" *The New York Times*, December 28, 1969.
42 Mike Pride, "Poets of the 60s: Established and New," https://www.pulitzer.org/article/poets-60s-established-and-new.
43 Oppen, *The Selected Letters of George Oppen*, 195.
44 Ibid., 188.
45 Ibid., 195.
46 Ibid., 196.
47 Ibid.,177.
48 Ibid.
49 See Natalie S. Robin, *Alien Ink: The FBI's War on Freedom of Expression* (New York: William Morrow & Co., 1992).
50 Oppen, *The Selected Letters of George Oppen*, 177-8.

Silver Spoons: Frances Stonor Saunders in Kansas

1. Christopher Lasch, "The Cultural Cold War," in *Towards a New Past: Dissenting Essays in American History*, edited by Barton Bernstein (New York and Toronto: Random House, 1968). Available here: https://www.joelwhitney.net/christopherlasch.html.
2. Patrick Iber, "Literary Agents," *The New Republic*, Jan 3, 2017, https://newrepublic.com/article/138946/literary-agents
3. Joining the CIA's National Student Association, Steinem signed up to diminish, divide and misdirect leftist students at Youth Congresses in Vienna and elsewhere.
4. It was poet Robert Lowell, she recalls later.
5. She didn't look at Latin America, Africa or Asia, and was criticized for not speaking other European languages. I reported some cases from these regions in *Finks*. In its archives at the New York Public Library in Manhattan, for instance, I read of how the Latin American magazine *Combate*, funded by the Free Europe Committee, a CIA front working in competition with the CCF, was delayed in its launch for a year because its CIA overseers wanted to censor and the editors resisted. Alas, the editors lost.
6. Black American artists Elizbeth Catlett and Charles White exhibited in Mexico when representation (and leftism) were suppressed/overshadowed by abstraction in the late 1940s. Catlett joined the Taller de Grafica Popular, and eventually took Mexican citizenship. David Alfaro Siqueiros used the Taller, in secret, as a staging ground for his failed 1940 assassination attempt on Leon Trotsky.
7. Former BBC staffer Peter Foges told me in a 2019 interview.
8. Peter Baker, "A Four-Decade Secret: One Man's Story of Sabotaging Carter's Re-election," *The New York Times*, March 18, 2023 https://www.nytimes.com/2023/03/18/us/politics/jimmy-carter-october-surprise-iran-hostages.html
9. Richard Crossman, who edited *The God That Failed*, the anti-communist tell-all.

Infiltrated: Malcolm X at the Audubon

1. Peniel Joseph, *The Sword and the Shield: The Revolutionary Lives of Malcolm X and Martin Luther King*, Basic Books, 2020, page 208.
2. *Who Killed Malcolm X?*, Docu-series, directed by Rachel Dretzin and Phil Bertelsen, US, 2020, 6 episodes.
3. Ibid., Episode 1.
4. Ibid.

5   Ibid., Episode 1.
6   Ibid., Episode 2.
7   Ibid.
8   Ibid., Episode 2 and 3.
9   Peniel Joseph, *The Sword and the Shield: The Revolutionary Lives of Malcolm X and Martin Luther King* (New York: Basic Books, 2020), 175.
10 *Who Killed Malcolm X?*, Episode 2.
11 Joseph, *The Sword and the Shield*; see also Clayborne Carson, *Malcolm X: The FBI File* (New York: Skyhorse, 2012).
12 Joseph, *The Sword and the Shield*.
13 Ibid.
14 Ibid., 133.
15 Ibid., 117-8.
16 Ibid., 137.
17 Ibid., 138.
18 Ibid., 116.
19 Ibid.
20 *Who Killed Malcolm X?*, Episode 3.
21 Ibid.
22 Ibid., Episode 4.
23 Ibid.
24 Ibid.
25 Ibid.
26 Ibid.
27 Ibid.
28 Ibid.
29 Ibid.
30 Ibid.
31 Ibid., Episode 5.
32 Ibid.
33 Ibid.
34 Ibid.
35 Ibid.
36 Ibid., Episode 6.
37 Ibid.
38 Ibid.
39 Ibid.
40 Ibid.
41 Ibid.
42 Ibid.
43 Ibid.

44 John Perrazzo, "Who Killed Malcolm X?" *Frontpage Magazine*, Feb 26, 2020, https://www.frontpagemag.com/who-killed-malcolm-x-john-perazzo/.
45 Malcolm X, "Message to the Grass Roots," delivered at a Northern Negro Grass Roots Leadership Conference in Detroit, in November 1963, *Malcolm X Speaks* (Merit Publishers, 1965).
46 *Who Killed Malcolm X?*, Episode 6.
47 Ibid.

Ars Politica: Octavio Paz at 100

1 Octavio Paz, *In Light of India* (New York: Harcourt Brace,1997) 199.
2 Eliot Weinberger, "Biographical Note," in Octavio Paz (Edited & Translated by Eliot Weinberger), *The Poems of Octavio Paz* (New York: New Directions, 2012), 577.
3 Paz, *In Light of India*, 15.
4 Jose Manuel Zamorano Meza, *Existential Octavio Paz or The Poetic Essence of Being*, Doctoral Thesis for University of British Columbia, 2012, 56 https://open.library.ubc.ca/media/stream/pdf/24/1.0073007/2.
5 Joseph Roman, *Octavio Paz: Mexican Poet & Critic* (New York: Chelsea House Publishers, 1994).
6 Weinberger, "Biographical Note," 578.
7 Octavio Paz, *On Poets & Others* (New York: Arcade Publishing, 2014) 8.
8 Octavio Paz, *Labyrinth of Solitude* (New York, Grove Press, 1985), 195.
9 Paz, *In Light of India*, 4.
10 Ibid., 199.
11 Ibid.
12 Ibid., 200.
13 Ibid., 200-1.
14 Ibid., 202.
15 Ibid., 203.
16 Weinberger, "Biographical Note," 580.
17 Ibid.
18 Meza, *Existential Octavio Paz or The Poetic Essence of Being*.
19 Peter Coleman, *The Liberal Conspiracy: The Congress for Cultural Freedom & the Struggle for the Mind of Postwar Europe* (New York: The New Press, 1989) 207.
20 Russell Cobb, *Our Men in Paris?*: Mundo Nuevo, *the Cuban Revolution & the Politics of Cultural Freedom*, dissertation, University of Texas at Austin, 2007, 122.
21 Paz, *On Poets & Others*, 126.

22 Stephanie Mencimer, "The Trouble with Frida," *Washington Monthly*, June 1, 2001.
23 Eliot Weinberger, Email to Author, October 3, 2013.
24 Enrique Krauze, *Redentores: ideas y poder en Latinoamerica* (Espano, 2012), 279.
25 Ibid., 279-80.
26 Ibid., 280.
27 Maarten van Delden, "Polemical Paz," *Literal Magazine*, Issue 7, https://literalmagazine.com/polemical-paz/.
28 Octavio Paz, "Poetry, Myth & Revolution," in *The Other Voice* (New York: Harcourt Brace Jovanovich, 1990), 68.
29 Ibid., 77.
30 Francois de Chateaubriand, *Mémoirs d'Outre-Tombe,* Joel Raupe, 1848, https://archive.org/details/MEMOIRESDOUTRETOMBE/page/n1/mode/2up.
31 van Delden, "Polemical Paz.
32 Clive James, "Borges' Bad Politics," *Slate*, Feb 7, 2007, https://slate.com/news-and-politics/2007/02/borges-bad-politics.html.
33 Krauze, *Redentores*, 281.
34 Ibid., 280.
35 Ibid., 294-5.
36 Ibid., 288.

For All Mankind: Diego Rivera in San Francisco and Detroit

1 Alfredo Cardona Peña (translated by Cardona-Hine Alvaro), *Conversations with Diego Rivera: The Monster in His Labyrinth* (New York: New Village Press, 2018), https://www.jstor.org/stable/j.ctvwrm5d1.
2 Patrick Marnham, *Dreaming with his Eyes Open: A Life of Diego Rivera* (Berkeley, CA: University of California Press), 128.
3 Ibid., 130.
4 Marisol Medina Cadena, "Inside Frida Kahlo and Diego Rivera's Life in San Francisco," KQED, Dec 3, 2020, https://www.kqed.org/news/11848986/inside-frida-kahlo-and-diego-riveras-life-in-san-francisco.
5 Diego Rivera, *My Art, My Life: An Autobiography*, with Gladys March (Courier Corporation, 2012), 114.
6 "The Rockefellers: Diego Rivera," PBS website, https://www.pbs.org/wgbh/americanexperience/features/rockefellers-rivera/ Their full exchange can be found at the website for the book *Black and White and Red All Over: Diego Rivera and the Battle of Rockefeller Center.*

https://xroads.virginia.edu/~MA04/hess/RockRivera/correspondence.html.
7   Michael Cavna, "Diego Rivera Google Doodle: Logo Celebrates the Legendary Mexican Muralist Who Career Was Larger than Life," *The Washington Post*, December 8, 2011, https://www.washingtonpost.com/blogs/comic-riffs/post/diego-rivera-google-doodle-logo-celebrates-the-legendary-mexican-muralist-whose-career-was-a-larger-than-life/2011/12/07/gIQAWca8dO_blog.html.
8   "Mural Theme Explained," Diego Rivera Mural Project website: https://riveramural.org/muraltheme/.
9   Marnham, *Dreaming with his Eyes Open,* 280.
10 "Mural Theme Explained." See Guide for Panel 3, and click on Paulette Godard.

Embodiment of the Enemy: Angela Davis in California

1   Angela Davis with Amy Goodman, "The New McCarthyism: Angela Davis Speaks in New York After Critics Shut Down Two Events," *Democracy Now!*, December 2, 2022, https://www.democracynow.org/2022/12/2/angela_davis_rockland_speech_protests.
2   Angela Davis with Amy Goodman, "The New McCarthyism."
3   *Free Angela & All Political Prisoners*, Documentary, directed by Shola Lynch, US, 2012, 102 min.
4   Ibid.
5   Ibid.
6   "A STATEMENT OF FACTS CONCERNING THE APPOINTMENT AND THREATENED DISMISSAL OF PROFESSOR ANGELA DAVIS, PROVIDED BY THE UCLA DEPARTMENT OF PHILOSOPHY, SEPTEMBER 29, 1969," https://oac.cdlib.org/ark:/13030/hb1x0nb4kq/?brand=oac4.
7   *Free Angela & All Political Prisoners.*
8   Ibid.
9   This was the so-called Loyalty Oath controversy from 1948 until the early 1950s.
10 *Free Angela & All Political Prisoners.*
11 Ibid.
12 Ibid.
13 Ibid.
14 Ibid.
15 Ibid.
16 Ibid.

17 Ibid.
18 Leo Branton.
19 *Free Angela & All Political Prisoners.*
20 Ibid.
21 Dan Baum, "Legalize it All: How to Win the Drug War," *Harper's Magazine*, April 2016. Quoted in Tom LoBianco, "Report: Aide says Nixon's war on drugs targeted blacks, hippies," CNN, March 24, 2016, https://www.cnn.com/2016/03/23/politics/john-ehrlichman-richard-nixon-drug-war-blacks-hippie/index.html

Militant: Leonard Peltier and Anna Mae Aquash in Pine Ridge

1   *From Wounded Knee to Standing Rock: A Reporter's Journey*, documentary, directed by Kevin McKiernan, US, 2019, 88 mins.
2   Unless otherwise noted, all quotes come from the film *From Wounded Knee to Standing Rock,*
3   Ned Blackhawk, *The Rediscovery of America: Native Peoples & the Unmaking of US History* (New Haven: Yale University Press, 2023), 419.
4   As a result, they are still engaged in litigation to get their federal recognition restored. See more here: https://narf.org/nill/bulletins/federal/documents/mishewal_wappo_v_jewell.html.
5   "Russell Means on Wounded Knee and the History of Native Americans in the US," C-SPAN, July 28, 2012, https://www.c-span.org/video/?c4068026/user-clip-russell-means-wounded-knee-history-native-americans-us.
6   "The Week Hundreds of Native Americans Took Over the Bureau of Indian Affairs," *Washington Post,* January 24, 2021, https://www.washingtonpost.com/history/2021/01/24/native-americans-occupied-bureau-indian-afffairs-nixon/.
7   While McKiernan cites poverty alleviation funds, Peter Matthiessen cites federal highway safety program funds: Peter Matthiessen, *In the Spirit of Crazy Horse* (New York: Viking, 1991) 61.
8   David Melmer, "Unsolved deaths debunked by FBI Case by case examination puts some rumors to rest," *Indian Country Today,* July 19, 2000, https://web.archive.org/web/20060506041458/http://www.indiancountry.com/content.cfm?id=747
9   Celestine Bohlen, "US Rejects Soviet Charge in Peltier Case," *Washington Post,* July 1, 1984, https://www.washingtonpost.com/archive/politics/1984/07/01/us-rejects-soviet-charge-in-peltier-case/b613d546-629d-4411-a10e-40979fd6ba3b/.

10   Yvonne Bushyhead, "In the Spirit of Crazy Horse: The Case of Leonard Peltier," Leonard Peltier Defense Committee, archived here: https://openyls.law.yale.edu/bitstream/handle/20.500.13051/7726/06_2YaleJL_Lib13_1991_.pdf?sequence=2&isAllowed=y.
11   Douglas O. Linder, "The Leonard Peltier Case," University of Missouri-Kansas City School of Law/Famous Trials, http://law2.umkc.edu/faculty/projects/ftrials/peltier/peltieraccount.html.
12   Dennis McAuliffe, "Last Stand for Leonard Peltier," *Washington Post*, July 4, 1995, https://www.washingtonpost.com/archive/politics/1995/07/04/last-stand-for-leonard-peltier/3e4fd676-3192-4e08-ae63-37e6d7cd07aa/.

Blood Memory: N. Scott Momaday on Rainy Mountain

1   *N. Scott Momaday: Words From a Bear*, documentary, directed by Jeffrey Palmer, US, 2019, 85 mins.
2   Ibid.
3   *Return to Rainy Mountain,* documentary, directed by Jill Momaday, US, 2017, 29 mins.
4   *N. Scott Momaday: Words From a Bear*.
5   Ibid.
6   Ibid.
7   Ibid.
8   N. Scott Momaday, "Morality of Indian Hating," *Man Made of Words: Essays, Stories, Passages* (New York: Macmillan, 1997), 68.
9   *N. Scott Momaday: Words From a Bear*.
10   Ibid.
11   N. Scott Momaday, *House Made of Dawn* (New York: Harper Perennial, 2010), 16-17.
12   Ibid., 21.
13   Ibid., 22.
14   *N. Scott Momaday: Words From a Bear*.
15   Momaday, *House Made of Dawn*, 131.
16   Ibid., 132.
17   Ibid., 134.
18   Ibid., 139.
19   Ibid.
20   "Wounded Knee 1973, Forty Years Later," C-SPAN, April 27, 2012 https://www.c-span.org/video/?306499-1/wounded-knee-1973-forty-years.

21 Kelsey Hill, "Sisters in the Struggle: The Journey From Wounded Knee," Al Jazeera, March 20, 2021, https://www.aljazeera.com/features/2021/3/30/sisters-in-the-struggle-the-journey-from-wounded-knee "Native men are four times more likely to go to prison than white men, while Native women are six times more likely than white women," writes journalist Kelsey Hill; activists call it the Womb to Prison Pipeline. "In addition, more jails continue to be built in Indian Country, enabling a further rise in incarceration rates."

22 "Anglos and Indians," Marshall Sprague, *The New York Times*, June 9, 1968, https://www.nytimes.com/1968/06/09/archives/anglos-and-indians-house-made-of-dawn-by-n-scott-momaday-212-pp-new.html.

23 George Oppen won that year for poetry; Norman Mailer's *Armies of the Night* for nonfiction; and an image of Coretta Scott King and Bernice King at Martin Luther King's funeral won for photography.

24 Sean Murphy, "Wonder & Exhilaration: N. Scott Momaday's *House Made of Dawn*," https://www.pulitzer.org/article/wonder-and-exhilaration-n-scott-momadays-house-made-dawn.

25 *N. Scott Momaday: Words From a Bear*.

26 Ibid.

27 N. Scott Momaday, "When the West was won and a civilization was lost," *The New York Times*, March 7, 1971, https://www.nytimes.com/1971/03/07/archives/a-history-of-the-indians-of-the-united-states-by-angie-debo.html.

28 *N. Scott Momaday: Words From a Bear*.

29 Ibid.

30 Ibid.

31 Susan Scarberry-Garcia, *Landmarks of Healing: Study of House Made of Dawn*, (Albuquerque, University of New Mexico Press, 1990), 2.

32 Momaday, *House Made of Dawn*, 139.

33 "Tucson Schools Ban Books By Chicano and Native American Authors," Brenda Norrell, *Truthout*, January 18, 2012, https://truthout.org/articles/tucson-schools-bans-books-by-chicano-and-native-american-authors/.

34 Stephen Caesar, "Tucson students confront loss of their Chicano studies,", *Los Angeles Times*, January 11, 2021, https://www.latimes.com/world/la-xpm-2012-jan-11-la-na-ethnic-studies-20120112-story.html.

35 "The Art of Criticism 1: Harold Bloom," *The Paris Review* no. 118, Spring 1991, https://www.theparisreview.org/

interviews/2225/the-art-of-criticism-no-1-harold-bloom. Find an excerpt here: https://devilslane.com/the-academic-virus-deliberately-designed-for-the-corruption-of-everything/.
36 *N. Scott Momaday: Words From a Bear.*
37 Ibid.
38 Ibid.

Anachronistic: Miguel Ángel Asturias on his grandparents' finca

1 Rita Guibert, *Seven Voices: Seven Latin American Writers Talk to Rita Guibert* (New York: Knopf Doubleday, 1972), xii; and cited in Russell Cobb, *Our Men in Paris?: Mundo Nuevo, the Cuban Revolution & the Politics of Cultural Freedom*, dissertation, University of Texas at Austin, 2007, 175, https://repositories.lib.utexas.edu/bitstream/handle/2152/3179/cobbd58005.pdf?seq.
2 Miguel Ángel Asturias (translated by David Unger), *Mr. President* (New York: Penguin Books), xxvi.
3 Ibid., xxiii.
4 Gerald Martin, "Cronología" in *El Señor Presidente*, Miguel Ángel Asturias, ALLCA XX, xxxix–li.
5 Gregory Rabassa, "The Life & Works of Miguel Angel Asturias," in *Asturias, Benavente, Bergon (*Nobel Prize Library, 1971), 169.
6 Ibid., 170.
7 Martin, "Cronología" in *El Señor Presidente*.
8 Rabassa, "The Life & Works of Miguel Angel Asturias."
9 Jimena Sáenz, *Genio Y Figura de Miguel Angel Asturias* (Editorial Universitaria de Buenos Aires, 1974), 110. (My own translation.)
10 Ibid.
11 Asturias, *Mr. President*, 103–4.
12 Ibid., 56.
13 Ibid., 85.
14 Ibid., 107.
15 Ibid., 93.
16 Ibid., 40.
17 While Asturias was there, you recall, Pablo Neruda had scrambled over the border in flight from Chile's Videla regime; in his exile to Europe, he borrowed Asturias's passport.
18 I cited this in *Finks*, and above.
19 Cobb, *Our Men in Paris?*, 172-3.

20 Ibid., 174.
21 Natalie S. Robin, *Alien Ink: The FBI's War on Freedom of Expression* (New York: William Morrow & Co., 1992), 314.
22 Gerald Martin, interview with the author, November 19, 2022.
23 Emir Rodríguez Monegal, "The Green Pope," *The New York Times*, February 28, 1971, https://www.nytimes.com/1971/02/28/archives/the-green-pope-by-miguel-angel-asturias-translated-by-gregory.html.
24 Ibid.
25 "Thoughts on the Novel Peace Prize," Hans Habe, *Encounter*, February 1974, 96-8, https://www.unz.com/print/Encounter-1974feb-00096/.
26 Martin, interview with the author, Nov 19, 2022.
27 Asturias, *Mr. President*, 116.

Clarification: Rigoberta Menchú in Oslo

1 Anders Riis-Hansen, "500 Years of Sacrifice Before the Alien Gods: An Interview with Rigoberta Menchú Túm," *Jewish Quarterly*, Vol 40, 1993, Issue 4, https://www.tandfonline.com/doi/abs/10.1080/0449010X.1993.10705958.
2 Thelma Cabrera, whose ticket was arbitrarily banned for trumped up charges against her vice-presidential running mate
3 *Rigobera Menchú: Daughter of the Maya*, documentary, directed by Dawn Gifford Engle, USA, 61 min, 2016.
4 Ibid.
5 Verguenza: Each is my alma mater, for undergrad and grad school, respectively.
6 *Rigobera Menchú: Daughter of the Maya*.
7 Ibid.
8 J. C. King, (25 July 1958), Subject: S. S. Springfjord, Memorandum for: Office of the General Council, Central Intelligence Agency, p. 1.
9 Rigoberta Menchú (with Elisabeth Burgos-Debray, Editor), *I, Rigoberta Menchú: An Indian Woman in Guatemala* (New York: Verso Books), 174.
10 Ibid.
11 Ibid., 157.
12 Ibid.
13 Ibid., 187.
14 Ibid., 188.
15 Ibid., 189.

16 Ibid., 211.
17 Ibid., 218.
18 *Rigobera Menchú: Daughter of the Maya.*
19 Ibid.
20 Lauren Carasik, "The Long Arc of Justice in Guatemala," *Al Jazeera*, April 22, 2013, https://www.aljazeera.com/opinions/2013/4/22/the-long-arc-of-justice-in-guatemala.
21 See "Truth Commission" report summary at the United States Institute for Peace website: https://www.usip.org/publications/1997/02/truth-commission-guatemala.
22 The Guatemala Genocide Case, The Center for Justice & Accountability estimates 70,000 in their web report here: https://cja.org/where-we-work/guatemala/. For the 75,000 death toll estimate, see Jennifer Schirmer, *The Guatemalan Military Project: A Violence Called Democracy*Philadelphia; University of Pennsylvania Press, 1988), 44.
23 *Rigobera Menchú: Daughter of the Maya.*
24 Menchú, *I, Rigoberta Menchú,* 284.
25 *Rigobera Menchú: Daughter of the May*a.
26 Ibid.
27 Ibid.
28 Ibid.
29 Ibid.
30 Ibid.
31 Ibid.
32 Ibid.
33 Ibid.
34 Larry Rohter, "Nobel Winner Accused of Stretching the Truth,", *The New York Times*, December 15, 1998, https://archive.nytimes.com/www.nytimes.com/library/books/121598cambodian-memoir.html.
35 *Rigobera Menchú: Daughter of the Maya.*
36 Mireya Navarro, "Guatemalan Army Waged 'Genocide,' New Report Finds,", *The New York Times*, February 26, 1999, https://www.nytimes.com/1999/02/26/world/guatemalan-army-waged-genocide-new-report-finds.html.
37 Greg Grandin, "Rigoberta Menchu Vindicated," *The Nation*, January 21, 2015, https://www.thenation.com/article/archive/rigoberta-menchu-vindicated/.
38 Menchú, *I, Rigoberta Menchú,* 284.

Unearthed: Jennifer, Efraín and the CIA in Guatemala

1. Patricia Goudvis, website page for *Dirty Secrets: Jennifer, Everardo, & the CIA in Guatemala* (1998) https://www.patriciagoudvis.com/dirty-secrets-1.
2. Ibid.
3. Ibid.
4. Ibid.
5. Ibid.
6. Ibid.
7. Ibid.
8. Ibid.
9. Jennifer Harbury, *Searching for Everardo: A Story of Love, War & the CIA in Guatemala* (New York: Grand Central Publishing, 1997), 6.
10. Ibid.
11. "Is it legal to cross the US border to seek asylum?" International Rescue Committee, July 1, 2022, https://www.rescue.org/article/it-legal-cross-us-border-seek-asylum.
12. Harbury, *Searching for Everardo*, 7.
13. Goudvis, website page for *Dirty Secrets: Jennifer, Everardo, & the CIA in Guatemala*.
14. Ibid.
15. Harbury, *Searching for Everardo*, 28-9.
16. Ibid.
17. Ibid., 43-4.
18. Ibid., 68.
19. Ibid., 78.
20. Ibid., 69.
21. Ibid., 75.
22. Ibid., 79.
23. Ibid., 88.
24. Ibid., 90.
25. Ibid., 101.
26. Ibid., 106.
27. Ibid.
28. Ibid., 113.
29. Ibid.
30. Ibid., 127.
31. Ibid.
32. Ibid., 154.
33. Ibid., 174.
34. Ibid.

35 Ibid., 178.
36 Ibid., 195.
37 Ibid., 195-6. Alas: this would not prove to be Nuland's most infamous case of involvement in something approaching a coup.
38 Ibid., 196.
39 Ibid., 199.
40 Ibid.
41 Ibid.
42 Ibid.
43 The president changed his position only when his family members were targeted by intelligence services, one killed.
44 Harbury, *Searching for Everardo*, 200-1.
45 Ibid.
46 Ibid., 201.
47 Ibid., 214.
48 Ibid., 234.
49 Ibid., 243.
50 Ibid., 251.
51 Ibid., 139.
52 Ibid., 279.
53 Ibid., 301.
54 Ibid., 314.
55 Patricia Goudvis, website page for *Dirty Secrets: Jennifer, Everardo, & the CIA in Guatemala*.
56 Ibid.
57 Tim Weiner, "CIA May Dismiss Chief Officer Involved in Guatemala," *The New York Times*, September 28, 1995, https://www.nytimes.com/1995/09/28/world/cia-may-dismiss-chief-officer-involved-in-guatemala.html?searchResultPosition=8. Tim Weiner, "More is Told About CIA in Guatemala," *The New York Times*, April 25, 1995, https://www.nytimes.com/1995/04/25/world/more-is-told-about-cia-in-guatemala.html.
58 Weiner, "CIA May Dismiss Chief Officer Involved in Guatemala"; "More is Told About CIA in Guatemala."

Hard Choices: Manuel Zelaya and Berta Cáceres on the Run

1 Jeremy Kryt, "Dispatch from Honduras: De Facto Regime Terrorizes Father of Slain Youth," *Earth Island Journal*, September 15, 2009, https://www.earthisland.org/journal/index.php/articles/entry/dispatch_from_honduras/.

2. Janet Gold, *Culture and Customs of Honduras* (Greenwood: 2009), 89-91.
3. Ibid., 89.
4. Dana Frank, *Long Honduran Night: Resistance, Terror & the United States in the Aftermath of the Coup* (Chicago: Haymarket Books, 2018), 13.
5. Ibid., 17.
6. Ibid., 35.
7. Ibid., 20.
8. Ibid., 14.
9. Ibid.
10. Ibid., 17.
11. Ibid.
12. Ibid.
13. Ibid., 18.
14. Ibid., 18-19.
15. Mark Weisbrot, "Does the US Back the Honduran Coup?" *The Guardian*, July 1, 2009, https://www.theguardian.com/commentisfree/cifamerica/2009/jul/01/honduras-zelaya-coup-obama.
16. Frank, *Long Honduran Night*, 20.
17. Ibid.
18. Ibid., 21.
19. Ibid.
20. Mary Anastasia O'Grady, "Honduras Defends Its Democracy," *The Wall Street Journal*, June 29, 2009, https://www.wsj.com/articles/SB124623220955866301.
21. Frank, *Long Honduran Night*, 22.
22. Ibid., 23.
23. Quoted in Frank but scrubbed from this website: http://cepr.net/blogs/the-americas-blog/newly-released-clinton-emails-reveal-state-department-s-celebration-over-honduras-flawed-elections-following-military-coup.
24. "Agrarian Reform in Honduras," FIAN International Website, 2015, https://www.fian.org/fileadmin/media/publications_2015/Agrarian-Reform-in-Honduras-2000.pdf.
25. Frank, *Long Honduran Night*, 72.
26. Paul Romer, "The World's First Charter City," TED Talks, March 2011, https://www.ted.com/talks/paul_romer_the_world_s_first_charter_city?language=en.
27. Frank, *Long Honduran Night*, 73.

28 Ibid.
29 Ibid., 75.
30 Ibid., 76.
31 Ibid., 77.
32 Ibid., 85.
33 Adam Davidson, "Who Wants to Buy Honduras?" *New York Times Magazine*, May 8, 2012, https://www.nytimes.com/2012/05/13/magazine/who-wants-to-buy-honduras.html.
34 Frank, *Long Honduran Night*, 101.
35 Ibid.
36 Ibid., 102.
37 Alas: this would not prove to be Nuland's most infamous coup. The neoconservative official was caught on audio leaked to the BBC in February 2014 plotting the replacement of Ukrainian President Viktor Yanukovich during the Maidan uprisings, famously exclaiming "Fuck the EU!" https://www.bbc.com/news/world-europe-26079957.
38 Frank, *Long Honduran Night*, 101.
39 Ibid., 103.
40 Ibid., 104.
41 Ibid., 106.
42 Ibid., 193.
43 Ibid., 189.
44 Ibid., 189-90.
45 Ibid., 191.
46 Ibid., 192.
47 Joe Biden, "A Plan for Central America," *The New York Times*, Jan 30, 2015, https://www.nytimes.com/2015/01/30/opinion/joe-biden-a-plan-for-central-america.html.
48 Dana Frank, "In Honduras, 'We're Supporting the Ax Murderers,'" [an excerpt from *Long Honduran Night*], *Jacobin*, Nov 24, 2018, https://jacobin.com/2018/11/long-honduran-night-dana-frank-us-honduras-juan-orlando-hernandez.
49 "Berta Cáceres," Goldman Environmental Prize Website, 2015, https://www.goldmanprize.org/recipient/berta-caceres/.
50 "Before Her Assassination, Berta Caceres Singled Out Hillary Clinton for Backing Honduran Coup," *Democracy Now!*, March 11, 2016, https://www.democracynow.org/2016/3/11/before_her_assassination_berta_caceres_singled.
51 Karol Suarez, Philip Wang, and Marlon Sorto, "Xiomara Castro becomes Honduras' first female president," CNN,

January 27, 2022, https://www.cnn.com/2022/01/27/americas/xiomara-castro-honduras-inauguration-intl/index.html.

52 Sonia Perez and Megan Janetsky, "Guatemalan president calls for transition of power to anti-corruption crusader Arévalo," *Associated Press*, August 29, 2023, https://apnews.com/article/guatemala-seed-movement-bernardo-arevalo-suspension-e553326fcc3ee118cce516633f904af4.

"Amplifier: Lorraine Hansberry in Midtown" was first published online in *Jacobin* on December 16, 2020.

"Nonsense of All These Years: Graham Greene in Vietnam" was first published in *The Baffler* on June 15, 2022.

"Wake Up, America!: Paul Robeson in Peekskill" was first published in *Jacobin* on July 18, 2022.

"Fifty Years of Disquietude: Gabriel García Márquez in *Mundo Nuevo*" first ran in *The Baffler* in December 2016; it was adapted from parts of Chapters 12 and 13 of my 2017 book Finks: How the CIA Tricked the World's Best Writers.

"Indestructible: George and Mary Oppen in Mexico City" first appeared on the Poetry Foundation website on January 18, 2021.

"Infiltrated: Malcolm X at the Audubon" was first published in *Jacobin* in July 2020.

"Ars Politica: Octavio Paz at 100" was first published in *Dissent* on March 25, 2014.

"For All Mankind: Diego Rivera in San Francisco and Detroit" was first published in *Jacobin* on October 25, 2022.

"Embodiment of the Enemy: Angela Davis in California" was first published in *Jacobin* on April 1, 2023.

"Militant: Leonard Peltier and Anna Mae Aquash in Pine Ridge" was first published in *Boston Review* on July 20, 2023.

"Anachronistic: Miguel Ángel Asturias on his grandparents' finca" was first published in *Public Books* on March 28, 2023.

"Hard Choices: Manuel Zelaya and Berta Cáceres on the Run" was first published in slightly different form in *Truthdig* on August 28, 2019.

Sean Jerd

Joel Whitney is the author of *Finks: How the CIA Tricked the World's Best Writers*, which *The New Republic* called a "powerful warning." His writing has appeared in *The New York Times*, *The Daily Beast*, *The Baffler*, *The Wall Street Journal*, *Boston Review*, *New York Magazine*, and elsewhere. He is a former features editor at *Al Jazeera America* and a founder and former editor-in-chief of *Guernica*, for which he was awarded the 2017 PEN/Nora Magid Award for Excellence in Editing. His essays in *The Baffler*, *Dissent* and *Salon* were Notables in Best American Essays 2017, 2015, and 2013.